GRAVE INJUSTICE

Fourth World Rising Series editors:

Gerald M. Sider
The College of Staten Island, CUNY

Kirk Dombrowski
John Jay College of Criminal Justice, CUNY

KATHLEEN S. FINE-DARE

Grave Injustice

The American Indian
Repatriation Movement
and NAGPRA

University of Nebraska Press

Lincoln and London

⊗

Library of Congress Cataloging-in-Publication Data
Fine-Dare, Kathleen S. (Kathleen Sarbinoff), 1953–
Grave injustice: the American Indian Repatriation Movement and NAGPRA /
Kathleen S. Fine-Dare.
p.   cm.
Includes bibliographical references and index.
ISBN 0-8032-2018-9 (cloth: alk. paper)—ISBN 0-8032-6908-0 (paper: alk.
paper)
1. Indians of North America—Antiquities—Law and legislation.   2. Human
remains (Archaeology)—Law and legislation—United States.   3. Human remains (Archaeology)—Repatriation—United States.   4. United States. Native
American Graves Protection and Repatriation Act.   I. Title.
KF8210.A57F56   2002
323.1′197073′09—dc21
2002020016

For Marion and Linda
And, especially, Byron

CONTENTS

Series Editors' Introduction

Grave Injustice is the fourth volume in Fourth World Rising, a series of contemporary ethnographies from the University of Nebraska Press. The series focuses on contemporary issues, including class, gender, religion, and politics: in sum, it addresses social and cultural differentiation among and between native peoples as they confront those around them and each other in struggles for better lives, better futures, and better visions of their own pasts. This focus thus represents a departure from many of the monographs produced by anthropologists about native peoples, which often have sought to reproduce either visions of ways of life now long past or else pasts refracted through current idealization. In the process, traditional anthropology has helped enshrine a backward-looking focus to native culture that has, at times, been influential in the way laws are framed and even in how native peoples come to see their own identity.

Ideas, especially when enshrined in law and lent the authority of governments, have power. And the idea that native cultures and societies are historical artifacts rather than ongoing projects has served to narrow the politics of native identity or indigenism worldwide. One purpose of this series is to change this focus and broaden the conception of native struggle to match its current complexity.

This is especially important now, for the last two decades have provided prominent examples of native peoples seeking to recast the public—ultimately political—basis of their native identity in ways other than the reproduction of often fanciful, even fictional, pasts. Our hope is that by offering a variety of texts focused on these and other contemporary issues, structured for classroom use and a general audience, we can help change the public perception of native struggle—allowing people to see that native cultures and societies are very much ongoing (and to a surprising extent on their own terms) and that the issues they confront carry important practical and theoretical implications for a more general understanding of cultural and political processes.

The primary geographical and topical emphasis of the Fourth World Rising series is the native peoples of the Americas, but the series will also include comparative cases from Australia, Africa, Asia, the circumpolar Arctic and sub-Arctic, and the Pacific Islands. Yet beyond its unique topical and contemporary focus, four critical theoretical and political features distinguish the series as well:

1. A focus on the struggles native peoples must fight, with the dominant society and with each other, whether they wish to or not, in order to survive as peoples, as communities, and as individuals, as well as the struggles they choose to fight.

2. A consideration of how the intensifying inequalities within and between native communities—emerging from social, cultural, and economic differences among native peoples—create unavoidable antagonisms, so that there cannot be any simple lines of cleavage between a dominant, oppressive, and exploitative state on the one side and its long-suffering victims on the other. Thus the series pays particular attention to gender, identity, religion, age, and class divisions among native peoples, along with differences in the goals and strategies that emerge from these struggles.

An emphasis on internal differences and tensions among native peoples is not at all intended to let the dominant states and societies off the hook for their policies and practices. Rather, this perspective calls to the foreground how internal complexities and divisions among native peoples and communities shape their struggles within and against the larger societies in which they find themselves. Indeed, it is precisely these internal differences among and between native peoples (and how these differences unfold over time and through native peoples' complex relations to one another) that give native people their own history and their own social processes that are, ultimately, partly separate from the history imposed upon them by the dominant society.

3. An emphasis on the praxis of native struggles: what works, and why, and with what intended and unintended effects; who benefits within native communities and who loses what, and why. The series monographs are thus not advocacy tracts in the conventional sense of that term, though they are undeniably political constructs. Rather, the emphasis on contemporary social processes and the political praxis of participants, advocates, and anthropologists serves as a stimulus for dialogue and debate about the changing pressures and possibilities for

particular native societies and the political situations confronting native peoples more generally.

4. An attempt to clarify the situation facing those whose concerns and fundamentally decent impulses lead them to want to help the victims of domination and exploitation. Such honorable commitments need to be developed in the midst of realizing that the radiant innocence of an earlier applied anthropology, and of many aid programs, along with the social world that sustained this innocence, has crumbled. It is no longer possible to say or to think "*we* will help *them.*" Now we must ask who is helped and who is hurt both by the success and by the frequent failure of aid programs, and why, and how.

The primary audience for this series is students in college courses in anthropology, political science, native and ethnic studies, economics, and sociology. Yet the series achieves its importance among a college and popular audience by being developed for a second audience as well. One of the major purposes of this series is to present case studies of native peoples' current struggles that have broader strategic relevance to those engaged in similar or complementary struggles and to advocates whose concerns lie more directly along the lines of what has worked in the past or in other areas, what has not, and with what consequences.

Hence this volume becomes part of a new way of both doing and teaching anthropology and native studies. On one level, the case studies seek to bring together activists, native peoples, and academics, not simply by dramatizing the immediacy of native struggles, but also by dispelling the notion that native societies derive their nativeness from being internally homogeneous and externally timeless. On a second level, the series as a whole helps those currently teaching native studies to pursue an engaged, contemporary perspective and a broad geographic approach—allowing for and in fact encouraging a global, contemporary native studies that is deeply rooted both in a fundamental caring for native peoples' well-being and in the realities of internal differentiation among native peoples.

Gerald Sider
Kirk Dombrowski

Preface

Enemy Ancestors

When I moved to Colorado in the early 1980s, I was told of two big attractions housed in the Mesa Verde National Park museum. One was "Esther," a mummified woman who had been removed from view before I made my first museum visit but who still figured prominently in the questions posed by visitors to park staff.

The second attraction, one quite popular with children and adults alike (and I was no exception), was a human skull with a stone weapon lodged deeply, and certainly fatally, near the orbital area. The exhibit was quite graphic in its display of Indian-to-Indian violence and was always completely surrounded by gawkers. It was finally removed from public view, sometime in the late 1980s, because of the growing concern over the ways Native American human remains and cultural objects were acquired by, curated, and displayed in museums.

Although I admit I was drawn to that skull from time to time and wondered about the appropriateness of its display, another far less sensational exhibit drew my attention even more. While most of the museum halls showcased the everyday and sacred objects of a people then called the Anasazi who had inhabited the area comprised by the park until sometime in the fourteenth century, this case exhibited the artwork of the Ute peoples for whom the park area had also served as homeland and hunting range presumably after it had been "mysteriously abandoned" by "the ancient ones." The term *Anasazi*, in fact, is an Athapaskan-derived term often translated as "enemy ancestor," supposedly reflecting the ways nomadic newcomers to the American Southwest created their own home away from home among persons whose very different ancestry was now incorporated into their own.

The Utes had always been a bit of a problem for park interpreters, who once described them in terms that implied that they had been not only latecomers to the Land of the Cliff Dwellers but perhaps violent usurpers. The Utes were viewed as being neither architects nor agriculturalists. They were thus considered to be much further away from being "civilized" than were their Anasazi neighbors who had graciously vanished, leaving "less-developed nomads" such as the Utes and Apaches to maraud the northern halls of Montezuma.

I would like to say that I am being facetious, but despite the fact that park interpreters no longer speak in such negative terms about the Utes (who still live adjacent to park lands), this viewpoint has persisted in many ways until the present day and continues to affect political and cultural relationships between the extremely varied peoples of the Southwest, both Indian and non-Indian. The viewpoint was made explicit in the exhibit of "Ute Beadwork" that showcased exquisite, detailed works of art that seemed to so contradict the opposite expectations that a disclaimer of sorts was posted for decades beneath the intricately beaded baby shoes and other lovely items. I wish I could remember exactly what the lettered card said, but the distinct question it posed was how such bloodthirsty savages could have made such beautiful objects. In spite of the pressure increasingly put on museums to remove offensive displays, the small lettered card labeling the Ute beadwork exhibit stayed put until the 1990s, when it finally disappeared, but not as a result of any official act of the museum. I will return to this story in a moment.

My interest in museums and the job of park rangers and exhibit labels to "interpret" for visitors the meaning of what they were viewing led to an article on the history and politics of the interpretive process at Mesa Verde (Fine 1988). Although some of the piece was critical of the ways in which interpreters had been instructed to speak about Indian peoples of the Southwest from the 1960s through the 1980s, a more important point that I made amounts to this: it is very difficult to choose sides against the federal government when so many of its employees are "on the side" of Indian people and use their park job to tell an alternative story whenever they can. Any government, of course, whether federal or tribal, is made up of human beings who follow the rules (or their perception of the rules) to widely varying degrees. While conformity and acquiescence to authority are no doubt the norm within powerful institutions, opportunities for one person to contest and perhaps even reverse the unfair exercise of power do exist. This book continues that theme by looking at ways some Native Americans and their allies have changed federal laws, state laws, local practices, "American culture," and both public and private morality by speaking out against one of the most taken-for-granted aspects of living in America, which is the acquisition, desecration, dispossession, and display of the cultural property and human remains of the first inhabitants of this hemisphere. There were many reasons for this, especially in North America, where the shallow time depth of European habitation made it necessary—psychologically, militarily, and otherwise—to collect the aboriginal past as a show of power, birthright, and organic connection to a new land. "Finders keepers" was not just a crude common law of possession but came to symbolize the wages of careful caretaking and productive use of the terrain through agriculture, mining, and ranching. It no longer mattered if the newcomers could demonstrate continuous residence going back for the centuries that they could plot in their Bibles. By hanging on to "Indian relics" and displaying them in their homes, the new Americans established a metonymic relationship to their own "enemy ancestors," to the peoples who farmed and lived on the same land many centuries earlier.

The idea that consumption-oriented, property-worshiping Americans should not collect and keep interesting objects, especially when located on their own land, is one that meets a great deal of resistance. I do not directly take up the moral implications of this act and these attitudes, as it is a complex one with no easy answers. For instance, a Dove Creek, Colorado, ranch family's display of arrowheads may in fact reveal much more suspicion and disrespect of academic archaeologists than it does of Native Americans. The movement chronicled in this book to *repatriate*—in other words, to bring home—objects and human remains that do not properly belong to their current owners is concerned with private collections as well as public ones. My focus, however, will be public museums, which can, in a way, be thought of as display cases in our national living room. Although on the surface it may seem that the collection and display of objects in public places may provide easier moral and practical answers than dealing with their counterpart in private hands, they do not.

In her excellent introduction to a collection of articles that traces various aspects of the repatriation movement since 1990, Choctaw historian Devon Mihesuah attempts with much success the nearly impossible, which is to categorize the diversity of opinion regarding "what should be done" with the remains of American Indians stored in museums. Coming up with no fewer than twelve distinct viewpoints organized into five broader categories—1) Indians, archaeologists, and pothunters; 2) Indians and social scientists; 3) Indians and Indians; 4) social scientists and social scientists; and 5) museums and Indians—Mihesuah succinctly demonstrates that there are far more players than "Us" and "Them," or "Whites" and "Indians," or "Feds" and "Academics" (Mihesuah 2000). Any one of these categories is so divided by the interests of class, economy, region, gender, and historical experience that attempts to locate the "bad guys" can only reach a dead end when they are not informed by a creative and honest retrospective of how things have come to be as they are and the realization that the current situation is replete with continuing injustices that must be addressed and corrected to the best of our varied abilities.

Sins of Omission, Changes of Heart

In the Andes of Ecuador thousands of people speak an indigenous language called Quichua or *runa shimi*, the "tongue of human beings," that has a past-tense verb ending, -*shkakarka*, which tells the listener that the act under discussion happened in the past but the speaker only just now realized it. The fact that this particular past-tense ending does not occur in English does not mean, however, that we are incapable of grasping its sense. Each of us is capable of understanding something that occurred before we learned of it, or having known of it, we only then grasp its meaning. We can revisit history and admit our inability (or our refusal) to see what might have happened that we missed so as to better understand its effects and meaning in the present. And as it was something in the present that shook up our memory, it is only fitting that we shake up the past for different meanings.

I am a college professor and have had students become very uncomfortable and even angry when they learn about postcontact American Indian history. Their feelings are engendered less because the events provoke such strong emotions (often of guilt) in and of themselves than the fact that they feel they were either lied to outright or by omission regarding what they see as a history they had a right to know as Americans. The reasons the "sins of omission" were made are deeply connected to the realities they cover up. Having been lied to, we can do little but lie in return, however innocently, unless we start learning what actually happened and attempt to turn our defensive guilt into -shkakarka realizations linked to education, lawmaking, reparations, and just plain rethinking.

Who Removed the Exhibit Label?

The removal of that unfortunate skull from the Mesa Verde museum exhibit in the 1980s, along with an increasing flood of events, laws, letters, and publications speaking to the questionable practices of museums, universities, and the federal, academic, and private actors linked to these institutions, led me to wonder why that hideous description of Ute artistry remained on display at the museum into the 1990s. I asked people I knew at the museum why the exhibit label was never changed, but they said nothing could be done as long as the "powers that be" refused to call for its removal or alteration. In other words, the then superintendent felt that the exhibit label was "historic"—that is, display-worthy, despite its offensive inaccuracy—and did not want it changed.

One day I went to see the case and was surprised to find the label gone, leaving a bare outline beneath the beaded shoes and bags. I made inquiries, but no one knew what had happened; the cardboard piece had "just disappeared" mysteriously, and everyone I spoke to gleefully hoped that particular sleeping dog would remain at rest. I persisted and finally learned that the culprit was neither a thief nor a low-paid rebel, but someone I will call "a highly placed fed in solidarity with Native American justice." This book was inspired by him and by all persons of whatever persuasion who seek to right the wrongs they either have known and lived for centuries or have been party to, knowingly or unknowingly. To borrow another phrase from Quichua: Tukui jatarishun—"let's all rise up together."

.

Acknowledgments

I am very grateful to a wide array of individuals who have supported me in the writing of this book in its various stages, but any errors located within belong only to me. Sujan Bryan, Kay Candler, José Cárdenas, Ruth Dare, Kirk Dombrowski, Cece Fine, Larry Fine, Linda Fine, Marion Fine, Rick Fine, Don Gordon, Keiko Ikeda, David Kozak, Carolyn Landes, Cassandra Leoncini, Norman Linton, the late Roger Peters, Jan Sallinger-McBride, Doug Richardson, Ashley Shultz, Jane Silveira, Carol Smith, and Karen Spear must be mentioned first, as this project would have suffered without their encouragement. Faron Scott has been especially important to me as a source of intellectual and emotional strength. I also owe a special debt to Linda Seligmann, without whose consistent friendship and intellectual generosity I might not have undertaken this work, and for her keen ability to make uncanny and crucial connections across time and space. Richard Handler has been singularly influential, for starting me down the path of critical museum studies long before it became fashionable and for providing level-headed encouragement throughout my rather strange career. I probably would never have pursued graduate work without the guidance and support of John Terrell, who first put into my consciousness the idea that museums might be sites of contestation as well as intellectual productivity as early as 1975 when I worked as a clerk at the Field Museum. I must also thank an unnamed reviewer of this manuscript, for providing many useful suggestions for improvement; Larry Zimmerman, for providing key suggestions at a crucial time; and Chris Kyle, for encouraging me to contribute to this series and for becoming an important colleague in many respects.

Those who graciously assisted my research at Fort Lewis College include Maggie Bull, Ken Charles, Mona Charles, Sean Cridland, Rachel Davenport, Philip Duke, Jim Judge, Susan Moss, and Susan Riches. Discussions with Rebecca Austin, Elizabeth Callard, Richard Ellis, Clark Erickson, Terry Fischer, Alan Goodman, Andrew Gulliford, Sharon Hatch,

Acknowledgments

Kristine Harper, George Hassan, John Isaacson, Dale Lehman, Debra Martin, Robert Preucel, Barbara Price, Alexa Roberts, Enrique Salmón, Bernard Schriever, Tom Shipps, Joseph Henry Suina, Rosemary Sucec, Nathaniel Todea, Carmelita Topaha, Carey Vicenti, Elayne Walstedter, Amanda Webb, Rick Wheelock, Amy Wise, Andelé Worthington, and Jim Zeidler have been extremely valuable concerning many aspects of the project. Key intellectual influences have come from the work of Kay Candler, Byron Dare, Claire Farrer, Richard Handler, Alice Kehoe, Leigh Kuwanwisiwma, the late Edmund Ladd, Beatrice Medicine, Tessie Naranjo, Deborah Poole, Gerald Sider, Terry Turner, Peter Whiteley, Norman E. Whitten Jr., and Larry Zimmerman. I also owe many thanks to the research staff at Mesa Verde National Park, particularly Liz Bauer, Art Hutchinson, Carolyn Landes, and Linda Towle. I am especially grateful to Sarah Olson for preparing the index and Jane Curran for her precise and communicative copyediting. The deepest debt of all I owe to Byron Dare, for his patient reading of all permutations of this work, his incisive suggestions for improvement, and for much more than I have life enough left to repay.

GRAVE INJUSTICE

Introduction: White Noise, Double Silence

In order to have all people understand how much land we owned, my father planted poles around it and said: "Inside is the home of my people—the white man may take the land outside. Inside this boundary all our people were born. It circles around the graves of our fathers, and we will never give up these graves to any man. . . . My son, never forget my dying words. This country holds your father's body. Never sell the bones of your father and your mother."

I pressed my father's hand and told him I would protect his grave with my life. My father smiled and passed away to the spirit land. I buried him in that beautiful valley of winding waters. I love that land more than all the rest of the world. A man who would not love his father's grave is worse than a wild animal.—Chief Joseph (Nez Percé), "My Son, Stop Your Ears," 1879

When I walked into that room, and got together with our ancestors, that was emotionally disturbing—I shed some tears. And then being there for a couple of hours, then, I guess, they told me that they were going back home. And we've been working on it ever since.—Pete Toya, War Chief, Jemez Pueblo, on seeing the Pecos collection at the Peabody museum, in 1996 (quoted in Goldberg 1999)

Pecos Homecoming

"Pecos" has a resonance to most Americans, evoking the Wild West and all its romantic lawlessness, as in "Pecos Bill," or the tamer realm of southwestern professional archaeology, as in "the Pecos Conference." In May 1999 the name reached American consciousness in a new way, as newspapers around the country reported a remarkable homecoming. After more than seventy years, the descendants of Pecos Pueblo (most of whom live today west of old Pecos in Jemez Pueblo; see Schroeder 1979) were able to repatriate the remains of nearly two thousand human beings and one thousand religious objects that had been excavated and sent to the Harvard Peabody Museum from 1915 to 1929 by the archaeologist Alfred V. Kidder (Baca 1999).

The actual Pecos repatriation process began in 1991 when the governor and tribal archaeologist of Jemez Pueblo conducted meetings with National Park Service representatives and other Jemez tribal members regarding the return of the long-alienated objects and remains as a result of the 1990 federal legislation that finally provided procedures for this longstanding dream. As Carey Goldberg reported in a *New York Times* article on 20 May 1999, the Pecos collection may be the largest taken from a single site in U.S. history, as Kidder sought to "lay the foundation for modern archaeological techniques" by peeling the site apart layer by layer (Goldberg 1999). What Kidder excavated, along with a few other items, had been stored and studied at distant locales in Massachusetts since at least 1929: the Peabody Museums located at Harvard University in Cambridge and the Phillips Academy in Andover. The repatriation negotiations that began in 1991 came to a close on 18 May 1999, when Barbara Landis Chase, head of Phillips Academy, read a formal statement expressing "sadness and regret for unintentional disrespect given by the expedition that exhumed the ancestors' remains from their ancient burial places. It is right, just and fitting to return with the greatest reverence and care the remains of the ancestors and burial and sacred objects into the hands of their descendants" (Walker 1999).

More than 130 crates were packed up for the 2,200-mile trip home that began on 20 May ("Jemez Remains" 1999). On 22 May, the 53-foot semitrailer truck in which the ancestral Pecos people journeyed was met by hundreds of their descendants at a site located in the Pecos Monument National Park. Many of these people walked over a hundred miles for three or four days to arrive for the private reburial ceremony, which had to be created on the basis of intense discussions (Goldberg 1999; Navrot 1999). In the words of Randolph Padilla, former governor of the Pueblo and coordinator for the repatriation activities, "We don't have a reburial ceremony. . . . We've never had to do that. We went back and forth with religious leaders to decide what to do" (Robbins 1999: 16). And what was done was simple, sad, and joyous. The walk to the burial site was led by the second lieutenant governor of Jemez, Ruben Sando, who carried the Pecos Pueblo governor's cane that had been given to the pueblo by Spanish administrators of what is now New Mexico. Near Sando walked Ada Romero, who sprinkled corn meal along the way. At the burial site, Sando is reported to have said that the "reburial symbolized a new beginning for the Jemez people. . . . Our ancestors and other tribes who were born here, played here, sang and danced along this beautiful Pecos River valley and mountain, who were taken away for so many years . . . are now home . . . I guarantee to all of you that they are joyously happy, as we all are" (Navrot 1999).

I am writing this book from a beautiful location that not so long ago was American Indian territory, most certainly that of the Southern Ute people who are now confined to a small reservation about fifteen miles away. A small river runs not twenty yards from my house, and along its banks grow enormous Ponderosa pine trees that have witnessed the movement of both Indian and non-Indian peoples into this area for at least the past two hundred years. The river and these trees compel me to write something that is neither mere narration nor mere complicity with the story as it has always been told. The critical philosopher Walter Benjamin, writing in response to the horrors of World War I, believed that history should be studied on the basis of present concerns and that it should "seize hold of a memory as it flashes up in a moment of danger" and as it articulates historical trauma. To not do so is to endanger "both the content of the tradition and its receivers. . . . Only that historian will have the gift of fanning the spark of hope in the past who is firmly convinced that *even the dead* will not be safe from the enemy if he wins. And this enemy has not ceased to be victorious" (Benjamin 1968: 255).

If we were to enter a door into United States experience that would reveal, in dense fashion, its history of interactions with Native Americans, what would it be? The answer is any number of events, symbols, or practices. One might, for instance, trace the knots of anger that survive in Navajo memories about the Long Walk or in Lakota histories of the Wounded Knee massacre or in Hawaiian stories of environmental and cultural degradation. One might gather the descendants of schoolchildren who attended one of the many Indian boarding schools that had as their goal the purging of Native American language and culture. One might ponder the deeper meaning of the University of Illinois's "mascot," Chief Illiniwek, and compare this symbol of the savage, noble or otherwise, to more than five hundred years of European identity construction based on their fantasies about Indians. One might continue the story of Pecos Pueblo as it ponders the meaning of the return of some

3

of its ancestors, many of whom were disturbed after eight hundred years of rest.

I have chosen, in my desire to illuminate a big picture, as if by means of a flashbulb going off in a darkened room, one single U.S. law to begin my story. This law, the Native American Graves Protection and Repatriation Act (NAGPRA) was passed in 1990 and marked a watershed in American awareness about its first inhabitants and their descendants (see appendix). What the reader must realize, as you would by exploring any of the topics listed above, is that the subject of this book is only the tip of an iceberg so vast that if you looked briefly through the glass you would gasp at the immensity of the events upon which this all rests. The question of *objects*, of course, is the central theme to this study of a law concerned with repatriation of human remains and associated objects that are funerary, sacred, and culturally significant. We briefly look at who has them, how they got them, who now wants them, and how the NAGPRA law facilitates or impedes their return. We are also forced to look at the fact that the alienation of objects ranges from a simple matter of malconveyance—some misunderstanding, some improper, uninformed gifting—to some sales made from desperation or greed, some manipulating, some elaborate coveting, much grave robbing, and a good bit of theft.

These objects, these human remains, these once living entities, these imprisoned spirits—however one views them—have accumulated to such a degree that it becomes difficult or embarrassing or shameful to answer the question "Why?" Why were they taken? Why were so many of them desired? In attempting to answer what should be a simple question, surely available in the accession records of museums, we step through the looking glass and for a moment feel like we are falling, weightless, disoriented into silence. Because to answer the simple how's and why's and why not's (Why not just give the things back?) means to return to Benjamin's notion of history and the *double silence* that occurs when one side cannot speak the truth because it does not have the power to do so, whereas the powerful side either does not have the information it needs to speak truthfully, or it must keep from speaking in order not to spill the beans of power (see Felman 1999: 211–13).

To open up the silences to answer the question of why thus means looking back into not only the past century and a half of American history, when most of the objects were acquired or purloined, but

4

into many more centuries of European history as it encountered, even especially among its own humanity, indescribable differences and then tried to boil these differences down to describable and manageable and possessable qualities and quantities. In defining itself, Europe tried to define and control and own the world. This was done through governmental policies and military conquests and also through trading companies, private enterprises, educational institutions, world's fairs, and museums. This was done, in part, by an academic discipline, called anthropology, that grew up in the belly of colonialism, both feeding it and trying to cut out pieces of its liver as it matured—but it was also done by history, by literature, by biology, by art history, by linguistics, and, most of all, by philosophy, the framework for all the other practices, for better and for worse.

To open up the silences, a whole interdisciplinary, academic set of pursuits has grown up, following the practices first laid down by early-twentieth-century critical theorists such as Benjamin. These practices today, viewed as a breath of fresh air by some, are variously labeled as postcolonialism, critical archaeology, critical museum studies, critical cultural studies, critical southern studies, or just plain radical relativism, the latter attached by those who smell "liberal," Satanic sulphur in all these critical this 'n' that's. What is more disturbing, however, than academic hot air is the specter of their temples—that is, museums—being gutted. This is more disturbing to some people than anything going on in Whiteclay, Nebraska, where Indians either drink themselves to death or are murdered by the squatters on their land.

It is widely believed and felt—and feeling cannot and must not be left out of these discussions, because the issues are deeply emotional—that the objects that may leave the museums as a result of the new laws were initially rescued from oblivion and that the fate of our entire world depends on their being retained for the good of not only science but of the people who need scientists and curators to tell them what these objects mean and who can care for them properly. The objects were beautiful, grotesque, quaint, pitiful—in short, out on a limb, in a bad way, orphaned, badly cared for, or just plain too typical of some important notion that they had to be taken, rescued, curated, cared for, and displayed as national or world patrimony. They might be a "type specimen," thus embodying a Platonic essence that should be accessible as a touchstone or a measuring rod. They might be pregnant with possibility, waiting in secret until a key could unlock their true meaning. They might just be one of a kind, reflecting if not the genius of an artist then the spirit of an entire, and vanishing, authentic people. They might simply be bones that needed to be kept carefully away until they can be thoroughly studied, using each new scientific technique that comes along. They might even be a piece of us, of our past, and some people believe we have already lost too much of it to give up any more without a fight.

Whatever went wrong was realized as being quite wrong at the time by those who were powerless to stop the process. Somewhere, sometime, they had been transformed from who they were in all their multiplicity into who they were told they were. Now those who possessed their objects and relatives' bodies had the means to prove it. Universal truth claims—whether made by Christians, Hegelians, or scientists—are just that: powerful conceptual machines backed by the facts of biology (we are one species, after all) that extend themselves to human experience by saying "You are us, but as yet you don't know it," just as the missionaries said "You have known God, but the devil has blinded your memory." For Christian missionaries, difference was thus easy to explain as the variety of ways a trickster like Satan could pull the wool over the pagan eyes. But for the children of the Enlightenment, difference posed a greater mystery, and they had neither world enough nor time to figure it out through direct experience. The objects would have to do.

The passing of the Native American Graves Protection and Repatriation Act in 1990 by the U.S. Congress marked the creation of a watershed in relationships between Native Americans (including Native Hawaiians) and universities, museums, and federal agencies across the United States. Ten years later it is apparent that the effects and varied meanings of NAGPRA have reached deeply into U.S. society, shaking up many worn-out, forgotten, or conveniently unarticulated assumptions about human rights, tribal versus national sovereignty, cultural property, and the politics of possession and representation. It has awakened the American and international conscience to the notion that perhaps there is a problem with taking Peruvian "ice princess" remains on the road or keeping mum about the location of the physical remains of Ishi for the better part of the twentieth century. It has contributed to absurd, if predictable, leaps between "Kennewick man" remains and alien culture heroes (of the *Star Trek* variety) and, more insidiously, between these same remains and the suggestion that maybe American Indians are not first, sovereign peoples at all. NAGPRA has been a wake-up call, but it is one to which most of us are still responding clumsily, stumbling groggily under five hundred years of guilt and amnesia. In ten short years the law has changed the very language we speak, as terms such as *Anasazi, remains, artifacts, objects, ruins, property*, and even *theft* have come under intense scrutiny, trickling down to the arena to which most Americans marginal to Native American peoples and societies gain their culture and historical understanding, the Discovery and Travel channels on their televisions.

On a more immediate level, passage of the law has created practical problems for tribal governments struggling to address the sad, frustrating, and expensive consultation and repatriation process. It has created an added layer of cynicism about American intentions as some museums drag their feet in meeting the law, therein placing the burden of action on the already strapped tribes. And what may be even worse, it has created new sources of conflict between and among Native American peoples themselves over issues of procedure, jurisdiction, affiliation, and interpretation. The law, which was designed to redress longstanding wrongs, has been nothing less than a nightmare for many of its participants, even as it stands as one of the most powerful human rights mechanisms in United States history.

The purpose of this monograph is to offer a partial retrospective and cautious prospective about the ways the issues surrounding NAGPRA implementation have grown in scope and complexity over the past decade, one that can suggest to the reader something about the importance of looking at American history and politics regarding indigenous rights in new ways as the Columbian encounter drags itself into another millennium.

By concentrating on the various cross-cutting motivations and players involved in NAGPRA repatriation, this monograph provides a case study of what the editors of this series call the "complex patterns of choice and necessity involved" in addressing any longstanding grievance in indigenous affairs worldwide. What it is hoped the reader will understand from this book is that NAGPRA is a cultural and political process as well as a legal "event," one that will be shaped for long years to come by a wide variety of participants who will find themselves moving back and forth across borders of alliance and solidarity. The book does not ask the reader to take a "side," although it cannot help but ask why the path to justice is as dark and murky as the labyrinth of storerooms in any major natural history museum. While it may be the case that the study of NAGPRA may tell us as much about ourselves as Americans as it does about the issue at hand, this book will be viewed by its author as a failure if it does not make us look away from the mirror and across to those holding it up for our gaze.

The book is divided into two parts, each emphasizing different key points. Part 1, "The Historical and Legal Contexts of the Repatriation Movement," illustrates the first key point, the processual nature of the law. Chapter 1, "Empire, Alienation, and the Museum Experience," examines the imperial and nation-building contexts for collecting and displaying the spoils of victory over the "savage" inhabitants of a nation founded in Puritanism, slavery, and capitalism. The next two chapters examine important elements of the Native American repatriation movement as it unfolded from the 1880s through the 1980s and contested the intersection of collecting, scientific practice, and the continued oppression of first peoples on the continent. These three chapters also illustrate a second key point, which is that repatriation activities did not just emerge in 1990 with NAGPRA but constituted the foundation for the creation of NAGPRA. A close examination of repatriation movement activities brings forward a third important point, which is that repatriation and reburial involve deeply religious, humanitarian, and human rights matters. In many ways, NAGPRA combines the intent of the American Indian Religious Freedom Act with that of the Archaeological Resources Protection Act and improves on both of them by providing ways to insert meaningful contestation of taken-for-granted cultural assumptions underlying the American legal system. Further, by addressing human rights issues, NAGPRA goes beyond the national and into the international realm of lobbying and political action.

Part 2, "Interpretation, Compliance, and Meaning of NAGPRA," examines the extra-legal aspects of the law in much more detail, emphasizing a fourth point, that a law can be a dense symbol laden with deep layers of cultural meaning, as well as a set of regulations. The symbolic aspects of NAGPRA allow it to be implemented in ways that expand American Indian law into more pluralistic dimensions and allow its intersection with international law. While chapter 4 continues the historical focus of chapters 2 and 3 that outlines the important events of the repatriation movement, it examines the NAGPRA process in more interpretive depth by focusing on a case study of the consultation process mandated by NAGPRA as it unfolded at the college where I work. The problems and concerns raised by this process are scrutinized in chapter 5, where eleven main concerns are outlined, ranging from the procedural to the interpretive and cultural. Issues of scientific authority, sovereignty, and cultural affiliation impasses are raised in this section, which suggests that NAGPRA may be as much nightmare as remedy. In chapter 6 it is suggested that NAGPRA is an imperfect solution to centuries-old injustices that embodies as many contradictions as it addresses. It opens old wounds, creates new problems, and reveals itself to be deeply implicated in the practices it supposedly critiques. Nonetheless, it has already brought home many ancestors, eased much suffering, and highlighted many concerns that North American first peoples have in common with indigenous peoples worldwide. For the law to be truly effective, however, it must be considered as much more than a type of cultural justice thrown out as a form of "appeasement" to the repatriation movement participants. It must be presented and developed as a form of economic distributive justice, one that entails the reallocation of resources so that the law can be implemented as it was intended, so that full justice can be achieved and the double silence filled with more than white noise. I conclude the book by considering how the repatriation movement has changed my own field of inquiry and practice, that of anthropology, and how it will forever be ingrained in the practices of my institution, a publicly funded, liberal arts college.

Part 1: The Historical and Legal Contexts of the Repatriation Movement

I

Museums and Objects of Empire

Whoever has emerged victorious participates to this day in the triumphal procession in which the present rulers step over those who are lying prostrate. According to traditional practice, the spoils are carried along in the procession. They are called cultural treasures, and a historical materialist views them with cautious detachment. For without exception the cultural treasures he surveys have an origin which he cannot contemplate without horror. They owe their existence not only to the efforts of the great minds and talents who have created them, but also to the anonymous toil of their contemporaries. There is no document of civilization which is not at the same time a document of barbarism. — Walter Benjamin, "Theses on the Philosophy of History"

While Boas might have questioned whether the tendency is inherent in museum display per se, it seems likely that in an ideological milieu befogged by evolutionary racialist assumption, such an object orientation often contributed to a degrading and distancing objectification of the "Others" who had made the objects, and who were themselves literally objectified in museum displays. — George W. Stocking Jr., "Philanthropoids and Vanishing Cultures"

Object Collecting and Empire Building

The story of the relationship of the United States of America to the continent's first peoples can perhaps be summarized in one phrase: Manifest Destiny. This well-worn concept not only refers to a divine mandate that America expand Christian influence across a continent full of "wildlife" and "savagery," but it has grown over more than four centuries to symbolize a wider variety of elements that have deep meaning to the American imagination. Perhaps the most powerful sense of the term is a millennial one that signals a new world order (one that still seems upside-down or backward to many) where insiders, or natives, are transformed into outsiders, or enemies, by newcomers who see themselves as the true Americans God destined them to be.

When this religious and cultural impulse is combined with the activities of empire building, much light can be shed on the reasons why millions of American Indian and Native Hawaiian human remains and cultural objects were obtained by museums and private collections. It takes not only territorial expansion, population growth, and ethnic cleansing to ensure the success of continental expansionism, but also some kind of "mass communication" to convince the public that the possession of territories, resources, bodies, and property of natives-turned-enemies is justified. As Edward F. Fry noted in a relatively early critique of museum practices, "The objects of art . . . that had once been commissioned or taken as spoils of war were recognized as the physical embodiment of a nation's history; and in most instances these works also, through their iconography, graphically related the historical events of a nation and its people" (Fry 1972: 104).

Seneca historian John C. Mohawk traces this acquisitive practice to the beginnings of early agriculture, when armed forces were deployed to acquire provisions for growing permanent settlements (Mohawk 2000: 30). He adds that the later growth of cities made plunder and other forms of aggression a necessity: "Civilizations sent armies in search of goods such as mineral deposits, fishing grounds, slaves, wood, agricultural produce, tribute, and any number of other sources of wealth. Plunder on such a scale gave rise to what we term imperialism: the form of organized theft practiced by civilizations with the capacity to apply military force to peoples less powerful than themselves" (32).

Although what Bruce Trigger (1989: 295) calls "conscious archaism" was present in societies from the Aztecs to the ancient Egyptians, Greeks, and Romans (i.e., using the remains of the past as religious symbols, "relics of specific rulers or periods of national greatness"), by the middle of the second century B.C.E. art collecting intensified, as Romans grew wealthy from the spoils gathered throughout their imperial domain (Etienne and Etienne 1992: 14–15). This practice continued with the Crusades, when medieval Christendom sought to get to Jerusalem, the center of the universe, often depicted in maps as Christ's navel. Frustrated by the power of Islam, the future Europeans traveled in ever-widening circles, hoping to acquire goods and grace through a back door by means of what came to be known as the Voyages of Discovery, which extended the Christian search for religious real estate to the rest of the globe (Greenblatt 1991: 45–51). This quest resulted in a commercial and social revolution that exploded in the fifteenth century (Mohawk 2000: 88–89, 104–5) and led to a "most unnatural craving" for gold and silver, whereby the "mercantile and the religious [would be] intertwined" for centuries (Greenblatt 1991: 64, 71).

Historian John Howland Rowe notes that before the Renaissance, "the writings by Europeans concerned with cultural differences can be summed up by saying that works of this sort were not numerous, and that the best ones were neglected or disbelieved" (Rowe 1974: 68–69). It was not until interest was renewed in the intellectual products of Greek and Roman antiquity that cultural contrasts became studied systematically, if unevenly, throughout Christendom (69). Although the first descriptions of ancient monuments are reported from the fourteenth century, the founder of the discipline of archaeology is said to be Ciriaco de' Pizzicolli, or Cyriacus (1391–1452), an Italian merchant who fought in the 1444 Crusade against the Turks. Deciding that monuments and inscriptions were "more faithful witnesses of classical antiquity than are the texts of ancient writers" (Etienne and Etienne 1992: 26), Cyriacus documented these observations in his *Commentary upon Ancient Things*, only a few pages of which survive (Rowe 1974: 71).

The possession of marvelous and authentic objects thus became an important sign of prestige throughout seventeenth-century Europe, when collectors such as Thomas Howard, the English earl of Arundel, mobilized a vast network to acquire sculptures and other antiquities. By the eighteenth century the "thing to do" for British subjects of means was to take the "grand tour" of renowned homes, castles, and museums of Europe. These tours were facilitated by the weakening of the Ottoman Empire, when more often than not Turkish officials looked the other way when antiquities were "exported" from their regions of origin, either in the pockets of tourists as souvenirs or in the cargo holds of ships groaning under the weight of Greek and Roman loot. A series of plundering scandals emerged in the 1800s, as the great powers of Europe looted each other's heritage.

By the late eighteenth century, archaeology and warfare were intertwined. Military expansion facilitated archaeological access to remote parts of the world, while archaeological activities helped justify the actions of imperialists who saw themselves as bringing civilization to the dark parts of the globe. Napoleon stole printing machines from the Vatican on his way to Egypt and used them to spread the good news of the emperor's respect for Islam and his various proclamations regarding the new French administration. The printing presses facilitated the work of Napoleon's Institut d'Egypte, formed in 1798 to conduct a wide array of scientific work. One expedition not only discovered the Rosetta Stone, which opened the door to the decipherment of hieroglyphics and the founding of "Egyptology," but facilitated the plunder of Egyptian art and culture (Boorstin 1983: 545–47; Trigger 1989: 39).

THE ELGIN MARBLES SCANDAL

A contemporary traveler who would like to see the Athenian Parthenon sculptures, those white icons of civilization so exquisite that the great poet Percy Bysshe Shelley was rendered mute in their presence, would have to buy a ticket to London, not to Greece. Why London? Because the sculptures have been in the British Museum since their removal from Greece by the English Ambassador Plenipotentiary of His Britannic Majesty to the Sublime Porte of Selim III, Sultan of Turkey in Constantinople, Thomas Bruce, seventh earl of Elgin and descendant of the famous Scottish freedom fighter Robert the Bruce. If this sounds confusing, it is. The reason that Bruce was ambassador to Constantinople and not to Athens was because Greece was part of the Ottoman Empire (with its capital at Constantinople) during this period of "severe international disorder" caused by the Napoleonic Wars (Rudenstine 2000: 30). Beginning in July of 1801, teams of workers carted away twelve or more pedimental statues, fifty-six frieze slabs, and fifteen metopes from the Parthenon. They made their way around the Acropolis, spiriting away the frieze of the Temple of Athena Nike, one caryatid from the Erechtheum, and countless other items (Etienne and Etienne 1992: 69).

Although Elgin justified the alienation of the sculptures on the grounds that they were badly cared for by the barbaric Turks and were furthermore in danger of being taken away by Britain's great rival, France, his predominant motivation, it appears, was to have them installed at his Scottish manor. For various reasons, including a cash-flow problem to repay debt, Elgin abandoned his plan to landscape his home with the booty, offering instead to sell the Elgin Marbles to the British government.

In 1816 a British parliamentary committee was created to evaluate

Elgin's request and to look into the circumstances of the acquisition of the Elgin Marbles. Elgin produced a letter to prove that he had received permission from the Ottoman Turks to remove the sculptures, but a careful search in the Istanbul archives by David Rudenstine (2000: 32–35) has turned up nothing but evidence that Elgin's documents were invalid. It appears, instead, that it was the lax policies of the Ottoman Turks regarding the protection of antiquities of their conquered territories (facilitated by bribes given to Ottoman officials) that "validated" the removal of the Elgin Marbles, and nothing more. Pillage of these monuments occurred unabated until 1805, when excavation and the removal of artworks were prohibited, although sculptures were to disappear from the Parthenon until 1811 (Etienne and Etienne 1992: 68, 74–75).

Native Americans in the European Imagination

> when they will not give a doit to relieve a lame
> beggar, they will lay out ten to see a dead
> Indian. — William Shakespeare, *The Tempest*

The point of discussing the Elgin Marbles is to indicate that the theft of cultural patrimony is not unique by any means to the United States. It is an ingrained practice of nation and empire building, one that is tied up with the need to create a future built on what is often little more than fantasies about the past. The "need" to protect ancient Greek objects from the perceived dangers of the modern world informed a parallel attitude regarding the possession of objects taken from the Americas. Although perceived as less magnificent than the Elgin Marbles, Native American museum specimens were nevertheless subjected to the same kind of scrutiny necessary to make good decisions regarding the antiquity, purity, creativity, or savagery of humans, and they were collected with increasing passion.[1]

One of the earliest published descriptions of Native American antiquities in the possession of a European appeared in London in 1656 in the form of a small catalog entitled "Museum Tradescantianum; or, A Collection of Rarities preserved at South Lambeth near London, by John Tradescant." On page 51 a "Black Indian girdle made of wampum peek best sort" is mentioned, which indicates that the owner was familiar enough with wampum to distinguish various grades of this precious and important class of objects. Another reference to wampum emerges in 1681 in the "Catalogue and Description of the Natural and Artificial Rarities" in the possession of Gresham College, London: "Several sorts of Indian Money, called wampam peage, 'Tis made of a shell, formed into small *Cylinders*, about a 14 of an inch long, and 1/5 over, or somewhat more or less: and so being bored as *Beads* and put upon *Strings*, pass among the Indians, in their usual Commerse, as Silver and Gold amongst us" (Bushnell 1920: 82).

European interest in Indians and their objects began with the mercantile voyages of the fifteenth and sixteenth centuries when living American Indians traveled—voluntarily or not—on return voyages to Europe. Upon arrival they were often displayed, in cities such as Paris, as living exotics or "wild men" who, as Michel de Montaigne argued in his famous essay "Concerning Cannibals," behaved in a more civilized manner than did the French, who were embroiled in bloody wars of religion that led to worse atrocities than merely consuming an enemy after his death. Amerigo Vespucci's accounts of life in the Americas were printed in several languages, and Thomas More's classic, *Utopia*, derived its inspiration from idealized Native American lifeways.

Perhaps the most influential writer to idealize Native American political freedom was eighteenth-century social philosopher Jean Jacques Rousseau, who lamented humankind's fall from a state of nature where inherent strength, freedom, and dignity were imagined to be the norm. The "noble savagery" exhibited by Indians was far superior, in Rousseau's view, to the state of decadence into which Europeans had fallen, exemplified by rigid social organizational rules and an exploitative division of labor (Rousseau 1952).

Native Americans and the American Project

As all schoolchildren in America are taught, the Puritans headed west in the seventeenth century to fulfill their destiny to create God's "city on the hill" and to escape cultural and religious persecution. In "New" England they encountered a wide variety of inhabitants who they attempted to bend to their spiritual will, much as their Crusader predecessors had the Muslim infidels. Captivity narratives from this time reveal the Puritan belief that "enemies in the wilderness" were placed on earth by God's "strange providence" to test the faith of the suffering Puritans. Indians were necessary as a reminder of all that the New England Puritans should not be, and of God's justice on an earth still inhabited by "merciless Heathens."

When John Locke thus pronounced in 1690 that "in the beginning, all the world was America" (Locke 1952: 35), he did so not out of the kind of admiration held by Rousseau for the ways Indians followed natural law, serving as models for democratic rule, but to point out the folly of owning property collectively on unimproved, unproductive land. Indians neither lived by the laws of grace nor those of capital, a theme that would result in their dispossession for the next two centuries as Locke's secular, Calvinist views were increasingly embodied in what Max Weber would call the "Protestant ethic and the spirit of capitalism." They would also be embodied in American ideals of progress, civilization, and Christian *lebensraum* (literally, "living room" expansionism, as it would come to be called in Germany), known in North America as Manifest Destiny.

The intersection of European immigrants with the American landscape and its Native peoples would be an odd crucible for the creation of American national identity, one marked by the simultaneous romanticization and denigration of the Indian presence on the continent. This contradictory and opportunistic tendency would manifest itself in various ways: through archaeological debates about the antiquity of Native Americans vis-à-vis all humankind; through a burgeoning tourist market that built itself around an invented West; through a national project to open up the frontier for agriculture and mining by brutally sweeping Native inhabitants out of the way; and through the building of museums that would house and exhibit the products of archaeological and looting activities. The idea today that any museums might be "emptied" of their holdings through repatriation seems like blasphemy to many, because of the ways these objects had gained a symbolic status "similar in function to that of the relics of Christian martyrs" (Fry 1972: 104). This quasi-religious status of museum holdings took on a large significance in the United States and Canada, which had no heritage on the North American continent other than what they could appropriate from American Indians or invent based on European traditions (see Handler 1985). The debates over property that emerged and that continue today have always been at the heart of the "American project" as they were, in Susan Scheckel's (1998: 9) terms, "simultaneously debates over what is proper to, and thus constitutive of, the nation."

Archaeology in North America

Arguably the first major expedition organized to collect objects of American "natural" history was Lewis and Clark's Corps of Discovery trek across the continent from 1803 to 1805 to solidify Thomas Jefferson's purchase of the vast Louisiana Territory from France. Animals, plants, geological specimens, and Native American artifacts gathered during the journey were eventually installed in Peale's Museum in Philadelphia so as to assert "the nation's control over the newly acquired area" (Conn 1998: 34). Thomas Jefferson's interest in the natural history of the Americas was a reflection of his belief that the physical conquest of the continent needed intellectual taming as well (34).

The scientific interests of eighteenth-century Enlightenment thinkers such as Jefferson, himself an amateur archaeologist (see Jefferson 1964; Hallowell 1960: 10–19), were developed more fully in the nineteenth century when North American archaeologists contributed to the discussions concerning the age of humanity in the Western Hemisphere (see Kehoe 1998). By the 1850s Europeans were coming to grips with the power of evolutionary theory, not only as elaborated in Wallace's and Darwin's theories of nonteleological change based on adaptation, but also as these biological theories were misused to support writers such as Herbert Spencer, who believed that competition was at the heart of all *social progressive* change. Bolstering these nonscripturally grounded views of human origins were the discoveries of geological sites where human remains were mixed with those of Pleistocene-epoch fauna (Meltzer 1983: 4–7). Humans were increasingly appearing to be older than the biblical date of 4004 B.C. calculated by Bishop Ussher.[2]

Although, as David J. Meltzer (1983: 5) reports, most archaeological activity in the United States prior to the 1860s was concerned with mapping and surveying the mounds and other earthworks found in river valleys, the search for evidence of Paleolithic (Stone Age) humans in the Americas dominated the activities of amateur, government, and university scientists during the final decades of the nineteenth century. The intellectual excitement generated by the European findings of remains predating Adam and Eve led to new types of practices that would culminate in the excavation, collection, and storage of hundreds of thousands of Native American skeletons and skeletal parts in museums.

The Exhibition and Curation of Power Relations

As Steven C. Dubin has cogently observed, "Museums have always featured *displays of power*: great men, great wealth, or great deeds." They have always been sites of controversy and cultural struggle, and they have always been about displaying, demonstrating, and "ratif[ying] claims of superiority" (Dubin 1999: 3). Many scholars who have studied the history of museums refer to these institutions both as places and as *processes* wherein history is not only "presented" through its displayed objects but is revised and even forgotten, as objects can never convey the complexity of "what really happened." In America, getting at the truth of things has always been colored by ambivalence about Native Americans. Were Indians the symbols of America's desire for freedom and suspicion of power and progress as defined by Europeans? Were Indians the impediments to progress, needing to be wiped out, only to be reconstructed in the tourist and national imaginary? In the view of historian Curtis M. Hinsley (1989: 170):

> After the Civil War, as the venue of destruction shifted to the trans-Mississippi West, a new cultural phenomenon emerged to help resolve the long-standing ambivalence: the museum process. The resolution was achieved by announcing and then demonstrating the end of Indian history. The museum process constructed a meaning of Indian demise within the teleology of manifest destiny; it indirectly addressed the insistent doubts of Gilded Age Americans over the import of industrial capitalism; and it did so by encasing, in time and space, the American Indian. Dehistoricization was the essence of the process.

Within this process, as Hinsley further explains, Native peoples underwent a series of representational transitions in Wild West shows, World's Fair exhibits, museum displays, souvenir shops, and publications. They were transformed from living communities to "life groups" in the museum exhibition hall, and from autonomous masters of their own destiny to market commodities and museum objects (Hinsley 1989: 170).

THE WORLD'S COLUMBIAN EXHIBITION, 1893

Those aspects of civilized society that most people take for granted today as "natural" and commonsense—museums, world's fairs, primitive art exhibits, tourism, and souvenir hunting—are the legacies of

Entry ticket: World's Columbian Exposition, Chicago, Illinois, 1 May–30 October 1893.

imperialism and nation-state building. The great public museums of Europe were born in the "age of empire," where the mentality of the Crusades met that of "imperial show and tell" (Willinsky 1998) mediated by the perceived necessity for the burgeoning natural sciences to gather data. The first catalog for the Pio-Clementine Museum in the Vatican was published in 1792, the British Museum opened in London in 1753, and the Musée Napoléon opened in Paris in 1801. In the words of Etienne and Etienne, "These museums were hungry for fine pieces whose prestige would contribute to the glory of the states that owned them" (1992: 66). Everything became a commodity in this context, even human beings, who were exhibited in living and dead states at the more than fifty international fairs held in the latter half of the nineteenth century. John Willinsky paints a vivid picture: "The Centennial Exhibition held in Philadelphia in 1876 featured pavilions divided into what were, in effect, racial zones, and the 1893 World's Columbian Exposition in Chicago split the world between the White City, as the pristine pinnacle of civilization, and the Midway Plaisance, as the baser home of such ethnological exhibits as 'Darkest Africa,' set amid the belly dancers and strip shows" (Willinsky 1998: 76).

"Native villages" became a common feature of American fairs after the Chicago Columbian exhibition and were built with the consultation of well-known anthropologists, some of whom brought students to the exhibits to offer them "an adventure in social Darwinism" (Willinsky 1998: 76). In other words, the exhibits of Native peoples from around the world were designed to commemorate "not only the triumph of the West in conquering the better part of the world, but also the growing gap between this achievement and the place of other peoples" (76). One could experience, by walking through the streets of the Midway, the living proof of Western progress and the defeat of the barbarians and savages who had not yet moved up the evolutionary ladder and who probably never would because of their presumed racial inferiority. These attitudes were impressed upon the fairgoers as they viewed the exhibits and read the copy that accompanied the photographic souvenirs that could be purchased at the events.

One such portfolio of photographs, *The Chicago Times Portfolio of Midway Types*, produced by the *Chicago Times* newspaper in 1893,[3] provides a disturbing glimpse into the mind set of the times. Along with Javanese "beauties," "Hindoo jugglers," and Cairo "donkey boys" are depicted a "group of Sudanese" from a region of Egypt "very obnoxious to Great Britain" and Samoans characterized as "voracious cannibals" (*Chicago Times* 1893). The description of Dahomeans and other Africans as "repulsive savages" on the Midway and the omission of the "colored American" from the rest of the exhibits of civilized life prompted public intellectuals Ida B. Wells and Frederick Douglass to write a pamphlet entitled "The Reason Why the Colored American Is Not in the World's Columbian Exposition," some ten thousand copies of which were distributed during the fair (Willinsky 1998: 76).

The *Chicago Times* portfolio is heavily weighted toward orientalist photos of Javanese, Turks, Bedouins, Egyptians, and lion tamers, but some photos of Native Americans are included, divided sharply between the idealized "Esquimaux" and the denigrated Sioux. Note the shift in tone in these photo captions, which become oddly distanced from what the actual photos reveal once the author moves from the relatively harmless Arctic savages to the warlike enemies of the U.S. Army:

No. 66: All the Esquimaux

The earliest arrivals at the World's Exposition were the Esquimaux, who came when the winter's snow was still on the ground and the winds that blew had the tone and touch of the North Pole, and gave to them a genial welcome. There were nearly thirty of these peculiar people and in the great Fair grounds they built their village near the entrance to the State Buildings and there presented to the public their manner of life. The village contained all the paraphernalia of domestic and hunting pursuits—huts, dogs, boats, weapons, etc., etc., and in their secluded spot they gave their exhibitions of life as lived in "the Land of the Midnight Sun." The people were small but plump. The illustration shows the little ones.

No. 67: *Esquimau mother and child*
The World's Exposition was specially marked by the birth of an Esquimau child, to whom was given, in honor of the event, the name of Christopher Columbus. His picture, and that of the mother, is given above. They are excellent likenesses of the happy pair.

No. 140: A professional scalper

Toward the west end of the Midway was a little encampment of Sioux Indians. Foreigners must have been surprised when informed that among this band were men who had waged a bitter war against the United States, and who, unpunished, tented upon the most famous arena of peace the world had ever seen. History is not so old, nor memory so weak, as to permit the Custer Massacre in 1876 to be forgotten; yet Chief Rain-in-the-Face, whose picture is above, was a prominent actor in that massacre. His presence secured him an admiring audience, the recollection of his atrocities being no bar to that sentiment of adulation that transforms murderers into heroes.

No. 185: *A gentleman of leisure*

Ghost dances, government Indian agents and the regulars of the army have been quiet for nearly a year, there came the opportunity, and a timely one, for the copper-colored wards of the nation to put in a few months visiting at the Exposition. Having no friends or relatives in Chicago, the Sioux kept house—that is their squaws did—on "their own hook." To this hospitality of theirs (with a string to it) the visitors to the Great Fair were indebted for the opportunity of seeing Indians who have been thorns in the sides of Uncle Sam, not the most insignificant of whom was that valiant and veteran scalper, *Lone Dog*, appropriately presented above. No apology is submitted for the scantiness of his wardrobe, for he was clothed in vanity, and took an infinite delight in checking off his record of atrocities in peace and war. With all credit to Herr Hagenback [a lion tamer at the fair] for his skill in taming the most ferocious of animals, he failed nevertheless, to try his ability on the Indians of the West, and has not, therefore, satisfactorily demonstrated the completeness of his powers. Lone Dog has returned to his agency to be a "good" Indian until he thinks it will pay him to be a bad one and so enhance the historic value of his portrait.

27

No. 199: Two squaws

Any superfluity of sentiment is wasted on the Indian. He prefers scalps to taffy, and fire-water to tracts. He is monotonously hungry to kill somebody, a white man, if possible, another Indian if the white man is happily absent. The Indian woman, or squaw, is a shade worse in human deviltry than the male. In the picture above mildness, docility, kindness, loveableness, seem impersonated. Yet the records of massacres, for centuries, show that the squaw is the apotheosis of incarnate fiendishness. These two, "Pretty Face" and "Mary Hairy-Chin," may never have scalped, nor built a fire around a prisoner, or flayed an enemy alive, but that does not signify that they would not do it if they had the chance. Serfs they always are; friends never; companionable in the inverse ratio of distance. They belong to no ethical societies, dress reform clubs or art cliques; nor are sewing bees or donation parties in their categories of enjoyments. Savages, pure and cunning, they gave to the Midway the shadows of characters that cannot be civilized, and the solemnity of appearances as deceptive as the veiled claws of the tiger.

28

No. 232: Sitting Bull's log cabin

Civilization is sufficiently advanced in the West to place log cabins among the curios of human habitations. Among the magnificent structures on the Exposition grounds proper, nestled two squalid huts—a reproduction of Davy Crockett's cabin and also of an Australian squatter's hut. The log homes of Lincoln and Grant have become tiresomely familiar in the newspapers, as if no other persons had ever lived in such structures. In view of this craze for the fantastic humbleness in dwellings, the placing of Sitting Bull's Cabin on the Midway was only a judicious catering to the popular craving for oddities. If Sitting Bull had been only an ordinary Indian instead of a noted warrior, very few people would have given any attention to his house; but the man who defied the great United States, who fought, defeated, and slaughtered its troops, who caused the government more trouble than any other savage has ever caused it—this man's house was as imposing as a castle to his admirers; but to his enemies was the rudest kind of cattle shelter. The difference between it and the frontiersman's dwelling was in the color and the diffused variety of the dirt of its occupants. As the home for the cunningest Indian politician of the century, it met all his demands, as he needed no other pictures, statuettes or knick-knacks, than scalps, war clubs, rifles, and papoose cradles.

I suppose it could be argued that the text of these photo captions was not typical of American attitudes at the time, but without more information about the anonymous author it makes more sense to view the wording as the kind of language Americans (and European visitors) were accustomed to hearing, particularly in a climate with fresh memories of Custer's defeat. I present this language in some detail for two reasons.

The first is to provide a sense of the "moral climate" of the times regarding American Indians that both influenced anthropologists and others who dealt with Indians on a "professional" basis and against which some anthropologists—including archaeologists—struggled. The reality is that one can choose any one of the great "humanitarian" figures of the times—Charles Darwin, John Wesley Powell, Alice Fletcher, Frank Hamilton Cushing, James Mooney, and even Franz Boas—and find evidence of both humanism and racism, as none of these figures was able to completely escape the intellectual climate of his or her milieu.

The second reason I provide some of the language from the 1893 Midway portfolio is to impress upon the reader the extent to which many Americans believed that Native people were not human beings. Instead, they saw them as curiosities to be collected and sold and as quaint, and sometimes gruesome, souvenirs to be displayed. That this attitude is typically and sadly American is borne out in the late-nineteenth- and early-twentieth-century practice of not only attending the lynchings, torture, and torchings of African Americans but also of procuring postcards, body parts, strips of fabric, and other souvenirs of the violent events (Allen et al. 2000).[4]

Acquisition of Native American Human Remains and Cultural Objects

By the early decades of the twentieth century enormous collections of Native American human remains and objects had been amassed. As Pawnee scholar Emma Hansen reminds us, these collections were given infusions by a few powerful collectors such as George Dorsey (Field Museum of Natural History), Clark Wissler (American Museum of Natural History), George Heye (Heye Foundation in New York City, now the National Museum of the American Indian), and Frank Hamilton Cushing (Bureau of American Ethnology)(Hansen 1998: 3). The devastating conditions under which Native Americans were reduced by the turn of the century "allowed for large numbers of objects, which were mistakenly viewed as ethnographic remnants of dying and disappearing cultures, to be purchased by private museum collectors. Even ceremonial bundles, once the keystones of spiritual life, found their way to museum collections" (3).

A Sotheby Parke Bernet catalog produced for an auction held 15 November 1980, reveals a minuscule amount of the kind of objects that have been in circulation and the enormous dollar values placed on them: Catlinite pipes, wood ladles, birch bark panels and boxes, quilled and beaded moccasins, bandoliers, twined bags, pouches, "possible" bags, pipe bags, cradleboards, rifle scabbards, saddles, horse costumes, horse blankets, children's clothing, beaded hide dresses and shirts, beaded leggings, beaded and quilled belts, women's elk tooth dresses, beaded and quilled vests, dolls, pictograph books and ledger drawings, silver and turquoise jewelry, rawhide playing cards, Zuni and Hopi wooden kachinas, button blankets, horn spoons and ladles, basket hats, knife sheaths, horn daggers, whalebone clubs, argillite totem poles, wooden model canoes and totem poles and figurines and rattles and masks and frontlets, and pages upon pages of weavings, pottery, and baskets (Sotheby Parke Bernet 1980). These objects, some of which were undoubtedly alienated without their original owners' permission, represent just one day's auction activity at Sotheby's, and they are just a pinhead's worth of what all has been accumulated in private and public hands for the past few centuries, particularly after museums became involved in the collection business.

Early anthropology was heavily involved in the collection process. The first "collecting party" sponsored by the Smithsonian Institution's Bureau of American Ethnology sent geologist James Stevenson and ethnologist Frank Hamilton Cushing to the Southwest with orders to "find out all you can about some typical tribe of Pueblo Indians" (Green 1990: 3). By September of 1879 the expedition had arrived at Zuni Pueblo, where Cushing lived for four and one-half years and gathered thousands of objects that were sent not only to Washington and Berlin but to privately contracted locations (4, 15).

According to art historian Edwin L. Wade, there is a strong convergence between the "end of the Indian wars" in 1890 and the massacre at Wounded Knee and the development of the tourist and ethnic arts market in the Southwest that was stimulated by the building of the Atchison, Topeka, and Santa Fe Railroad. Indian fairs were invented, pothunting was stimulated, and anthropologists were sent out to purchase huge lots of art objects for museums (Wade 1985: 170–72). This history is no secret to most Americans, especially those who are Southwest prehistory buffs. What is not well known is that it was not just pottery and "curios" that collectors were after, but Indian skulls, bones, scalps, and sometimes whole heads and bodies. Many of the remains of Cheyenne men, women, and children slaughtered at the Colorado Sand Creek massacre of 1864 were sent to the Army Medical Museum, discussed below. Other remains from this massacre, such as scalps and women's pubic hair, were strung across the stage of the Denver Opera House (Thomas 2000: 53, 56–57).

REGULATIONS OF THE INDIAN OFFICE

In a few very brief, shocking pages, Suzan Shown Harjo of the American Indian Ritual Object Repatriation Foundation discusses the United States government policies that contributed in a major way to this dehumanizing treatment. One policy centering around the suppression of religious activities was linked to the nation's mission to civilize, Christianize, and deculturalize American Indians, which had begun in earnest by the end of the nineteenth century and involved collusion between the federal government, the military, and Christian organizations. In 1884, the secretary of the interior published a document called *Regulations of the Indian Office*, which not only mandated a Christian and English-only education for Indian children but "bann[ed] all traditional religious activities, ceremonies and dancing," including the Sun Dance, the activities of medicine men who disrupt civilizing practices, and any "ceremonies involving any exchange or elimination of property" (Harjo 1995: 5). Violations of the *Regulations* indicating that Indian leaders were "hostile" to the American government or its policies resulted in the deaths of many leaders, such as Sitting Bull, Big Foot, and Black Kettle; the imprisonment of leaders such as Geronimo; the massacre of men, women, and children at places such as Sand Creek, Washita, and Wounded Knee; and the "confiscation of sacred objects, funerary items and any cultural or personal property" (5). These objects, as Harjo further notes, were often transferred to agents, soldiers, and their families, who then sold or transferred them to other collectors.

"INDIAN CRANIA STUDY"

The second practice mandated by the U.S. government that filled museums was the collection of Indian bodies and body parts for various reasons, all of them somehow linked to "scientific research." Institutions such as the Army Medical Museum, founded in 1862 by Surgeon General William A. Hammond, initially wanted Indian bodies to advance the study of infectious diseases. By 1867–68 field medical doctors and officers were enjoined to "send 'Indian specimens' " to "augment the collection of Indian crania" (see Echo-Hawk and Echo-Hawk 1994: 25–26; Gulliford 2000: 16). Collections were amassed in both the United States and Europe based on the Smithsonian–Army Museum agreement, which "set in motion a decades-long practice of decapitating Native people, weighing their brains and shipping them as freight to Washington DC, for more 'study.' The crania were 'harvested' from massacre sites, battlefields, prisons, schools, burial grounds (including scaffolds, caves and water, basketry and pottery vessels) and even from hours-old graves. One officer reported waiting 'until cover of darkness' and departure of 'the grieving family' before 'I exhumed the body and decapitated the skull . . . which is transmitted forthwith' " (Harjo 1995: 4).

Harjo's piece provides other examples that leave no doubt that "some Indian people may have been murdered for their heads" and that the macabre treatment of Native American remains continued throughout the twentieth century in carnival displays, in research laboratories, and on the desk of a physical anthropologist in 1984, who was using the skull of a known Modoc chief as an ashtray (Harjo 1995: 4). Although, as Harjo reports, the complete report of the "Indian Crania Study" has been lost, the Smithsonian now has some of the Army Museum's records in its Anthropological Archives. We know that about one-fourth of the Smithsonian's collection of Native human remains is made up of around "4,500 crania, half of them obtained from the Army in 1898 and 1904" (4).

A Closer Look at Museum Possessions

Native American artifacts have always served as fine art investments, personal souvenirs, war booty, "power objects," research material, and "bait" to attract the wealthy donors who are the lifeblood of museums. In the case of the Smithsonian's Bureau of American Ethnology, twenty-five years' worth of collecting enterprises beginning in 1879 "removed thousands of objects of material culture from the pueblos, especially Zuni and the Hopi villages—an average of more than five artifacts per person at Zuni between 1879 and 1884—with profound effects on local economies and social structures" (Hinsley 1989: 176).

One only has to walk through the storerooms of Chicago's Field Museum or the University Museum of the University of Pennsylvania, as I have, to be stunned by the quantities of objects arrayed on shelves, curled around textile rollers, stored in drawers, and, increasingly, kept in climate-controlled vaults. It must be remembered, however, that by no means was every object in these institutions "stolen" or robbed from a grave. The manufacture of objects for trade and sale restructured the economies of entire tribes in response to the fur trade, and the boom in ethnic arts marketing that coincided with the end of the Indian wars brought even more objects into commercial circulation, many of them ending up in museums.

The quantity of the manufactured objects is overwhelming enough, but what concerns us here more directly is the quantity of human remains acquired by museums in the form of whole skeletons, part skeletons, skulls, a few soft tissue body parts (such as Ishi's brain, located in 1999 in a Smithsonian vault), and mummies.[5] As mentioned above, the 4,500 crania located in the Smithsonian are only about one-fourth of the whole story.

One of the first articles to bring this situation to the attention of the public was published in *Harper's Magazine* in 1989. The author of the piece, Douglas J. Preston, worked at the time as a writer and editor at the American Museum of Natural History in New York City and was drawn to the story, literally, by an overwhelming smell of mothballs coming from a storage room next to his office. He decided to investigate:

The mummies were stored in the defunct South American hall, a cavernous room with a tiled floor and fine, old oak cabinets. Most of the mummies were stacked along the back wall in a solid tier of black tin crates; several in the center of the room were in glass cases—apparently they had once been on display.

It was that morning when I first began to understand that the American Museum collected not only the art and artifacts of other cultures but bodies too, along with bones, skulls, whole skeletons—in a sense, collected *people* of other cultures. It is such a large collection that storing it is a headache. One curator had sacrificed half his office for the keeping of thousands of human skulls, each in its own little cardboard box. Lining the halls outside the anthropology department's offices were rows of lovely nineteenth-century cabinets;

in many of them, behind rippled glass, I glimpsed stacks of human
bones and mummified body parts. (Preston 1989: 66)

Preston read museum reports to learn how these human remains
were acquired and thus began the process of making public the story,
which was continued ten years later as notices emerged in the *Federal
Register* detailing the acquisition, affiliation, and intent to repatriate the
dead. For instance, one group of mummies was acquired in the 1870s
by an archaeologist who had been sent on an expedition to open an
Aleut mausoleum in the Bering Sea to bring back whatever remains he
could find to contribute to research on "early man" in the New World.
This collection—two men, two women, and a child—was added to
what became 600,000 such specimens estimated by the Native American
Rights Fund to be housed in collections throughout the United States
(Preston 1989: 67). More than 18,000 human remains were estimated
to be in the Smithsonian Institution alone, 700 of which (including
associated burial goods) were returned to the Larsen Bay Tribal Council
of Kodiak Island, Alaska, in 1991 (Native American Rights Fund 1991).

It is instructive to read the words of biologist Aleš Hrdlička in order
to get a sense of the attitude of those within the scientific community
who were presumably not directly concerned with the sale of human
remains for private gain. In a report he wrote for the Smithsonian's
Bureau of American Ethnology entitled *Skeletal Remains Suggesting or
Attributed to Early Man in North America* (1907), Hrdlička summarizes what
is known up to that point regarding human antiquity in America based
on analysis of human remains found in Louisiana, Canada, Mississippi,
Florida, Colorado, South Carolina, California, Illinois, Mexico, New
Jersey, Kansas, and Nebraska. Some remains were deliberately excavated
from mounds, while others were encountered inadvertently during the
digging of mines, foundations, and apple cellars. One skull, known as
the "Rock Bluff Cranium," was donated to the Smithsonian in 1866 after
it was found near a river in Illinois. The letter that accompanied the
skull was written by a Mr. McConnell of Jacksonville, Illinois, who was
eager to take part in the scientific activities going on around the country
regarding the identity of what some referred to as the "Mound Builder
race," distinct from the "Aztec," "Esquimaux," or "Indian" races:

I have sent to you by express a small box containing a human skull
of an unusual shape and formation. It is evidently not deformed, but

a natural skull, and from its shape and the place where it was found it is believed not to have belonged to any race of men now known to exist, and it is conjectured it may have belonged to a preadamite race, if there was any such race . . . I have never met with such a formed head, either living or dead, as this, and for this reason I send it to you, supposing from your opportunities in this branch of science you might determine if I am right in supposing this specimen not to have belonged to any one of the present races now extant . . .

In the neighborhood of this quarry and indeed all along the Illinois river are found many mounds called in this country Indian mounds, but evidently (they) have no connection with the present race of Indians. (Hrdlička 1907: 20, 28–29)

These old Smithsonian reports are sometimes more interesting for the insights we gain into the mind-set of the times than they are for their scientific accuracy. Hrdlička's descriptions are as meticulous as his criticism is scathing when some amateur botches an excavation or speculates wildly about unknown matters. This was, after all, "science," and Hrdlička was interested in establishing the identity, age, and evolutionary placement of the specimens accurately, carefully recording the extent to which the face juts out relative to a Negro, to an Indian, or to "a zoologically lower or otherwise substantially different type of humanity" (Hrdlička 1907: 60). In examining the "loess man" of Nebraska, Hrdlička quotes from Henry Fairfield Osborn's assessment of the remains as published in *Century Magazine* in January 1907 (p. 373):

The parts of the older four crania found beneath the clay layer are of the same type, it being probable that difference in age may account for the slight differences in the development of the supraorbital ridges . . . Estimating the back of the skull as of the same height as that of the normal Indian skull . . . we still have a very low cranial capacity and a type of skull resembling that of the Australian negro, which is virtually the lowest existing type known at present. While the supraorbital ridges are not more pronounced than that of the Australian negro, the forehead is even more receding and flattened. In other words, the portions of the cranium preserved indicate, so far as they go, a man of small cerebral capacity, having a brain inferior to that either of the Indian or the typical mound builder. (Hrdlička 1907: 71)

After studying the skeletal remains found in Nebraska and the reports of others who had also studied them, Hrdlička arrives at the conclusion that they "are in no way exceptional when compared with similar dimensions in skulls of Indians" (Hrdlička 1907: 97). This leads him to conclude more generally regarding all of those examples under review in his book, that "the somatological evidence bears witness against the geological antiquity of the remains and for their close affinity to or identity with those of the modern Indian" (98). This might have put an end to the organization of amateur and professional grave robbing, but Hrdlička has this to add:

> There may be discouragement in these repeated failures to obtain satisfactory evidence of man's antiquity in America, but there is in this also a stimulus to renewed, patient, careful, scientifically conducted and checked exploration: and, as Professor Barbour says in one of his papers on the Nebraska find, "the end to be attained is worth the energy to be expended." A satisfactory demonstration of the presence of a geologically ancient man on this continent would form an important link in the history of the American race, and of mankind in general. The Missouri and Mississippi drainage areas offer exceptional opportunities for the discovery of this link of humanity if such really exists. (98)

In other words, after careful study of all available evidence, the preeminent physical anthropologist of his day issued a mandate for more collecting, more curating, and more alienating of Native American human remains.

Theories of Difference and Inferiority

The historical context of the attitudes that underlay these collecting activities is of interest to us, particularly because many of these attitudes prevail in American society today. Just as the late twentieth and early twenty-first centuries reflect an obsession with the Bering Strait and competitive hypotheses of human origins in the Americas, nineteenth- and early-twentieth-century science was motivated by the desire to prove or disprove that it was the ancestors of living and historically known Native Americans who built great architectural features such as the mounds of the Mississippi and Ohio valleys and the cliff dwellings found later in the Southwest. In many ways these researchers were still attempting to answer the question posed by John Locke in 1690: Are Indians nothing more than lazy collectivists and thus a throwback to the time before the wheels of historical progress were set in motion? Or are Indians historical beings, the creators of their own destinies? To understand this strange set of scientific and philosophical questions, we must look at the prevailing theories regarding human difference at the time, most of which haunt American existence today.

We are accustomed to drawing a line between two basic explanations for human diversity around the globe: one created by God's hand (creationism) and the other a result of gradual change independent of God's continued involvement with the world (evolutionism). But in the nineteenth century more views abounded, which can be labeled as *polygenesis, monogenetic degeneration, and monogenetic evolution*.

POLYGENESIS

As the term implies, *polygenesis* (also known as pluralism and strongly underlain by hereditarianism, or the idea that biology creates destiny) was the unorthodox view that different human "types" represented not only different "races" but different species of humanity, each a result of *separate acts of creation* by God. This viewpoint was supported by attempts to explain the unfamiliar, extinct fossil remains in geological layers by positing something called *catastrophism*, or the idea that the world was destroyed and re-created several times by God's hand.[6] This viewpoint was developed aggressively in France but was always less accepted than theories based on the conventional explanations of difference as a result of something that happened after God's initial, singular acts of creation, or *monogenesis*.

MONOGENETIC DEGENERATION

Degenerationists believed in monogenesis but said that human differences are a result of the degeneration of some people away from God's original grace. This process began in the Garden of Eden when the possibility of true human oneness was destroyed by Adam and Eve's disobedience, and humans were cast out to fend for themselves. Those who stayed close to God's word, believing that he would bring a savior one day to redeem them from their original sin, retained most of the original features of God's creation, including white skin. Those who

38

drifted away, spiritually and geographically, lost their souls and gained darker skin, a stigma of their distance from the Center.

A version of this "wandering" theme (one related to the Jewish theory of Indian origins, which had been forwarded since the sixteenth century) was developed by the Mormons, who believe that some Native Americans strayed further from God's will than others, as indicated by their "curse" of a dark skin. These violent "Lamanites," or rejecters of the gospel, succeeded in defeating the "Nephites," or the fair-skinned wanderers from Israel. Those Nephites who survived hid tablets that would become the book of Mormon. According to this world-view, a bloody war took place on this continent some four hundred years after Christ's birth, in which the ancestors of today's Indians nearly exterminated the more enlightened and lighter-skinned aborigines (see Mooney 1973: 790, 792–93; Smoak 1986: 275–81; Walton 1970: 65–98).[7]

Many other theories abounded regarding the cause of degeneration, such as alcoholism and the negative influence of European practices on Indian innocents. But whatever the reason, the role of science was to save the remnants of the past glories of Native American societies for the benefit of all humanity. However connected living Native Americans might be to these monuments, their presumed lack of memory of this connection (postulated by people who had, in fact, rarely if ever asked them about such memories) and their purported lack of skill in protecting and preserving these "antiquities" removed them, in the view of colonizers, not only from contemporary stewardship but from the right to (re)claim the territory throughout which these monuments were spread.

MONOGENETIC EVOLUTIONISM, OR SOCIAL DARWINISM

The third viewpoint regarding human differences, *monogenetic evolutionism*, better known as *social Darwinism*, was by comparison an enlightened one for the time. This view—held by anthropologists Lewis Henry Morgan, Frank Hamilton Cushing, and Matilda Coxe Stevenson, and by geologist John Wesley Powell, the head of the Smithsonian's Bureau of American Ethnology—postulated that all peoples possessed the basic psychic and moral components of God's unique creation of humankind. Some humans might have proceeded more rapidly along the path to Civilization (the term being defined in relation more to mechanical, technological, aesthetic, and governmental arts than to a "quality" of being), but the others would inevitably catch up. The reasons for the lag were varied, and many of them were environmental in nature, but the presumption was that they would, indeed, "become like us." At the time, this seemed like a good thing, never mind the assimilationist and even genocidal implications, especially in comparison to the darker views of the degenerationists and the polygenists. "Social," "Cultural," "Civilizational" evolution was a good thing, an optimistic thing, a progressive thing. And best of all, it conformed not only to God's plan but to that of the empire builders.

Another way that evolutionary monogenism was interpreted was through the idea of *diffusion*, or the notion that the world's great creations (e.g., writing, pyramids) were invented in one crucible and then spread to the rest of the world. Although it may seem that the Bering Strait hypothesis (the idea that Native Americans migrated from Asia across a narrow waterway to the American continents) is a type of diffusionism, the proponents of this idea have more often than not argued *against* the varieties of diffusionism that deny feats of engineering and intellectual and artistic creations to Native Americans. In defense of Native American authorship of New World creations, "Bering Strait-ists" argued vigorously against the idea that it was Celts, Japanese, Egyptians, Polynesians, or aliens from space who created the petroglyphs, hieroglyphs, pyramids, pottery, cliff dwellings, and art works of the Americas. By the late twentieth century, nineteenth-century racist diffusionism was largely forgotten as the source of Bering Strait orthodoxy, which now had racist overtones in a new political and intellectual climate that pointed out the Eurocenteredness (if not the bad science) of that view (e.g., V. Deloria 1997: 67–91).

Museum Practices under Late Imperialism

The State

Ours is a government of liberty by, through, and under the law
A great democracy must be progressive
or it will soon cease to be great or a democracy.

Aggressive fighting for the right
is the noblest sport the world affords.

In proper government results worth having can only be

achieved by men who combine worthy
ideals with practical good sense.

If I must choose between righteousness and peace I choose righteousness.

—Theodore Roosevelt; the words are carved on the inside wall of the
main rotunda of the American Museum of Natural History, New York
City

"You're a race of scientific criminals," he charged. "I know I'll never
get my father's bones out of the American Museum of Natural History.
I am glad enough to get away before they grab my brains and stuff
them into a jar!"—Minik Wallace, to a reporter before sailing back to
Greenland to be rejoined with his family, 1909

How can one prove or disprove theories about human origins, prehistoric territorial rights, and human equality? In the early twentieth
century, one attempted to disprove them using the same "data" that one
used to prove them—that is, human remains and associated objects
pulled from graves. The German-born scientist Franz Boas, known
widely as the "father of American anthropology" and an adamant opponent of the misuses of science to prove the alleged inferiority of non-
European peoples, himself ordered the excavation of grave sites in order
to get the proof he needed for his crusade against scientific racism
and took part in the sale of Native American human remains (Thomas
2000: 58–60). Despite participation in practices that today would be
labeled highly unethical and racist, including a scandal involving the
death of several Eskimo men and women who had been brought to New
York for research purposes (Claiborne 1992; Harper 2000), Boas wrote
vehemently against the prevailing idea that race determines culture,
morality, and intelligence.

In Boas's view, which had been shaped by the German distinction between scientific practice aimed at understanding human and historical
affairs (*Geisteswissenschaft*) and scientific practice that aimed at studying
natural phenomena (*Naturwissenschaft*), one should carefully study living
human beings in great linguistic, cultural, geographical, and historical
depth before making pronouncements about their purported "nature."
Social evolutionary theories that placed human beings on a simple con-
tinuum from "savage" to "civilized" based their claims not only on poor

observations but, what was worse, on bad scientific assumptions. Boas's version of scientific practice, based on long-term, fieldwork-grounded experience, revealed that so-called savages were in possession of the same range of humanity exhibited by all peoples. In other words, in any population one would find philosophers and pragmatists, innovators and dullards, tyrants and tremblers.

The fact that Boas sought such evidence in the record of a people's graveyards is controversial, as today what seems to be careless disregard for the feelings of the living took a back seat to his desire to obtain a variety of head shapes and physical features for scientific investigation. This was because, as Boas also demonstrated in his measurements of European head shapes before and after immigration to the United States, experience plays a powerful role in the development of human beings as a result of interactions with the cultural, physical, intellectual, and emotional environment (see Baker 1998; Boas 1928).

Why Boas, himself a lifelong victim of anti-Semitism, could not forward his theories on the basis of firsthand knowledge of living people is answered by the spirit of the times in which he lived and the inability of even the most educated and enlightened to pull free from it. This lesson is a hard one to learn, and it is being absorbed only incrementally in these times of late imperialism, where the United States still maintains dominant relationships over peoples within its geographical borders and without.

I have spent some time discussing these views not to justify the activities of the evolutionists (practices and beliefs that would disintegrate from enlightened optimism to downright racism and genocide, as indicated above), nor to provide a seal of approval to all of Boas's activities, but to point out the complexity of historical truth and the ways that such practices as the collecting of bones can cut two ways. Graves were desecrated and bodies collected as much to defend Native American claims to the continent as to refute them. This argument is very much alive today, as curators of these objects and human remains decry with passion the unreflective removal and repatriation and reburial of these objects before they can yield information that will be of benefit to Native Americans themselves (see AAPA 2000; SAA 1986, 2000). Some Native Americans have agreed, in part, with this view and have asked that scientific analysis take place on the remains of their relatives before they are reburied. Others believe that there is nothing to be learned that can undo the rest of what has occurred to them since well before the nineteenth century. For them, the claims of science have been nothing more than justifications for theft and stalling tactics to keep museums filled with the spoils of war. Manifest Destiny disguised as natural history filled American museums with the objects that those in power as well as the general public longed for to prove that science—and its imperialist underwriters—now held the whole continent in its hands. American Indians and Native Hawaiians would spend the better part of the twentieth century expending effort to get their ancestors' bodies and grave goods returned to them, a right to which they were entitled not only under English-based American common law, but as partners in treaty contracts, which have the force of international law behind them.

Yet as we have seen with the case of the Elgin Marbles from Greece, powerful nation-states can be very resistant to international law, sentiment, or persuasion. Although Elgin was disappointed at the purchase price of the sculptures (£35,000), he received eternal fame when his name was attached to them, leaving the impression that they had arrived at their rightful home (Etienne and Etienne 1992: 74). The Greeks have asked for the return of the sculptures since the early nineteenth century, when village elders tried to convey to those unearthing the sacred objects that misfortune would fall upon them all if the objects were not returned (Etienne and Etienne 1992: 79). Requests for the repatriation of the Elgin Marbles have been made repeatedly by the Greek government, the European Parliament, and international organizations. To poet Yannis Ritsos, however, the reason to return the sculptures is a simple one: "These stones cannot do with less sky" than that afforded by their homeland (Hitchens 1997: 139). To this day, however, British Museum officials say that the return of the Elgin Marbles is impossible, because to do so would destroy the cultural heritage of all mankind and, more to the point, would serve as the "thin edge of the wedge" that would result in the gutting of the British and, by extension, all European museums (Hitchens 1997: 139; Osborne 1999).

The outcry that emerged over the vandalism and theft at the Acropolis in Greece marked the beginnings of a consciously expressed sentiment in Europe that the powerful may not have the right to strip the less powerful of their heritage. This sentiment has been turned into action in various instances, as European Jews have struggled to regain their possessions taken during World War II, and Greece has mobilized international support (including a large segment of the British public) for the repatriation of Periclean artwork. The arguments for returning cultural property to its rightful owners seem simple to many. Why not return objects wrongfully taken? What is all the fuss about?

There are several arguments raised in opposition to repatriation. First, it is claimed that return of these objects starts a slide down a slippery slope where no request can be refused, and museums will cease to exist. This reasoning connects with a morally grounded rationale claiming that magnificent works of art *transcend* mere nations or cultures (see George Kubler's argument in note 2). As artistic genius is an individual quality that exists beyond or even in spite of the limitations of the nation-state, true ownership resides in humanity itself, which counts on the protection of *world patrimony* so that all of us may be enlightened and instructed (and entertained, although this obvious motivation is rarely mentioned out loud) by the intellectual and aesthetic power of valuable and beautiful objects. It has ever been thus, so the argument goes, that the world improves itself: by protecting its wonders so as to uplift the common rabble. In these days of lowbrow entertainments that draw men and women back down to apish sentiments, there is only one thing that can keep humanity on the path to progress: the products of civilized minds with their civilizing influences.

These objects should therefore not be viewed as "stolen," but instead as being in the safekeeping of those who would provide controlled access to all of it, for all of us, you and me and him and her, all over the world. A version of this view can be found in the Principles of Archaeological Ethics of the Society for American Archaeology, which includes the promotion of "stewardship of archaeological resources" (*www.saa.org/aboutsaa/ethics/prethic.html*).

The fear that motivates many of the attitudes and policies of archaeologists and others is that if sites, human remains, and cultural objects are left unprotected by those with the wisdom and resources to properly protect them, they will be lost forever to humanity. The rationale, which we have already seen expressed in British Museum policy regarding the Elgin Marbles, goes something like this: *the obligation for one nation to protect world patrimony is greater than that of another to reclaim it.* This view is evident in the wording of various international conventions and recommendations regarding the treatment of cultural property drafted in the twentieth century. While it is beyond the scope of this book to explore international mechanisms in detail, it is important to at least mention the most relevant of them now.

INTERNATIONAL CONVENTIONS

Although various types of international legislation were passed concerning the preservation of American Indian cultural patrimony and cultural treasures beginning with the 1782 Act for Preventing Fraudulent Dealings in the Trade with the Indians in Canada and the 1783 Ordinance for the Regulation of Indian Affairs in the United States, the first really significant international convention appeared in 1954. In this year the United Nations Educational, Scientific and Cultural Organization (UNESCO) issued the Convention for the Protection of Cultural Property in the Event of Armed Conflict, which opened up a "new engagement of the international community with the perfection of means for protecting and defining patrimony" (Lux 1999: 61; translation mine).

UNESCO issued other recommendations concerning the safeguarding of cultural sites, but it was the 1970 Convention on the Means of Prohibiting and Preventing the Illicit Import, Export and Transfer of Ownership of Cultural Property that made the first sizeable impression on the international museum community (Lux 1999: 62–63). Other conventions were to follow in the 1970s regarding the protection of world and specifically American "cultural and natural heritage." According to Lux (1999: 64; translation mine), the 1972 Convention Concerning the Protection of the World Cultural and Natural Heritage "definitively instituted the aesthetic values and subjective characteristics of world patrimony." One passage of this convention refers us back, however, to the paternalistic attitude mentioned above: "Considering that cultural property is the product and witness of the different traditions and of the spiritual achievements of the past and thus is an essential element in the personality of the peoples of the world . . . it is indispensable to preserve it as much as possible, according to its historical and artistic importance, so that the significance and message of cultural property become a part of the spirit of peoples who thereby may gain consciousness of their own dignity" (Lux 1999: 64; quoted from Document 17/C107, UNESCO, Paris, 1972).

While these 1970s conventions raised consciousness about the ways museums acquired their objects and resulted in a wave of changes to museums, the paternalistic language embedded in the problematic idea of "world patrimony" has hindered addressing the practices of cultural property repatriation under international law. We now turn to the United States and to the national and state-based legal mechanisms that emerged alongside the never-flagging attempts of Native peoples to have their ancestors' remains and cultural property returned to their descendants.

2

History of the Repatriation
Movement, 1880s to 1970s

After the [South Dakota] Home Guard killed the Ghost Dancers
[16 December 1890], [Riley] Miller and Frank Lockhart scalped,
stripped, and left the corpses (men, women, and children) where
only wolves could find them. Miller shipped his fresh Indian artifact
collection to Chicago during the 1893 World's Columbian Exposition
and went into partnership with "Omaha Charlie" . . . They opened
a 500-piece Indian relic sideshow on the midway. The principal
attraction: a dried Indian baby. The grisly relic attracted hordes of
people who filed past the unfortunate child, nestled in a glass box.
Thousands of curious people pressed their hands and noses to the
scratched glass, and parents lifted children to catch a glimpse of what
the billboard called the "Mummified Indian Papoose, the Greatest
Curiosity Ever on Exhibition." —Renée Sansom Flood, *Lost Bird of
Wounded Knee*

A large portion of this book focuses on the Native American Graves
Protection and Repatriation Act (NAGPRA), the 1990 federal repatriation
law that has made a big difference in how museums and other institutions with museumlike functions deal with Native American human
remains, Native American objects, Native American knowledge, and
Native Americans themselves. This difference, in some ways, has been
so profound that people have begun to speak of NAGPRA as more than
a mere law, but as an era. It is important to recognize from the outset,
however, that this law was passed as a result of persistent hard work on
the part of Native Americans and Hawaiians as their demands for justice
were expanded from particular cases to state laws and then on to federal
law with international ramifications. The creation of NAGPRA was just
the latest stage in a diverse and century-old repatriation movement. To
get a sense of the development of this movement I return to the story
begun in chapter 1.

A Century of Dishonor and Ethnic Cleansing

On 29 December 1890, the United States Army opened fire on women, children, and men on a bitterly cold day at Wounded Knee Creek, South Dakota. It is estimated that over 346 Lakotas were killed during this massacre, around 150 of whose bodies were dumped into a mass grave. By contrast, around 30 men were lost from the Seventh Cavalry, and 37 were wounded (Flood 1995: 45; Lathrop 1986: 257; Thornton 1987: 152–54). The Indian bodies were stripped of their possessions, many of which ended up at the 1893 World's Columbian Exposition in Chicago and in museums in the United States and Europe (Flood 1995: 52–54; Thornton 1987: 154–55). If you travel about seventeen miles north of the infamous Nebraska town of Whiteclay to the southwestern section of the Pine Ridge Reservation, you can visit the Wounded Knee graveyard and read the names of the victims on carved stones.

The air of sadness that blows gently through the site opens to the casual visitor just a tiny window into the massive and ongoing grief and trauma still suffered by Wounded Knee descendants and their relatives today. Wounded Knee is not "over"; it serves as a reminder of all the unfinished business in Indian Country as Native Americans struggle with poverty, neglect, unemployment, low wages, racism, poor health, and high death rates from suicide, alcohol-related illnesses, automobile accidents, and many other forms of violence, often, but not exclusively, at the hands of non-Indians.

To many non-Indians, Wounded Knee represents something else. If they are "Indian wars" buffs they will tell you that the battle served as revenge for the defeat of Custer and the Seventh Cavalry at the Little Big Horn in 1876, a hundred years after the Declaration of Independence was signed. They may also tell you that the soldiers fired on sick, starving, and freezing Indians in overreaction to the threat they perceived in the Ghost Dance, a revitalization movement designed to bring back all the living things decimated by western expansion and white aggression. Others, if they know the history well, will tell you that like many violent acts against Indians, there was really no point or rationale for what happened at Wounded Knee. Young and bored, many of them drunk, the soldiers responded to a shot while attempting to disarm Chief Big Foot's band of Minnecojous. American Horse, a Lakota "friendly" who supported the U.S. government, provided this testimony to Congress regarding what he saw that day:

> When the firing began, of course the people who were standing immediately around the young man who fired the first shot were killed right together, and then they turned their guns, Hotchkiss guns, etc., upon the women who were in the lodges standing there under a flag of truce, and of course as soon as they were fired upon they fled, the men fleeing in one direction and the women running in two different directions . . .
>
> There was a women [sic] with an infant in her arms who was killed as she almost touched the flag of truce, and the women and children of course were strewn all along the circular village until they were dispatched. Right near the flag of truce a mother was shot down with her infant; the child not knowing that its mother was dead was still nursing, and that especially was a very sad sight. The women as they were fleeing with their babes were killed together, shot right through, and the women who were very heavy with child were also killed. All the Indians fled in these three directions, and after most all of them had been killed a cry was made that all those who were not killed or wounded should come forth and they would be safe. Little boys who were not wounded came out of their places of refuge, and as soon as they came in sight a number of soldiers surrounded them and butchered them there. (Mooney 1973: 885–86)

The year 1890 is therefore viewed by some as a trope, symbolizing the final defeat of American Indians at the hands of the United States of America. Ever since the first decade of the nineteenth century, when Lewis and Clark warned the Indians of the West that they were "clearing a path" for settlement by handing out peace medals to men they treated as children, the United States made consistent and determined attempts to cleanse the West of its aborigines as it built an empire that stretched from sea to sea. Whole nations of Native peoples were forced by Andrew Jackson to march from their homes east of the Mississippi during what was known as the Trail of Tears and to settle in Indian Territory, or what became Oklahoma. Fifteen percent of the population of the Chickasaw and Choctaw people died during this forced death march, as did fifty percent of the Cherokees, Creeks, and Seminoles (Stannard 1992: 122–

25). Indian Territory was then progressively reduced in size as oil was discovered, and business ventures, once again, took precedence over promises and justice (see Debo 1940, 1941).

The Trail of Tears, the Navajo Long Walk, and the defeat and imprisonment of Chiricahua Apaches are fairly well known to most Americans (see Brown 1970), but as David E. Stannard reminds us, there were hundreds of massacres throughout the continent that served to reduce the Native American population by perhaps 95 percent in some areas and reduced many tribes to extinction: "Massacres of this sort were so numerous and routine that recounting them eventually becomes numbing—and, of course, far more carnage of this sort occurred than ever was recorded. So no matter how numbed—or even, shamefully, bored—we might become at hearing story after story after story of the mass murder, pillage, rape, and torture of America's native peoples, we can be assured that, however much we hear, we have heard only a small fragment of what there was to tell" (Stannard 1992: 126).

As discussed in chapter 1, the latter part of the nineteenth century produced a host of connected phenomena that seemed to kick into high gear as soon as the Indian wars were declared over: tours of "savage life" were organized by enterprising businessmen, both "out West" following the railroads and "back East" at World Fairs; commerce in Indian goods intensified; museums were built; reservations were established, some of which served as mere holding tanks for Indians who had been removed from their homelands; Indian sovereignty was eroded and treaties broken; anthropological studies were conducted to "salvage" what was seen as vanishing ways of life; Hollywood films were made depicting the hero as Indian fighter; sports teams took on often caricatured images of Indians as mascots; federal Indian policy oscillated between treating Indians as protected children and as obstacles to progress in need of assimilation to mainstream American life; and the collecting of Indian artifacts and human remains to fill museums, tourist shops, and the homes of the wealthy took on frantic and obsessive proportions. These activities and processes were to continue well into the twentieth century, with the result being that most Americans thought that Indians were dead, dying, or irrelevant to mainstream American life.

The "decade of NAGPRA" in the 1990s therefore did not appear from nowhere. But it is more than a response to the American Indian Movement that developed in the 1960s, more than a reflection of the parallel critique of anthropology that emerged at the same time, and more than a sign of the triumph of fundamentalist nativism in American life. And while certainly the 1990 NAGPRA cannot be viewed apart from its relationship to earlier legislation on issues of repatriation and religious freedom, its origins go back to the biological and cultural holocaust that occurred when 80 to 90 percent of the population of the Americas died before Lewis and Clark set out with the Corps of Discovery. They died from the ravages of disease spread by European hosts: traders, conquistadors, missionaries, and refugees from European settlements. When Lewis and Clark remarked about the silence as they traveled past abandoned earthworks, it was because they were passing by thousands and thousands of graves, many of which would be desecrated and claimed for science, agriculture, nation building, and progress as the nineteenth century unfolded.

I am aware, as I write these words, that some readers will label this version of history unnecessarily revisionist or sensationalist, who will wonder of what relevance to a discussion of a law can be the rehashing of events over which no one in the present has any responsibility, much less any control. My response is that without laying the historical groundwork of the dispossession, desecration, and delay of the repatriation process, the reader may forget (or indeed be unaware) that the debate about the law, about the objects under consideration for return, about the "slippery slope" that taking any kind of action might send us down, is not just between "Indians" and "scientists" or, for that matter, Indians and whites. If we begin at the outset in this way, by boiling down history into these two stereotypical camps, we will not be able to form any opinions or make any decisions about the law that are informed by other than a "we say"/"they say" rhetoric (see Zimmerman 1997b for a discussion of the complexity of the so-called sides). The contexts and the means by which Native American human remains and objects were acquired has everything to do with the discussions about their return. The cultural legacy of mourning over these remains is a real one that has been transmitted for several generations, and it has everything to do with the decisions about their treatment and repatriation. Finally, the abused epithet "It's just politics," which is hurled out whenever anyone tries to discuss unequal power relations as if to defuse and discredit all such talk, has everything to do with the discussion about the just return of human remains and cultural objects stored in museums.

The history of Indian-white relations on this continent has been one characterized by a great dying, by a concomitant dispossession, by an unspeakable and ongoing mourning, and by resultant unfathomable inequalities of access to life, liberty, and the pursuit of happiness. Some Indians are more aware of these phenomena than others; most non-Indians are unaware of them entirely. Some Indians have attempted to deal with the situation by rejecting many Western practices and beliefs either by fighting the system or dropping out of it. Other Indians have become scholars and scientists, archaeologists and ethnographers, park rangers and attorneys so that they might confront the system from within and work on behalf of their people. Many (probably most) non-Indians never think about Indians at all or do so within the framework of stereotypes and racism. Other non-Indians try to understand aboriginal America from what they hope is an "Indian perspective," seeking its romance and wisdom in ways that sometimes earn them the labels of "white shamans" or "wannabes" or "anthropologists," even if they have had no anthropological training. Yet other non-Indians become scholars and scientists, archaeologists and ethnographers, or park rangers and attorneys so that they might confront the dominant system from within to work on behalf of Indian people as advocates or brokers.

NAGPRA will mean something different to all of these kinds of people and will be reflected in the extreme diversity of opinions found within each of the broad categories presented above. But in the end, despite all of these opinions, the facts must be remembered: American Indian lives and cultures were nearly exterminated as a result of European contact in the second half of this millennium; American Indian physical remains and cultural objects were taken by the hundreds of thousands and put in private homes, private collections, and public collections; many of those currently in possession of these objects believe that they have a right to keep them, under concepts of property that they believe to be true and universal; and most of those who wish to conduct scientific research on these objects or to curate them in their museums sincerely believe that they are doing so for the good of all humankind. It is equally true that those who believe themselves to be the actual, political, spiritual, or ethnic descendants of these human remains and the rightful owners of the alienated property are convinced that they have rights to the return of these remains and objects not only under United States law but also under international law. In their view, and in the view of those who identify themselves as being in solidarity with their cause, the rights to repatriation of American Indian ancestors and ancestral property take precedence over notions of scientific authority, world patrimony, or a possession-based "finders, keepers" stance.

"Being Indian" in the United States

When most Americans think of Indians, or Native Americans, or North American Indians, or First Americans—never being quite sure what to call "them," and almost certain to feel guilty resentment when they don't get the name right—they tend to do so in four broad, interrelated ways, each of which has its origins in the cultural and historical phenomena discussed in chapter 1.

INDIANS AS A "MINORITY"

First, and probably most conventionally, Indians are viewed as an "ethnic group" that, like African Americans, Asian Americans, Hispanics, and other such designated "minorities," is always struggling for rights and recognition. This way of viewing American Indians is based on the criteria of "racial" difference, cultural deviance from a putative American norm, and some vague idea of demographic percentages. This mode of conceptualization carries perhaps a modicum of guilt, but this guilt is less connected to the causes of this group's marginality than to a belief that a certain amount of charity is the American (Christian) way. More sophisticated thinkers look at the intersection of race, class, and ethnicity as they seek to understand Indian travails, but the class component in Native American identity formation has not been studied to the same extent as it has with other cultural groups, a fact that may be linked less to the neglect of researchers as to the poverty of class analysis when it comes to understanding American Indian experiences on this continent.

INDIANS AS "SPECIAL"

A second way to view American Indians is that they possess a special kind of marked difference, one created by their historical relationship to this continent and to the historic struggle of the United States to create its own national identity. Within this mode, Indians are seen as either noble, innocent victims of American progress or as atavistic throwbacks to a more savage, if pristine, era (one can hear echoes of Locke and Rousseau in here). This special status of Indians is transformed many times into versions of those qualities that are linked with the "noble savage" and that hundreds of thousands of Americans scramble to touch, own, or learn from as they endure their own struggles with a dehumanizing, consumer-oriented society. Sympathy for Indian causes attached to this way of thinking about them is necessarily, however, tinged by large doses of paternalism and pity.

INDIANS AS DESERVING OF NEGATIVE TREATMENT

A third way of viewing Indians—one less common but related to the first two and encountered in various pockets of the United States where Indian hating is a grim art—is to see them as lower than animals and as deserving of whatever negative consequences their alcoholic, gambling, neglectful, violent, marginal, and lazy lifestyles have brought them. As moral incompetents, as savages, as children, as illiterates, as a wasteful scourge, they have no business making claims on anything like the Black Hills or on priceless museum objects since they cannot be trusted to do anything but convert valuable objects to pawn. Indians bleed the nation of its resources and collectively lower the standard of living for all. This attitude may emerge directly, when a young Indian man is beaten to death and his body is stuffed in a trash can on the Pine Ridge Reservation, or indirectly, when the news media fail to report the death of a young Lakota woman who is beaten and dragged miles behind a car.

"INDIAN" AS A LEGAL CATEGORY

None of the above views, of course, is accurate, although oddly the second has more to recommend it because at least it recognizes some kind of vague historicity. In the United States, being Indian is also a legal form of identity and status that has been shaped by years of federal Indian policies, laws, and practices. For those Americans who have had some introduction to Indian law, the definition of an Indian takes on new complexity, for the criteria are only partly those of biology.

One important legal definition is derived from the Indian Reorganization Act of 1934, which recognizes three classes of person as Indian, including "Eskimos and other aboriginal peoples of Alaska" (48 U.S. Stat. 984, quoted in Baca 1988: 230):

1. All persons of Indian descent who are members of any recognized Indian tribe now under federal jurisdiction. There are 570 federally

recognized tribes as of the year 2000; 150 remain unrecognized but nevertheless exist (Baca 1988: 230; Deloria and Lytle 1984: 150; Frazier 2000: 70).

2. All persons who are descendants of such members residing within the boundaries of an Indian reservation (as of 1 June 1934), "regardless of blood" (Deloria and Lytle 1984: 150).

3. All other persons "of one-half or more Indian blood, whether or not affiliated with a recognized tribe, and whether or not they have ever resided on an Indian reservation" (Deloria and Lytle 1984: 151).

However, as Stephen L. Pevar points out in the American Civil Liberties Union ACLU handbook, *The Rights of Indians and Tribes*, "many federal laws use the word 'Indian' without defining it." Further,

> This allows federal agencies to decide who is an Indian under those laws. Some agencies have been accused of defining Indian too narrowly, thereby depriving people of benefits that Congress intended them to receive. . . . These varying legal standards have caused confusion and inconsistency.
>
> As an example, a person may qualify as an "Indian" for educational benefits and not qualify for health benefits. The Census Bureau takes a simple approach to these problems. The bureau lists every person as an Indian who claims to be one. (Pevar 1992: 12–13)

The ACLU handbook further states that the situation is complicated by the fact that each distinct Indian tribe has its own criteria for membership eligibility. While most tribes require at least one-fourth "tribal blood" for membership, others ask for only one-sixteenth. The Southern Ute tribe is one that requires one-fourth Ute blood, which presents problems to the many members who possess one-half blood and marry outside the tribe. Even if their spouses live on the reservation and raise their children as Southern Ute, these children must marry full-bloods or else see their own children lose access to tribal membership.

The result is that one person could be recognized as an Indian by the U.S. federal government but not by her own tribe, while another person could be recognized by his tribe but be ineligible for benefits from the U.S. government if that tribe is not federally recognized. As noted legal scholar Felix S. Cohen puts it in his *Handbook of Federal Indian Law*,

> The term "Indian" may be used in an ethnological or in a legal sense. . . . If a person is three-fourths Caucasian and one-fourth

Indian, it is absurd, from the ethnological standpoint, to assign him to the Indian race. Yet legally such a person may be an Indian. From a legal standpoint, then, the biological question of race is generally pertinent, but not conclusive. Legal status depends not only upon biological, but also upon social factors, such as the relation of the individual concerned to a white or Indian community. The individual may withdraw from a tribe or be expelled from a tribe; or he may be adopted by a tribe. He may or may not reside on an Indian reservation. . . . Indeed, in accordance with a statute reserving jurisdiction over offenses between tribal members to a tribal court, a white man adopted into an Indian tribe has been held to be an Indian, and the decided cases do not foreclose the argument that a person of entirely Indian ancestry who has never had any relations with any Indian tribe or reservation may be considered a non-Indian for most legal purposes. (Cohen 1971: 2)

Because legal definitions themselves do not rest on firm or consistent criteria, including those of biology, and because the details of American Indian history and law are rarely taught in the American classroom, it is easy to see why discussions about Indian rights and justice readily disintegrate into confusion among the American public. Most Americans still define Indians as a very tiny "minority group" that not only is vanishing but that makes ridiculous demands regarding issues such as sports team mascots, "tomahawk chops," and ancient bones.

INDIANS AS SOVEREIGN PEOPLES ENTITLED TO SELF-DETERMINATION

The truth is that American Indians are not a "minority group" based on purported racial demographics or distance from mainstream cultural values. Rather, most American Indians are members of sovereign nations located within the boundaries of greater North America. While they sometimes bear physical characteristics that lead some to label them as a separate "race," and while they may share some common assumptions about the nature of reality that lead many to talk about "Indian ways" as if "being Indian" meant one big subculture, the more accurate historical, experiential, and politically economic fact remains that "being Indian" means numerous things. In its most legal sense, "being Indian" is established in the "Commerce Clause" of the U.S. Constitution, "which stipulated that the federal government alone would be responsible for

56

regulating trade with 'Indian Tribes' in the same fashion it does so with foreign nations and between the 'various states' of the union. Also at issue is Article I, Section 2 of the Constitution, which defines 'Indians not taxed' as comprising a polity (or polities) separate from that of the United States, and Article I, Section 10, which precludes the federal government from entering into treaty agreements with any entity other than another fully sovereign national entity" (Churchill and Morris 1992: 13).

This is but a starting point, however, as "being Indian" can also mean the following:

Being accepted as an Indian "by the community in which he lives or from which he comes" (Baca 1988: 230).

Holding oneself to be an Indian (230).

Carrying dual citizenship (if one chooses) as a member of an Indian tribe or "dependent domestic nation" (see *Cherokee Nation v. the State of Georgia* in Spicer 1983: 186–87) and as a citizen of the United States of America.

Possessing viewpoints and interests and experiences often quite distinct from those of mainstream North Americans and yet not exclusive of being able to behave and converse as a member of the "dominant culture" if one so chooses.

Being reminded on a daily basis that one is the historical and ongoing recipient of patterns of treatment at the hands of a more powerful system that links one to all other peoples who have received like treatment.

Striving not so much for inclusion within the "American system" as for the right to self-determination and independence (see Van Slambrouck 1999: 3).

Being a person within the context of one's own people. As Deloria and Lytle point out (1984: 15) "being Indian" may carry, as does the concept of land, a religious connotation, one that is crucial in understanding the importance of the repatriation movement and the difficulties many tribes are having with NAGPRA, as it is impossible to separate issues of "property" from those of culture, well-being, human rights, and identity.[1]

"Being Indian" is therefore a cultural, historical, social, political, and experiential form of identity that cannot be reduced to categories such as *race, minority, ethnic group,* or *vanishing breed*. It can also mean something far more complex, as many self-identifying Indian people desire inclusion in the broader society and simultaneous separation from that society via cultural autonomy. In addition, the fact that more than 54 percent of the total Indian population in the United States lives in urban areas means that ever-increasing numbers of Indians identify themselves as "mixed-bloods," an extremely complex category of identification that often leaves the Indian side of the equation open to dispute (Krause 1999). What Circe Sturm (1998) has called "blood politics" in relationship to the often painful complexities of black/Indian ancestry must be figured in to any nuanced discussion of "Indian identity" as well (also see Brooks 1998). In short, *where*, *when*, and *how* is an Indian are just as important questions as *who* one is.

The question of Indian identity and the special status of Indians as accorded by U.S. federal law is an important way for us to begin our discussion of the key historical events that contributed to the twentieth-century repatriation movement and to the 1990 NAGPRA, to which we now turn our attention.

The "Civilizing Process" before the 1920s

Although the First Amendment of the U.S. Constitution states that "Congress shall make no laws respecting an establishment of religion, or prohibiting the free exercise thereof," this freedom was not accorded to Native Americans, who have been persecuted for their religious practices and beliefs since their first contact with Europeans in the fifteenth century. On 22 July 1790, Congress passed the Trade and Intercourse Act, which not only licensed trade with Indians and "provided for the punishment of crimes committed in the Indian country," but which also established a process to instill the American way of life into the Indians (Horsman 1988: 33). President Thomas Jefferson talked a great deal about the importance of bringing civilization to Native Americans, urging "the instruction of the Indian men in agriculture and the Indian women in spinning and weaving" as well as, in some cases, intermarriage (34–36).

This promotion of "White standards of civilization and education, in the hope that the Indians would be absorbed into the general stream of White society" (Prucha 1988: 40), would become embodied in the Indian reform movement, which was connected with one of the most devastating federal policies, the Dawes Severalty Act of 1887, which took away collective Indian territories, enormously reduced the Indian land base, and disrupted tribal governments in exchange for private property, agricultural instruction, and assimilation. As Pevar (1992: 5) reports, only 50 million acres of collectively owned Indian land remained in 1934 of the 140 million acres that existed in 1887, a reduction of nearly two-thirds. A real estate ad issued in 1909 demonstrates not only the mechanics of allotment-based divestiture of Southern Ute lands but also the capitalist and Lockean ideology that justified it:

FREE ORCHARD HOMES IN SUNNY COLORADO
16,000 Acres of Government Land
FIRST SEGREGATION OF THE
SOUTHERN UTE INDIAN RESERVATION
TO BE OPENED FOR ENTRY
DRAWING AT IGNACIO, COLO., JULY 15, 1909
Under the auspices of the State Land Board, by authority of the
Department of the Interior under the terms of the Carey Act, at
ONE DOLLAR AND SEVENTY-FIVE CENTS PER ACRE
EXCLUSIVE OF WATER RIGHTS

Not merely good farm land, but the very finest fruit land in Colorado, where apples pay annually from $200 to $600 per acre, and where the surrounding land is highly improved and producing orchards are worth from $500 to $2,000 per acre. A WONDERFUL OPPORTUNITY FOR YOU.

REMEMBER Registration commences a week before the opening.
Drawing at Ignacio, Colo., July 15, 1909.
Write for beautiful booklet.
AMERICAN COLONIST and TRUST Co. *Exclusive General Agts.*
MAIN OFFICE, DENVER, COLORADO
THE SOUTHERN UTE INDIAN RESERVATION

Down in Pine River Valley, twenty miles east of Durango, Colo., on the Denver and Rio Grande railroad, the landscape gardeners who are adding to the acreage of irrigable land and increasing the great family of husbandmen and fruit growers, are about to redeem 16,000 acres of the most fertile soil in the West. This land has lain idle since the beginning of time, and for a half century its progress has been checked by the fact that the government set this land aside for the Southern Ute Indians as their reservation.

The romance of the red man enters into the story of Pine River

Valley. In 1868 the government set aside the whole western half of Colorado as the reservation for the Ute Indians. Four years later, when the tribes showed a lack of harmony and utter hopelessness of ever reaching it, the Northern Utes and the Southern Utes, with nothing in particular in common between them, divided up, the Southern Utes taking the pick of the reservation, which includes Pine River Valley.

It is an established fact that the Indian is lazy. He was too lazy to develop the rich soil of the valley that has long been an unclaimed reward for enterprise; but this same Indian did not overlook the boundless possibilities of the climate, the abundance of game—the quail, the grouse, the deer, bear and the elk. He picked that part of the state which appealed to him most, and he landed in Pine River Valley.

But it would have been all right for the Indian to remain there if he had developed some of the resources that lay at his feet. When it was shown to the congress of the United States that 16,000 acres of rich, loamy soil lay undeveloped in the western part of Colorado, the congress did not hesitate to take it away from the reservation and give it to the state of Colorado to sell at $1.75 an acre, with the provision that the Indian fund get the benefit of the proceeds. Congress further required of the state that the land be opened for settlement providing the state guaranteed that the private capital would reclaim it by putting enough water on the land to transform it into a veritable garden.

The march of civilization is across Pine River Valley. The Indians failed to make the best of the resources, would not stay on the reservation, liked other game because it required some wandering to find it—and now the government and the state, guaranteeing the proper development of the tract by[?] private capital, will on July 15 open the land to settlement.

There is a moral in that story of Indian lassitude and white man enterprise, and the moral will be all the more forcibly shown when after the land is disposed of, along in July, they transform what was once a mere hunting ground of the Indians into a new farming and fruit community, where crops and fruit will form the nucleus for new cities and new industries and wealth.

. . . This is unquestionably a wonderfully unique opportunity for the settler to secure a tract of land at the first net cost from the government and state, located in the very midst of the unquestioned greatest fruit growing district in America; and were it not for the fact that this was Indian land and was held by them until this time, the land would have many years ago been filed upon and would now be selling for from $100 to $1,000 per acre, as is the land in the immediate vicinity, which is privately owned.

. . . Any man with average intelligence can learn how to irrigate his land in a day. The men who cannot learn in two days are mostly confined in insane asylums.

. . . The price of the land is $1.75 per acre, of which 50 cents is to the state and $1.25 to the Indian trust fund. The price of the water-right is fixed by the State Land Board at $45 per acre, which is actual cost of the water on the land. The first payment of 25 cents on the land must be made at the time of filing.

CHEAP RATES FOR WEEK OF OPENING

July 15, 1909

For information, write F. A. Waldleigh, A. C. P. & T. A., Denver, Colo. Drawing at Ignacio, Colo., July 15, 1909. Write for beautiful booklet.[2]

Although the allotment policy was always said to be for "the good of the Indians," it is clear from the language in the above advertisement that it was the interests of land speculators and settlers that were facilitated by allotment. The manner in which it was done was calculated to soothe any feelings of doubt or guilt on the part of prospective buyers who might wonder if they were entitled to formerly Indian land at such cheap prices. "Not only are you entitled," the advertisement declares, "but you are stepping onto moral high ground by turning this formerly wasted and barren land into the productive zone intended by the forces of God and civilization."

Native Americans would not accept the allotment policy without protest. In 1901 a leader named Crazy Snake of the traditional faction (the "Snakes") of the Creek Nation organized an unsuccessful rebellion in protest of allotment. After being imprisoned along with his followers for organizing a rival government that refused to accept allotments, Crazy Snake continued to actively lobby against allotment (Bad Wound 1999a: A1).

Most Americans do not realize that church and state were close allies in the implementation of United States federal Indian policy, as the government funded missionary societies to carry out a civilization "program" centered around instilling Christian beliefs, practices, and ethics (Adams 1995: 6, 23). In 1882 Interior Secretary Henry M. Teller ordered that all "heathenish dances" end, and in 1884 the Bureau of Indian Affairs (BIA) published "Regulations of the Indian Office," which outlawed all traditional religious ceremonies. Indians found wearing braids, performing the Sun Dance, or otherwise participating in ceremonies deemed to be a "great hindrance to civilization" were to be imprisoned for thirty days. It was, in fact, the U.S. government's attempt to suppress the Ghost Dance Religion that resulted in the 1890 massacre at Wounded Knee (O'Brien 1993: 28). By 1910 the Plains Indian Sun Dance would be directly outlawed (Bad Wound 1999a: A3).

Assaults on religion occurred on two other fronts as well: in the boarding school classrooms, where Indian children were pressured to convert to Christianity and forgo their Native beliefs and language (Adams 1995: 164–73), and at the gravesites, where Native American burial and bereavement practices were altered not only because of their greater frequency due to disease, murder, and dispossession, but also because of (largely, but not entirely, Protestant) Christian pressure to halt pagan practices. In addition, and most relevant for our discussion, serious and sustained grave looting was carried out by non-Indians for purposes of revenge and robbery. Cases were also reported of unscrupulous and desperate Indians who looted their own ancestors' graves in order to obtain wampum or other articles for trade with Europeans (Axtell 1981: 110–28).

THE FEDERAL ANTIQUITIES ACT OF 1906

As looting of graves became widespread on federal and tribal lands, the government passed the Antiquities Act (16 U.S.C. §§ 431–33) to protect archaeological sites in these areas. Dead Indians and their associated objects buried on these lands were thereby declared "archaeological resources," "objects of historic or scientific interest," and "federal property" that could be excavated, disinterred, sent to museums, and otherwise "managed" only with the proper federal permits in hand (Tsosie 1997: 68). While the act served to greatly reduce amateur archaeological looting on public and Indian lands, it reinforced the idea that the Native American past belonged not to Indians but to scientists (Thomas 2000: xxxv). According to one estimate, by 1990 at least 14,500 Native American bodies were in the hands of federal agencies such as the National Park Service, the Bureau of Land Management, and the Fish and Wildlife Service. In addition, the federal government seized Blue Lake and the land surrounding it from Taos Pueblo and declared it federal wilderness. The 1906 Act cannot therefore be seen as working on behalf of Indian peoples or protecting their burial sites (Hill 1996: 85; Tsosie 1997: 68).

The 1920s: Ambiguous Reformers and Indian Activists

The first waves of American Indian political activism began to be felt in the 1890s, when BIA employees sought civil service status (Deloria and Lytle 1984: 37). Various actions to defend Indians' legal rights against states took place in the early years of the twentieth century, and in the 1920s the Indian Defense League took action to get eastern tribes' treaty rights recognized by the U.S. and Canadian governments. Protests of the governments' noncompliance with the Jay Treaty and the Treaty of Ghent took various forms, including nonpayment of customs duties and annual reenactments of the Jay Treaty signing (Nagel 1996: 160).

Non-Indian reformers were very active in the 1920s, as they sought to both improve conditions for Indians and facilitate their assimilation into the dominant society. Early Indian rights organizations included the Women's National Indian Association, an interdenominational group founded in 1879 that was "dedicated to treaty-keeping, education, and eventually to missionary and social welfare activities" (Hertzberg 1988: 305). The Indian Rights Association was founded in 1882, followed in 1883 by the influential Lake Mohonk Conference of the Friends of the Indian. The National Indian Defense Association was the only national non-Indian organization that opposed the General Allotment (Dawes) Act of 1887, but on other issues, such as Indian citizenship, opinion was more evenly divided (Hertzberg 1988: 306).

The Alaska Native Brotherhood was founded in 1912 to fight for Native Alaskan rights and succeeded in establishing relationships with other Native and non-Native reform groups. What became the American Indian Association of 1922 began as the Society of American Indians in 1911. This organization was founded by several Indian leaders, including Santee Sioux physician Charles A. Eastman, based on the idea of sociologist Fayette A. McKenzie of Ohio State University that a "race leadership" could build a "race consciousness" that would be of benefit to all humanity (Hertzberg 1988: 307–8). Although the organization was in decline by the end of World War I, it helped develop many of the issues that would revitalize the Indian reform movement in the

1920s, particularly in response to various threats to Indian lands that came in the form of congressional bills. The most well known of these organizations was the American Indian Defense Association, founded by John Collier in 1923, which reflected growing sentiment that favored the preservation of Indian cultures rather than their extinction through assimilation (Deloria and Lytle 1984: 41; Hertzberg 1988: 308).

The first (and only) Indian vice president of the United States (elected with Herbert Hoover), Charles D. Curtis (Kansas–Kaw/Osage) wrote the text for what was to become the Indian Citizenship Act. This act passed in 1924 and conferred citizenship to those Native Americans who had not received it under the General Allotment Act (although a number of nations, such as the Hopi and Onondaga, refused to acknowledge the Citizenship Act as binding). It also gave Indians the right to vote (Bad Wound 1999b: A3; Churchill and Morris 1992: 15). A new organization emerged in 1926 to encourage Indian political participation, the National Council of American Indians. By the end of the decade the reform of governmental policies was well under way, largely in response to the 1928 Meriam Report, issued by a group of independent experts from the Brookings Institution at the behest of the secretary of the interior (see Meriam et al. 1928). The Meriam Report provided detailed recommendations for change in the ways Indian affairs were administered by the U.S. government in order for Indians to live healthy lives with decency. This represented a departure from other reports, which had largely recommended that more money be allotted so that existing programs might function more efficiently. By contrast, the Meriam Report suggested that the government needed to change its orientation toward the Indian people it served (Deloria and Lytle 1984: 53–54).

In October of 1929 the Lake Mohonk Conference of Friends of the Indian met to discuss the Meriam Report and outlined the following priorities: Indian education, health and family life, employment, law and order, and the establishment of an Indian claims commission (Hertzberg 1988: 309–10). Whereas the legislation in 1930 was centered around the Indian past in the form of erecting markers to commemorate treaties or battles, the administration of Franklin D. Roosevelt shifted the focus onto the Indian future (Deloria and Lytle 1984: 53–54).

The 1930s: The Indian New Deal

In 1932, Roosevelt selected the skilled and controversial reformer John Collier as commissioner of Indian affairs. Thus began one of the most remarkable (and, in the minds of many, harmful) chapters in American Indian legal history in the United States, as the "Indian New Deal" was carried out under a commissioner committed to transforming institutions rather than merely making them more efficient (Deloria and Lytle 1984: 55). Two of the seven principles that Collier and his staff formulated have relevance to the repatriation movement:

> Second, the Indian societies, whether ancient, regenerated or created anew, must be given status, responsibility, and power. . . .
>   Fourth, each and all of the freedoms should be extended to Indians, and in the most convincing and dramatic manner possible. In practice this included repeal of sundry espionage statutes, guarantee of the right to organize, and proclamation and enforcement of cultural liberty, religious liberty, and unimpeded relationships of the generations. (Collier 1947: 261–62)

On 12 February 1934, Collier's Indian Reorganization Act (IRA) was introduced to Congress for consideration. As Deloria and Lytle (1984) discuss in much detail, the rapidity with which Collier introduced his radical vision of federal Indian law made it vulnerable to scrutiny and eventual gutting. What passed as the IRA (or Wheeler-Howard Act) in June of 1934 nonetheless terminated the policy of allotment and made it possible for Indians to establish tribal governments based on the U.S. model with their own constitutions (Spicer 1983: 212–17). Not all Indian groups liked this model, despite claims that the IRA gave greater powers to Indians to hang on to their land base as well as encouragement for them to set up their own businesses. John W. Ragsdale Jr. (1997–98: 441) notes that "some have criticized Collier for drawing too heavily on the Anasazi and Pueblo world views and generalizing to the neglect of variations in the visions of other tribes." In the case of the Lakotas, the "democratic" IRA form of government allowed for the replacement of traditional leaders "by educated, but largely landless mixed-bloods," a situation that would have disastrous consequences by the 1960s for the Lakotas at Pine Ridge and would continue to divide many reservations between "traditionals" and "progressives" (Churchill and Morris 1992: 15).[3]

According to Hazel Whitman Hertzberg, "During the remainder of the 1930s the energies of the Indian rights movement were devoted primarily to the operations of the Indian Reorganization Act." Most Indian rights organizations were "regional rather than national in scope," and many Indian reformers worked for the BIA (Hertzberg 1988: 311–12), which itself increasingly became a target of tribal protests (Nagel 1996: 160). During this time period the Navajos endured the BIA livestock reduction program, which continues to have serious ramifications. In addition, the federal government set in motion the seeds for a Hopi and Navajo territorial dispute, causing major conflicts that continue to the present and that have significantly affected the NAGPRA process (Brugge 1994: 30–33).

Nevertheless, the legacy of the IRA was significant in some ways for Indian self-determination, as it allowed tribes to retain the rights they were granted by treaties, prevented states from passing legislation that would infringe on these rights, and built up the economic base of tribal entities by expanding the federal services available to Indians (Deloria and Lytle 1984: 184).

THE HISTORIC SITES ACT OF 1935

President Roosevelt signed the Historic Sites Act as part of the New Deal and to indicate that the federal government was concerned over the preservation of cultural objects, as stated in the original 1906 federal Antiquities Act. The 1935 act established a board of up to eleven citizens to advise the federal government regarding national parks, historic sites, buildings, and monuments. The secretary of the interior was to choose the eleven members, and preference was given to those with academic expertise (Price 1991: 26). In terms of relevance to NAGPRA, the 1935 act establishes the historic centrality of the National Park Service in federal preservation activities. (In the late 1990s the choice of the National Park Service as the administrator of NAGPRA was questioned; see chapter 5). According to Barbara Bad Wound (1999c: A6), the first successful repatriation effort took place in 1938 when the sacred Midipadi Bundle was returned to the Hidatsas.

The 1940s: World War II and the Aftermath

On 18 July 1942, the Six Nations declared war on the Axis powers as a form of protest against the United States government, which disregarded sovereignty and imposed the draft on Native Americans (Bad Wound 1999d: A6).[4] The era of World War II, which began for the United States on 7 December 1941, spelled the end of the Collier administration. By the time the war broke out, Collier had alienated and angered Congress because of his unwavering opposition to assimilationism. Collier resigned as BIA commissioner in 1945, but not before calling together an influential meeting of Indian Affairs personnel in 1942 for the purpose of strengthening ties between North and South American Indians. The employees turned down this idea but agreed that there was a need for a national organization, made up of representatives selected by the tribes themselves, that would allow them a stronger voice in the American political and cultural arena (Hertzberg 1988: 312; Thomas 2000: 194).

On 15 November 1944, delegates from over fifty Indian nations met in Denver to form the National Congress of American Indians (Bad Wound 1999d: A6). The NCAI continues to be one of the most influential Indian rights organizations in the United States and has contributed a great deal to discussions regarding repatriation matters. As Nagel (1996: 160) points out, the Indian activism of the postwar period was often directed against federal public works projects such as dams "that threatened Indian land holdings and sacred areas." A movement away from national and toward local concerns, while addressing the needs of communities, threatened the kind of solidarity that Collier had tried to establish with Indian causes. By the late 1940s many in the United States equated "activism" with "communism," and any opposition to state and corporate interests was seen as threatening to the "American way." The 1940s also saw the reduction of BIA services to Indians as the main office moved from Washington to Chicago during the war, and many BIA employees resigned to work in areas more closely related to the war effort. Reservations were emptied of young people—just at the age for entering tribal government—as thousands of men and women enlisted or went to work in war-related industries, bringing many tribal enterprises to a standstill (Deloria and Lytle 1984: 190).

Nevertheless, Indian communities were changed by the many returning veterans—more than 25,000 Indian men and women had joined the services—who had fought in World War II, with the Navajo code talkers contributing significantly to victory in the Pacific arena. Wartime experiences contributed to a desire for more training and education, which was facilitated by the GI Bill (Nagel 1996: 118–19). In the view of sociologist Joane Nagel, the second World War had a "transformative impact" on Indian consciousness as "American Indian veterans and wartime workers returned to the reservation with a recognition of common problems, a new vision of justice and rights for American Indian individuals and communities, an enhanced sense of personal and political efficacy" (118). These veterans were to play an active role in the National Congress of American Indians, in voting rights struggles in states, and in the increased urbanization of American Indian life.

In 1946, the Indians Claims Commission (ICC) Act was passed by Congress as a means to settle pending tribal land claims and treaty disputes. Mandated to last ten years, the ICC extended to 1978 and "was presented with 370 petitions representing 852 claims made by more than 200 tribes and Indian groups" (Nagel 1996: 119). Although a dark period followed with the advent of termination policies, the ICC served to mobilize many communities to take political action in ways that would enhance tribal experience in making repatriation claims a half-century later.

Not everyone views the ICC Act in a positive light. According to Deloria and Lytle (1984: 264), every Indian community was to have received notice of its right to file claims under the act. In fact, very few received such notice, particularly in the eastern United States. In addition, the ICC Act was much more narrowly focused than John Collier had intended when he first proposed it as part of the IRA (Deloria and Lytle 1984: 57). To Churchill and Morris, the ICC Act was passed as little more than a gesture "probably provoked in large part by the fact that the U.S. was preparing to hang nazis at Nuremberg for having engaged, among other things, in 'wars of aggression and conquest.' In actuality, the Commission was not empowered to return land to any Indian nation, no matter how illegally it was adjudged to have been taken" (Churchill and Morris 1992: 15). Rather than return land outright, the commission provided only monetary compensation, whether the Indians making the claim wanted money or not, based on the estimated price per acre of the land "at the time it was taken" (Churchill and Morris 1992: 15).

Canadian First Nations peoples had been treated as second-class citizens since the inception of the Canadian nation-state. Nonetheless, the fact that Native peoples had the highest rates of military enlistment during World War II brought attention in the postwar period to their claims for equal treatment under Canadian law and for increases in budgetary allotments to Indian Affairs. In 1880 Indian Affairs was designated as a separate department within the federal government but was demoted in 1936 to a branch within the Department of Mines and Resources. In 1949 the Indian Affairs Branch was moved to the Department of Citizenship and Immigration, and in 1951 modest changes to the Indian Act were made as a result of government hearings held in 1948 and 1949 (Sanders 1988: 278–81). Nevertheless, although Inuit people were given the right to vote in federal elections on 30 June 1950, this franchise was not extended to Indians unless they signed a waiver agreeing to give up their tax-exempt status (which the Inuit did not have) in exchange for the vote (Bad Wound 1999d: A6).

The 1950s: Termination

In 1948 the National Congress of American Indians met in Denver to discuss the so-called termination policies that were being forwarded in Congress to dismantle the reservations, "emancipate" Indians from federal control over their lives, and place them under state jurisdiction. This "emancipation" was viewed by many with alarm, as it looked more like "ex-termination" of federal protections over Indian territories and sovereignty. The new BIA commissioner, Dillon S. Myer, had been in charge of the War Relocation Authority from 1942 to 1946, which operated and then dismantled the "relocation centers" (concentration or internment camps) where Americans of Japanese descent were held. To him, according to David Hurst Thomas, the reservations were like Japanese internment camps: "short-term facilities to incarcerate the inmates." Just as the end of World War II removed the need for internment camps, so the end of the Indian wars made reservations and federal trusteeship unnecessary in the view of Myer and other powerful conservative congressmen known as the "terminationists" (Thomas 2000: 194–95).

In 1953 termination became official policy through House Concurrent

Resolution 108 and later through Public Law 280 (1954), passed under the Eisenhower administration. The idea was not only (once again) to assimilate Indians into mainstream America, but also to save the government money by dismantling the Bureau of Indian Affairs. Between 1953 and 1963 federal responsibility ended for 109 tribes, each of which "was ordered to distribute its land and property to its members and to dissolve its government" (Churchill and Morris, 1992: 15–16; Pevar 1992: 7). In 1959 hundreds of Indians marched to the BIA headquarters in Washington DC to express their opposition to the termination policy (Bad Wound 1999e: A6). The termination policy came to an end in 1968 under the Johnson administration (after it had been ignored by Kennedy) and then was further undermined by a series of pieces of legislation that were designed to return to the idea of tribal economic development that had been central to the Indian Reorganization Act (Pevar 1992: 8).

The 1960s: Preservation Laws and Civil Rights Struggles

In their influential study of American Indian self-determination and sovereignty, The Nations Within, Vine Deloria Jr. and Clifford M. Lytle designate 1945 to 1965 as "the barren years," when "self-government virtually disappeared as a policy and as a topic of interest, [and] Indian affairs became a minor element in the American domestic scene" (Deloria and Lytle 1984: 190). To most Americans, Indians were just another minority group, and their special, long-standing historical relationship to this continent had largely been forgotten. But Indians themselves had not forgotten. In 1949 the Hopis sent a letter to President Truman, asserting their rights as a sovereign nation, and in 1959 sent a delegation to the United Nations (Matthiessen 1991: 39). Other groups, such as the Iroquois Nation, had also asserted their independence and struggled on their own against state infringements on their rights. In 1961 a Declaration of Indian Purpose was prepared at the American Indian Chicago Conference, at which eight hundred people from ninety tribes gathered to address their spiritual and cultural rights and to call Indian people to action. In 1964 the first school under the control of a sovereign nation—run by an all-Navajo school board and board of directors—was opened, the Rough Rock Demonstration School in Chinle, Arizona. In 1966 the Alaska Federation of Natives was founded, in 1967 the American Indian Law Center opened at the University of

New Mexico Law School, and in 1969 the Navajo Nation opened the first four-year college controlled by an Indian tribe (Bad Wound 1999f: A6). In 1968 the Indian Civil Rights Act was passed. It was designed to extend Bill of Rights protection to reservation Indians but served mainly, according to Churchill and Morris (1992: 16) to make "native governments a functional part of the federal system." It was not until 1978 that American Indian religious freedoms were addressed directly. What is more significant for purposes of the present discussion is that the 1960s saw an increase in U.S. legislation designed to address environmental, historic, and cultural preservation.

RESERVOIR SALVAGE ACT OF 1960

The Reservoir Salvage Act, which supplements the Historic Sites Act of 1935, allows archaeologists to remove "relics and specimens" from federal dam construction sites after conducting an archaeological survey (Price 1991: 26). Only sites of "exceptional significance" were to be preserved, a policy that, according to Hill (1996: 86), led to the growth of "many of the current collections of ancient Indian objects" in museums around the United States.

NATIONAL HISTORIC PRESERVATION ACT OF 1966 AND TCPs

The "philosophical base and administrative structure" of today's cultural resource management practices—often referred to today as "compliance archaeology" (McGimsey 1999: 11)—had its beginnings with the 1966 National Historic Preservation Act. According to attorney Rebecca Tsosie, the act finally fulfilled an 1896 Supreme Court finding that the government had a "public purpose" not only to designate but also to preserve "historic sites" (Tsosie 1997: 71). The act authorizes "the Secretary of the Interior to expand and maintain a National Register of Historic Places, to designate National Historic Landmarks, and nominate historic properties for inclusion in the World Heritage List" (Collins 1992: 97). The act also specifies the establishment of State Historic Preservation Offices (SHPOS). According to McGimsey (1999: 11), the need for historic preservation grew rapidly after World War II because of the many construction projects associated with urban development and the creation of the interstate highway system.

In 1986 regulations were added to the National Historic Preservation Act stipulating that Indian tribes (and their "traditional cultural leaders") be given "the opportunity to participate as interested persons" if traditional cultural properties (TCPs) were to be affected by undertakings on federal lands. This requirement was strengthened in 1992 by an amendment providing that "a Federal agency shall consult with any Indian tribe or Native Hawaiian organization that attaches religious and cultural significance" to a TCP that falls under the act. The amendment also stipulated that significant Native American or Hawaiian cultural properties could be included in the National Register (see Parker and King 1990; Trope 1996b: 32).

There are various problems with this act, the central one being that it places the burden of proof for cultural relevance or sacredness on the tribes, who often consider this information not for public consumption (Price 1991: 26–27; Tsosie 1997: 72).

NATIONAL ENVIRONMENTAL POLICY ACT OF 1969

Although no archaeologists were involved in the steps that led to the passage of National Environmental Policy Act (NEPA), and although nowhere in this environmental protection law are archaeologists specifically mentioned, it nevertheless establishes the base for making archaeology part of every plan for a federal project. This is because of the language found in section 101(b)(4), which states that it is the responsibility of the federal government to "preserve important historic, cultural, and natural aspects of our national heritage." It was hoped that the law would therefore force action, rather than be "simply another pious statement" (McGimsey 1999: 11). According to Tsosie (1997: 73), however, NEPA is "purely a procedural statute," in that its main purpose is to make sure that federal agencies "make informed decisions when engaging in development projects" based on environmental impact statements (EISs) and environmental assessments (EAs) (Price 1991: 29; Trope 1996b: 32). Making informed decisions does not mean ensuring that the environment or cultural heritage will be, in the end, protected. Again, being informed in regard to Native American sites means placing the burden of demonstration on tribes regarding the specific location of places deemed private and trusting that those privy to the information, such as ethnologists and archaeologists, will not disclose sensitive information (Tsosie 1997: 73).

In sum, although the 1960s laid down some federal groundwork for protecting sites of national and historical significance (other relevant laws include the Department of Transportation Act of 1966 and the Administrative Procedures Act of 1966, according to Price 1991: 27–28), these laws were insufficient in that they put the burden of proof on Native Americans regarding sacred sites, and they emphasized preservation—and then only in exceptional circumstances—rather than repatriation of burial remains and Native American cultural property (Price 1991: 28, 117).[5]

What is perhaps most important about the decade of the 1960s is that a rapidly growing number of state statutes and laws regarding antiquities, historic preservation, and the protection of American Indian human remains and burial objects were passed. Some of these laws include the Minnesota Field Archaeological Act in 1963, the Texas Antiquities Code in 1969, and the Georgia Protection of American Indian Human Remains and Burial Objects Code in 1969 (Lux 1999: 177). I return to the discussion of state statutes in chapter 3.

THE REPATRIATION MOVEMENT IN CANADA IN THE 1960S

Here at Cape Mudge we set up the Nuyumbalees Society to get a museum going and bring back the potlatch regalia. . . . Nuyumbalees means "the beginning of all legends." The legends are the history of our families. . . . It has all worked out pretty well. All our stuff that was brought back from Ottawa is in glass cases in the museum according to the family that owns them. That's what the masks and other things mean to us: family ownership. We are proud of that!—Harry Assu, *Assu of Cape Mudge: Recollections of a Coastal Indian Chief*, 1989

As mentioned above, the post–World War II era in Canada was one of assertiveness for First Nations peoples who sought first- rather than second-class status. Various kinds of reorganization of the Indian Affairs Branch took place in the 1960s, and Natives were granted the right to vote in 1960. In 1967 the federal government financed an Indian pavilion at Montreal's Expo 67. Not only was the funding itself unusual, but the government gave full control of the pavilion's contents to Native people, who produced an aboriginal account of Canadian history through "pictures, print, and sound" (Sanders 1988: 281).

Another major action took place in 1967 when Kwakiutl Natives began negotiating with the National Museum of Canada for the return of confiscated and stolen potlatch materials. The potlatch (an elaborate ceremonial mechanism central to the workings of political power, familial status, and socioeconomic redistribution) was outlawed by the Canadian Parliament in 1885, and the government began prosecuting Indians for performing potlatch ceremonies in 1913. In 1921 Nimpkish chief Daniel Cranmer (1888–1959) held a large potlatch at Village Island. As a result, Indian agent William Halliday decided to enforce the law and obtained forty-five convictions. Twenty-two individuals received suspended sentences in exchange for turning over their potlatch regalia, including blankets, whistles, rattles, copper plaques, masks, bowls, boxes, and headdresses. These items were shipped to the National Museum of Canada in Ottawa and to the Museum of Man in Hull, while some were sold to the Museum of the American Indian in New York. The government gave the Indians a total of $1,495 for these 750 objects, said to be worth more than $35,000 (Clifford 1991: 227–29; Hill 1996: 84–85; Jacknis 2000: 266–69).

By 1951 the anti-potlatch law had been dropped, which resulted in the open resumption of its practice. Various construction projects were undertaken in the 1950s to provide institutions for Native dances, performances, and cultural exhibitions. By the end of the 1950s, requests for the return of potlatch materials were under submission, and in 1967 the federal government responded, saying that the materials could be returned when the Natives had museums in which to house them. In 1979, the U'Mista Cultural Society of Alert Bay, Vancouver Island, and the Nuyumbalees Society at Cape Mudge Village on Quadra Island opened their doors to the return of the sacred potlatch items (Clifford 1991: 228–29; Hill 1996: 85–87). Nevertheless, the repatriation has not occurred without controversy, as potlatch items are not viewed as communal property but as belonging to individual chiefs and their families. The ways that this has reinscribed status differences and created local conflicts is largely hidden under the romantic vision of repatriation and its connection to the beauty of Northwest Coast art (Jacknis 2000: 274–77; see www.schoolnet.ca/aboriginal/umista2/index-e.html).

The 1970s: Red Power, Religious Freedom, and Cultural Property Issues

By the end of the 1960s, Native American political activism at the national level had been revitalized. Indians began to use their voting power and political voice to achieve recognition in American society at a time when other protest movements were developing in a nation torn apart by the Vietnam War and stimulated by the civil rights and feminist movements (Nagel 1996: 161–62).

Johnson, Champagne, and Nagel (1999: 287) trace the initiation of the "rhetoric of Indian self-determination" to Melvin Thom, a Paiute from Walker River, Nevada, who cofounded the National Indian Youth Council (NIYC) and became its president. In the early 1960s Thom spoke of the need for Indian people to seek justice without compromising their sovereignty or identity as Indian people. Another significant act on the road to self-determination was the Zuni decision to manage BIA programs themselves, contracting the agency on a local basis only. In 1969 President Nixon urged other tribes to follow the Zuni model in seeking self-determination (Champagne 1997: 32).

In the mid-1960s the NIYC organized a series of "fish-ins" primarily in various northwest locations to protest the restriction of Indians from waters to which they were entitled to fish on the basis of long-standing treaty rights (Deloria and Lytle 1984: 198–99; Nagel 1996: 161–62). The occupation and "illegal" fishing of rivers became good practice for a series of other organized movements that took place in the 1960s and early 1970s, such as the occupations of Alcatraz Island off the coast of California, of Fort Lawton and Fort Lewis in Washington, of Ellis Island in New York, and of the BIA office in Washington DC. By far the most significant of these actions was the occupation of Alcatraz Island by a variety of urban Indian students from UCLA, UC Santa Cruz, San Francisco State College, and UC Berkeley, between 20 November 1969 and 11 June 1971. Although it did not organize the Alcatraz occupation, the American Indian Movement took center stage in the national consciousness about Indian activism (Johnson, Champagne, and Nagel 1999: 297–305; see also Mankiller and Wallis 1993; Nagel 1996).

The American Indian Movement was founded in 1968 in Minneapolis and soon thereafter opened chapters in Cleveland, Denver, and Milwaukee. Initially an Indian rights organization, AIM expanded its scope and influence after the Alcatraz occupation, particularly through its skillful use of the news media to publicize Native American causes (Nagel 1996: 166–67). No fewer than seventy takeovers of property were effected between November 1969 and 1978, a nine-year period referred to as the Alcatraz–Red Power Movement (ARPM) (Johnson, Champagne, and Nagel 1999: 303).

The issues over which AIM and other Indian activist groups struggled included treaty rights, water rights, fishing and gathering rights, mining leases, jobs, housing, education, protection from police violence, legal rights, aid to juvenile offenders, racism, corruption in tribal governments, and religious rights. A variety of new Indian organizations emerged in both the United States and Canada to address legal aid, analysis of pending legislation of relevance to Indian Country, and Indian rights. The Native American Rights Fund (NARF) was established in Boulder, Colorado, in 1970, and it still serves as an important clearinghouse for legal information and provides legal assistance to Native Americans (see their Web site at *www.narf.org*). In the fall of 1972—the same year that the *American Indian Law Newsletter* was founded—eight Indian organizations (including the National Indian Brotherhood of Canada) met in Denver to plan a "Trail of Broken Treaties—Pan American Native Quest for Justice" caravan that would culminate in Washington DC to present demands for a new administrative framework for Native American affairs. The group occupied the BIA building (renamed the Native American Embassy), causing damage to files and, ultimately, to the BIA itself, which had to be reorganized following the shakeup. The movement for Indian rights became divided as a result, and conflicts between Indian groups heightened, culminating in the seventy-one-day siege of Wounded Knee, South Dakota, in 1973 (Hertzberg 1988: 320–22; also see Matthiessen 1991).

THE REPATRIATION MOVEMENT IN THE UNITED STATES

At this point in our story we must take a turn toward repatriation, representation, and cultural property issues. The 1970s saw a growing discussion regarding the general role of museums in possessing, displaying, and representing Native American cultural objects and human remains. A panel discussion on the role of museums in acquiring, curating, and representing Native American human remains and cultural objects was held in 1971 in Aspen, Colorado, as part of the Second Convention of Indian Scholars. The kinds of issues that were to culminate in NAGPRA thirty years later were raised during this discussion, as well as issues that are not included in the law but that have remained alive and have become attached to NAGPRA practice. Some of these issues include who should be in charge of displays, why Indians should be employed in museums, who the appropriate persons should be to design educational programs centered around Native American cultures, and how a tribe can set up its own museum and gain title to the objects in it.

Perhaps the most important issue to emerge through the discussion concerned objectionable museum practices, particularly regarding what is placed on exhibit. John White (Cherokee), who worked in the Education Department of Chicago's Field Museum of Natural History discussed what occurred when the museum exhibited human remains that had been excavated from burials found in an Illinois state park: "Opposition to this was immediate, and the result was that the Field Museum had a 'death feast' for the remains. There were about 100 Indians there, and they had a 'give-away.' They brought down a wooden casket and the Winnebagoes took it back to their reservation and reburied it in a mound. Maybe we should go and excavate Christ Church Cemetery in Philadelphia or Boston, and check to see how people were doing at the time they were buried. It seems clear that there is a real feeling growing on this point" (Second Convocation of Indian Scholars 1974: 201–2).

This "real feeling" was to take the form of action. In 1970 the American Indian Student Association at the University of Minnesota submitted a grant proposal to the National Science Foundation to excavate a pioneer cemetery in order to draw attention to the double standard regarding scientific justification for grave digging. In 1971 the Narragansets of Rhode Island conducted a ceremony to rebury remains that had been removed from a tribal cemetery by an anthropologist (Bad Wound 1999g: B4). In 1972 Indians picketed the museum of the State Historical Society of Iowa, which resulted in the governor ordering the removal of Indian remains from exhibition. In 1976 the Canadian Union of Ontario Indians performed a citizen's arrest of an archaeologist for failing to comply with the Canadian Cemeteries Act of 1976 (Hill 1996: 86).

The actions of Native Americans in the 1970s regarding the excavation, ownership, treatment, and display of indigenous human remains and cultural objects were not merely symbolic. From 1971 to 1977 California issued a moratorium on the excavation of all Indian burial sites abandoned for less than two hundred years. Articles on repatriation began emerging in journals, including Comanche anthropologist James D. Nason's piece entitled "Museums and American Indians: An Inquiry into Relationships," published in 1971. In 1972 Lloyd Kiva New (Cherokee) became chairman of the federal Indian Arts and Crafts Board and pushed for Indian control of museums and other cultural institutions (Bad Wound 1999g: B4).

The Six Nations peoples were particularly active in the 1970s. In 1974 the Council of Chiefs issued a statement prohibiting the sale of religious objects such as wampum beads and false face masks, and in 1975 several thousand wampum beads were returned to the Onondaga Nation from the Buffalo and Erie County Historical Society (see chapter 3 for a more detailed discussion of wampum repatriation). In addition, forty-five sacred masks were loaned to the traditional Longhouse people for ceremonial use (Hill 1996: 86).

AMERICAN INDIANS AGAINST DESECRATION

The end of the era of the Alcatraz–Red Power Movement signaled a shift in Native American activism, one that worked concertedly for repatriation. In March of 1978 several hundred Native Americans began a protest march that began in San Francisco and ended in Washington DC in July. The purpose of the Longest Walk was to bring attention to a backlash against treaty rights that had picked up support in Congress (Nagel 1996: 175). The protest was peaceful and had as one of its outcomes the formation of American Indians against Desecration (AIAD), an organization that was to figure prominently in the push for repatriation laws (Hammil and Cruz 1989). According to AIAD director Jan Hammil (Mescalero Apache), the need for the organization was made apparent during the Longest Walk when the participants visited museums, universities, and laboratories along the way and "found the bodies of our ancestors stored in cardboard boxes, plastic bags and paper sacks. We found our sacred burial places stripped and desecrated, the bodies and sacred objects buried with our dead on display for the curious and labelled 'collections,' 'specimens' and 'objects of antiquity' " (Hubert 1988: 2).

According to Hammil,

AIAD was formed in 1980 for the purpose of addressing and challenging the archaeological treatment of Indian remains, and the desecration of sacred Indian burial sites. Although the focus of attention by AIAD and other Indian organizations had been limited to local, state and national boundaries, Indian people have been aware for some time that excavations and international trading practices between universities and museums had resulted in thousands of Indian remains and sacred objects being shipped and stored in facilities throughout Europe, thereby making the treatment of American Indian burials and the violation of traditional Indian religious beliefs an international problem (Hammil 1995: 1).

AIAD would set the tone and agenda for repatriation efforts in the 1980s and 1990s through its presence at archaeological conferences held by groups such as the Society for American Archaeology and the World Archaeological Congress and through its efforts to change the display practices of museums such as the Pitt Rivers in Oxford (Hubert 1988).

CANADIAN FIRST PEOPLES' ACTIVISM IN THE 1970S

Native political action in Canada in the 1970s was stimulated by the production of what was called the "white paper" on revised Indian policy, which contained provisions that angered and mobilized many aboriginal groups. Some of these provisions were similar to those found in the U.S. Termination Act, and Canadian aboriginals resisted vehemently the idea of ending Native reserves. In 1975 the Subarctic Athapaskans issued the Dene Declaration of nationhood, and in 1978 the National Indian Brotherhood issued a demand for a constitutional amendment to recognize treaty rights and political engagement. As mentioned above, a series of demands for the return of cultural objects took place in the mid-1970s, culminating in the return of potlatch materials in 1979–1980. Although it is beyond the scope of this book to discuss Canadian First Nations activism in any detail, it must be pointed out that the North American Indian movement in many ways is just that, a movement that did not recognize the latecoming boundary between the United States and Canada (see Johnson, Champagne, and Nagel 1999: 285–90).

AMERICAN INDIAN RELIGIOUS FREEDOM ACT OF 1978

The intent of the American Indian Religious Freedom Act (AIRFA) is to make explicit the right to religious freedom that should be guaranteed to Native Americans under the U.S. Constitution but that has been violated time and again throughout American history. It was also seen as a final blow to the ethnocidal philosophy of the termination policy and an affirmation of ideas of Native American self-determination. In other words, it was seen as the ultimate legislative remedy to the past sins of the U.S. government regarding Indian peoples and their right to practice their own traditions and beliefs. Robert S. Michaelsen (1933: 133) offers this regarding what must take place for the law to be effective:

> What I am suggesting is that the law be seen for what it can do to enhance human life, to encourage the expression of the human spirit, and to improve relations among people. This no doubt entails as an ultimate objective a shift in values from a stress on self-seeking and possessiveness to an encouragement of openness and sharing. I suggest as an intermediate step the exploration of all facets of the law to discover those aspects of it which can expand our and the courts' understanding of the meaning and potential of the Free Exercise Clause and of the unique relationship between the U.S. government and American Indians in such a way as to advance movement toward that ultimate objective. Thus law may advance liberty.

According to Richard Hill Sr., however, AIRFA has "turned out to be one of the biggest disappointments in federal-Indian relations" (1996: 87). Because NAGPRA is viewed as a remedy to this unsuccessful legislative remedy, it is important that we spend some time looking at its intent and the reasons for its failure.

According to anthropologist Alfonso Ortiz (San Juan Pueblo), Native American activism for the right to practice their own religions began in 1906 when President Theodore Roosevelt signed the order that annexed Blue Lake, the primordial ancestral home of the Taos Pueblo people, to the Carson National Forest. It was not until 1970 that the Taos people were able to regain this holy place, when President Nixon signed the legislation returning Blue Lake and the 48,000 acres surrounding it to the Taos people. This act was highly significant, according to Ortiz, because "it marked the first time the federal government returned a significant parcel of land to its original owners in the name of indigenous religious freedom" (Ortiz 1996: 26).

The success of Taos Pueblo opened the door to religious activism on many other fronts in the 1970s. The sorts of practices against which Native Americans lodged protests included the arrest under the 1976 Bald Eagle Protection Act of Cheyenne and Arapaho people for using eagle feathers in religious ceremonies; the exposure and destruction of medicine bundles by customs officials who disallowed the transport across state lines of the sacred plants and animals contained within the purified bundles; the arrest of members of the Native American Church for the transport and use of peyote in religious ceremonies; the forcing of Native American prison inmates to cut their hair; the prevention of Native American access to Native American sacred lands on federal and state property; the dispossession of sacred objects from Native Americans; the denial of equal protection under laws that otherwise prohibit grave robbery and the desecration and mutilation of the dead in the United States; the refusal to return sacred objects necessary for ceremonies to Native American petitioners; and the denial of proper burial rites to Native American remains (Echo-Hawk and Echo-Hawk 1993: 67–68; O'Brien 1993: 28–29).

Following an important meeting of Native American traditional leaders in New Mexico and testimonies given by Native Americans and Hawaiians concerning violations of religious freedom, the American Indian Religious Freedom Act was introduced to Congress by Senator James Abourezk in December of 1977 and signed into law on 12 August 1978 by President Jimmy Carter after a long battle in the House of Representatives.

Some of the issues that were raised during House debate—such as whether the act would conflict with the Equal Protection and Equal Establishment Clauses of the Constitution, and whether the act would be more a statement of policy rather than a procedure that could be upheld—would come back to haunt the implementation of this rather ineffectual law (O'Brien 1993: 29–30). In a succinct retrospective on the law, Vernon Masayesva, former tribal chairman of the Hopi Tribe, concludes that AIRFA has been "practically meaningless" in its attempts to protect American Indian religious freedoms, largely because although "procedural niceties" are observed when federal bureaucrats talk to Indians onsite about their concerns, the decision documents say very little about the real impacts of federal projects on Indian religious rights.

Very few federal agencies modified their practices to accommodate Native American religious practices, and cases tried in court under AIRFA have not met with much success. Nonetheless, things looked hopeful in the beginning. Jimmy Carter mandated that a detailed report be prepared based on extensive consultation with traditional leaders regarding religious beliefs and practices, and a series of detailed recommendations was produced in the 1979 report that was delivered to the secretary of the interior; these recommendations are still under debate. Some of the issues raised in the report include the relationship of museum possession of sacred objects to Indians' religious freedom; the obligation of museums to consult with Indians before exhibiting, labeling, conserving, and storing sacred objects; and the necessity for putting a halt to the traffic in stolen cultural objects (Hill 1996: 87; Michaelsen 1993: 120).

When actual cases were tried, it became clear that, ironically, the application of the law has often served to *reduce* rather than expand the free exercise of religious practice for Indians, particularly in the higher courts (Michaelsen 1993: 123). This has happened when it was interpreted that although the government must *consult* with Indians regarding a potentially harmful practice, it need not *defer* to them in making the final judgment (e.g., the 1988 *Lyng* case; see Michaelsen 1993: 122). This has happened when it was interpreted that Native practices should not impede the government's control over *its* land (e.g., the 1989 *Manybeads* case; see Michaelsen 1993: 123). And it has happened, and will continue to occur, when the courts think of land as mere property and do not understand the ideas of stewardship, caretaking, and fluidity involved in Native American ideas of religious observance centered on their relationship to the land.

Another crucial point made by Vernon Masayesva is that AIRFA requires culturally biased proof of the violation of free exercise of religious belief in ways Christians and Jews, for instance, are never required to produce. The "bizarre" test requires that Indians show three things:

1. That the religious practice is central to their religion. ("How," Masayesva asks, "do people define which practices and beliefs in their religion are central and which are not?")

2. That the religious belief or practice is indispensable to their religion. ("How can any people tell which practices or beliefs are indispensable?" Masayesva wonders. "Can Catholics do without the Vatican?")

3. That the practice or belief cannot be done elsewhere. (Here is where the kind of relationship to the land comes in that Jews and Christians are not asked to demonstrate, as their practices are oriented more heavenward).

In being asked to pass these tests, Indians are required not only to answer questions that those holding other religious faiths are never asked to prove in courts of law, but also to render the kind of private information that can endanger their religious practices more directly than can the issue that brought them to court in the first place (Masayesva 1993: 134–35). In his dissent from the *Lyng* decision, Justice Brennan made this comment regarding the irony of a Supreme Court decision that "sacrifices a religion at least as old as the Nation itself, along with the spiritual well-being of its approximately 5,000 adherents, so that the Forest Service can build a six-mile segment of road that two lower courts found had only marginal and speculative utility, both to the Government itself and to the private lumber interests that might conceivably use it" (*Lyng* 1988: 564, quoted in Michaelsen 1993: 125–26).

ARCHAEOLOGICAL RESOURCES PROTECTION ACT OF 1979

This influential piece of legislation can be viewed as an updated version of the Antiquities Act of 1906. Nevertheless, the Archaeological Resources Protection Act (ARPA) differs from the Antiquities Act in three important ways. First, unlike the 1906 act, ARPA specifically mentions human physical remains in its concept of the "archaeological resources" over a hundred years old that are protected by it. Second, ARPA specifically requires that AIRFA regulations be considered when excavating on public lands. This means that Indians must be given notice of excavations being carried out, even on non-Indian lands, if the work might cause damage or disturbance to Indian religious or cultural sites. (Although Indians have control over excavation permits on their lands, it is the federal land manager who issues permits on federal non-Indian land.) Third, the penalties for violating ARPA are much more severe than those under the Antiquities Act, with fines ranging from $10,000 to $100,000 and prison sentences from one to five years, depending on such factors as the value and cost of restoring the resource and whether or not the offense has occurred more than once (Price 1991: 30–31).

As Rebecca Tsosie points out, despite the increase in penalties and explicit reference to AIRFA, ARPA differs but little from the Antiquities Act. First, like the 1906 Act, ARPA refers to Native American human remains and cultural patrimony as "archaeological resources" that are the property of the entire United States. Second, the fact that ARPA issues excavation permits means that it still condones the destruction of Native American sites. Although AIRFA and the stated concerns of Native peoples are to be taken into consideration when issuing permits, the last word remains with the federal land manager, not with the Indians. In the end, ARPA supports traditional U.S. property claims and scientific research interests rather than the concerns and values expressed by individual tribes (Tsosie 1997: 69).

Indian activism and U.S. federal legislation through the 1970s laid the groundwork for the intense legal and political activity of the 1980s that would lead to the "decade of NAGPRA," discussed in the next chapter. In addition, state statutes regarding Native American cultural property and burials continued to be passed, including the Alaska Historic Preservation Act (1971); the Mississippi Antiquities Code (1972); the Colorado Historical, Prehistorical and Archaeological Resources Statute (1973); the Colorado Land Use Act (1974); the Rhode Island Antiquities Act (1974); the California Archaeological, Paleontological and Historic Sites Code (1976); the Iowa Reinterring Ancient Remains Code (1976); the California Native American Historical, Cultural and Sacred Sites Act (1976); and the Pennsylvania Historical and Museum Commission Policy on the Treatment of Human Remains (1978) (Lux 1999: 177–78).

3

History of the Repatriation
Movement, 1980s

In the United States today, an estimated 300,000 to 2 million human remains of indigenous peoples, including many remains of our South and Central American and Pacific relatives, are housed and put on display in the federal, state, and private museums of the United States. . . . It is well known, for example, that the United States National Museum—Smithsonian Institution—warehouses the remains of some 18,000 of our peoples. Despite repeated requests over many years, only 21 remains, to date—those for which there is full documentation of blatant theft—have been returned to their peoples for proper reburial. . . . Beyond the issue of the remains of our ancestors, literally millions of our cultural objects—many of great spiritual importance and critical cultural significance to the traditional lives and values of our peoples—lie in boxes or vaults in these institutions. The theft and unconsented collection, cataloguing, and warehousing of our cultural patrimony continues unabated. Many sacred items, too, routinely are defiled by open and public exposure and display in the purported interest of educating the majority population.—Rory Snowarrow Fausett, "Indigenous Cultural Rights as Human Rights"

The Indian Wars Continue

The burst of energy evident in Native American political activism in the late 1960s through the 1970s was stimulated by Native American demographic growth and cultural revival across the North American continent. Table 1 provides a census enumeration of American Indians in comparison to the total United States population from 1890 to 1980. Recall that the Indian population at the time of European contact has been estimated at approximately 18 million souls living north of the Rio Grande, and perhaps higher (see Stannard 1992: 267–68). The drop to a mere 248,253 in the United States by the year 1890 is horrifying.

According to Thornton, although the recovery apparent in the Amer-

Table 1. Comparison of American Indian and Total U.S. Populations

Date	American Indian		Total United States	
	Size	Change from Previous Decade (%)	Size	Change from Previous Decade (%)
1890	248,253		62,947,714	
1900	237,196	-4.5	75,994,575	20.7
1910	276,927	16.8	91,972,266	21.0
1920	244,437	-11.7	105,710,620	14.9
1930	343,352	40.5	122,775,046	16.1
1940	345,252	0.6	131,669,275	7.2
1950	357,499	3.5	151,325,798	14.5
1960	523,591	46.5	179,323,175	18.5
1970	792,730	51.4	203,302,031	13.4
1980	1,366,676	72.4	226,545,805	11.4

Source: Russell Thornton, *American Indian Holocaust and Survival* (Norman: University of Oklahoma Press, 1987), 160.

ican Indian population from 1920 to 1980 was not uniform across all tribal groups, and although there are many problems with census reporting, there are several reasons that may contribute to the increases, both structural and demographic, including improvements in health care, migration, and intermarriage. In a 1983 series reprint published by the *Denver Post* entitled *The New Indian Wars*, the authors talk about the gains made by the people of "The Great Turtle Island" by 1980, when the American Indian population had increased 450 percent since 1900: "They are more numerous, healthier, more prosperous, and more confident since any time since the guns fell silent on Wounded Knee. . . . Infant mortality among Indians has been cut by three-fourths, and the number of Indian mothers who die during childbirth has dropped 87 percent. Some 10,000 Indian professionals—lawyers, doctors, nurses, teachers, accountants, and engineers—are making an impact on American life. Indians are not the poorest Americans anymore. Though far behind white America, they rank ahead of blacks, Hispanics, and Asian-Americans in several socio-economic categories" (Farrell and Richardson 1983: 3–4).

By 1998 the population had grown even more, according to a report released by the United States Census Bureau on 26 October 1998, for

American Indian Heritage month. From 1980 to 1990 the American Indian population had increased by another half million from 1,364,033 to 1,878,285. By 1 August 1998, it was estimated that 2.4 million American Indians, Eskimos, and Aleuts lived in the United States, comprising nearly 1 percent of the total population. The report states that the increase from 1990 to 1998 constitutes a 14 percent increase as compared to an 8 percent increase in the U.S. population as a whole. It is projected that at this rate of growth, the American Indian, Aleut, and Eskimo population will grow to 3.1 million by 2020, a faster rate than that of African Americans or whites, but slower than that of Asians and Pacific Islanders (United States Census Bureau 1998).

While one-third of American Indians, Eskimos, and Aleuts lived below the poverty line in 1995 (it has been calculated that one in seven lived on less than $2,500/year), there was an increase of 93 percent in the number of businesses they owned from 1987 to 1992, increasing from 52,980 to 102,271 (whereas the rate of increase for all U.S. firms was 26 percent). The rate of increase of receipts from American Indian-, Eskimo-, and Aleut-owned businesses increased 115 percent during the same time period (compared with an increase of 67 percent for businesses as a whole in the United States). In 1992 there were 95,040 American Indian–owned, 4,493 Eskimo-owned, and 2,738 Aleut-owned firms (United States Census Bureau 1998).

Nonetheless, the "Indian wars" continue, according to Farrell and Richardson, because of the following problems:

Bad economic deals, deception, and malfeasance. Although the federal government is obliged to protect Indian land and resources, Native Americans are not provided with the kind of technical information needed to develop resources on their own lands. They are also still persuaded to give up their lands to business interests (railroad, mining, etc.) on the basis of shady deals and misrepresentation.

Government waste. Federal Indian programs are plagued by inefficiency and corruption. Farrell and Richardson (1983: 4) estimate that nearly 70 percent of every dollar designated for Indian affairs is spent by the bureaucracy before it reaches the people. Money is poured into poorly designed plans that show few results.

The high costs of self-determination in the face of continued government paternalism. Because Indian reservations often are marginal economies within a global system, the prospect of Native American freedom from the trust relationship with the federal government may result in the need for the kind of quick economic development that may be costly to the environment, to health, and to cultural integrity. Income tends to flow off reservations rather than be invested on the reservation.

The continued attacks on Indian water rights. In 1980 more than fifty tribes were involved in expensive litigation to obtain water rights to which they are entitled.

Lingering and pervasive social inequality in a nation that is still deeply racist. In spite of the progress discussed above, Native Americans still lag far behind the average American in terms of income, life expectancy, and educational achievement. Wounded Knee lies in what was the poorest county in America in 1980—Shannon County, South Dakota—located on the Pine Ridge reservation. In 1980 Native Americans led the nation in unemployment, child mortality, violent death, and alcoholism. The 39 percent unemployment rate on Indian reservations in 1980 was four times the national average, and the median family income was two-thirds of that for white American families. Twice as many Indians died of diabetes, influenza, and pneumonia than did average Americans; six times as many died from tuberculosis; and three times as many infants died before their first birthdays (Farrell and Richardson 1983: 12). In 1980, 60 percent of all Indian housing was substandard, 55 percent of the Indian population had a high school diploma (68 percent was the rate for white Americans), and Indian college graduates earned 75 cents for every dollar average Americans earned. By the 1990s the statistics would not have changed much.

Lingering and debilitating "absence of will" in American society to seek solutions for Native Americans. Farrell and Richardson quote attorney and scholar Sam Deloria: "Until there is a strong public consensus in this country that the nation will no longer tolerate a policy where Indians pay with their poverty while others use their resources, Indians will remain poor" (Farrell and Richardson 1983: 70). White guilt over the matter often assumes the form of either trying to help Indians become assimilated into Euro-American culture or doing nothing at all out of a sense of hopelessness.

This sense of hopeless inevitability was based, in part, on predictions that came from reports stating that Indians were on the verge of disappearance. The 1928 Meriam Report, discussed in chapter 2, is seen by many as a turning point for more enlightened government policies toward Native Americans. Nevertheless, the report stated that most American Indian communities were headed for decline if not extinction:

> The economic basis of the primitive culture of the Indians has been largely destroyed by the encroachment of white civilization. The Indians can no longer make a living as they did in the past by hunting, fishing, gathering wild products, and the extremely limited practice of primitive agriculture. The social system that evolved from their past economic life is ill suited to the conditions that now confront them, notably in the division of labor between the men and the women. . . .
>
> This advancing tide of white civilization has as a rule largely destroyed the economic foundation upon which the Indian culture rested. This economic foundation cannot be restored as it was. . . .
>
> Those states which have a considerable number of Indians who have already lost their lands and have not been developed to a reasonable standard of efficiency, will ultimately realize the price they paid for taxes on Indian property. The price is a body of Indian citizens, unassimilated, poverty stricken, and diseased; a liability to the community, not an asset. (Meriam et al. 1928: 6, 87, 96; also see Nagel 1996: 5)

It is clear today that some of these predictions were premature, as American Indian culture and communities have become revitalized in important and growing ways. This is not to say that there is not grave concern among Native Americans regarding the decline of what they define as traditional culture and the rapid disappearance of Native languages. But the overwhelming reality is what Nagel calls a "general renewal and reaffirmation of American Indian ethnicity" across the continent (Nagel 1996: 7). This process is occurring at both individual and collective levels and transcends the boundaries of nation-states. It is Joane Nagel's opinion that this process is a result of "the interplay of politics and ethnicity" throughout the historical periods sketched in chapter 2 of this work. Nagel argues convincingly that this resurgence in American Indian ethnicity is, ironically, a direct result of the many policies that sought to destroy it.

The political mobilization of the 1960s that was a direct response to the attempts at assimilation in previous eras developed into the Red Power movement of the 1970s, "a period marked by the highest rates of Indian protest activism in the twentieth century" (Nagel 1996: 12–13).

While Vine Deloria half-jokingly remarked that an interest in Indians cycles around every ten years or so, catching the eye of dominant society before fading back into its subconscious, this time the attention of non-Indians was not going to wane, even if much of it was centered around Kevin Costner and Russell Means. One might cynically say that the era of Red Power disintegrated into the era of Casino Power, but there has been far more to it than that. Indian cultural revival was not going to occur without the return of Indian sacred objects and human remains, the struggle for which made the 1980s and 1990s a "new ball game" for museums and academic institutions.

Confrontation and Legal Responses to Cultural Property Alienation

As Gordon L. Pullar (Supiaq/Alutiiq) noted in a conference held by the Society for American Archaeology concerning the changing relationship between Native Americans and archaeologists, the 1980s "brought special focus to the issue of Native American relationships to archaeologists and who had the right to decide what. The emotion of protecting graves of ancestors was central to this debate. I was in many meetings where the debate raged, usually framed as a conflict between the needs of scientific research against the rights of native people to protect their burials" (Ferguson, Watkins, and Pullar 1997: 251).

We are devoting more attention to the 1980s because of the fact that repatriation issues play a much bigger role in Native American cultural and political struggles during this era than they did in any previous decade. It was also during the 1980s that critiques from anthropologists, archaeologists, historians, art historians, and museum specialists on practices relating to the possession, treatment, curating, and representation of Native American material objects became an important new interdisciplinary subfield, as critiques of the authority of science and social science met the critiques of Native American intellectuals and activists who have long been calling for new attitudes and practices to emerge regarding the treatment of sacred phenomena. Finally, the 1980s saw a transition from sieges, occupations, and other types of more direct political protest to legal actions at federal and international levels. It had taken nearly a hundred years for the repatriation movement to reach fruition. Before we examine state and federal laws drafted in response to the repatriation movement, we look at two examples of repatriation struggle that spanned the twentieth century, that of the Six Nations Iroquois Confederacy for the return of wampum and that of the Zunis for the repatriation of their Ahayu:da (War Gods).

REPATRIATION OF WAMPUM TO THE SIX NATIONS

As Richard Hill Sr. points out in a piece prepared for *Mending the Circle*, the handbook produced by the American Indian Ritual Object Repatriation Foundation, many claims for the return of cultural property were made before any federal repatriation laws were passed (Hill 1996: 83). Hill, a Tuscarora special assistant at the National Museum of the American Indian and lecturer in Native American Studies at the State University of New York at Buffalo, demonstrates this claim by providing a detailed chronology of removal and repatriation practices. One of the first entries in Hill's chronology is the following: "1891. Onondaga Chief Thomas Webster sold four wampum belts (Hiawatha, George Washington Covenant, Sighting of the First Palefaces, Chaplain) in his possession to General Henry B. Carrington, U.S. Census Agent, for $75. Carrington later sold the belts to Dr. Oliver Crane, who in turn sold them to John B. Thatcher, mayor of Albany for $500 in 1893. For his actions, as wampum were considered communal property of the Onondaga Nation, Chief Webster was removed from office in 1897" (84–85).

The alienation and return of sacred wampum to the Six Nations is a good place to begin our discussion of repatriation issues for three reasons. First, even if most of us do not know much about Hopi Taalawtumsi or Zuni Ahayu:da, we have heard of wampum because of its presence in the foundational narratives of American and Canadian nation building and treaty making. Second, a discussion of wampum reminds us that Native American concerns are hemispherical ones that extend into Canada, Mexico, and beyond (although this book is largely limited to a discussion of the United States, as NAGPRA does not have jurisdiction beyond U.S. borders). Finally, the fact that the Onondaga Nation struggled for nearly a century to retrieve the four wampum belts further underscores Hill's point that repatriation issues have been around for over a century.

In chapter 1 I presented some information regarding the possession of wampum in English collections as early as the seventeenth century.

Wampum is an Algonquian-derived word referring to cylindrical white or purple ("black") shell beads that averaged about one-eighth inch in diameter and one-fourth inch in length. These beads were strung or woven together into various shapes that served a variety of functions, including identification and ornamentation, ambassadorial mechanisms for treaty ratification, intertribal messages, compensation and exchange, history recording, and accompaniments for the dead on their journey to the beyond (Bushnell 1920: 80–83; Orchard 1975: 71–87). While some controversy exists concerning the extent to which wampum was manufactured before European contact, the fact remains that wampum did, does, and shall always carry a great deal of significance for the Iroquois. It was also prized by outsiders, some of whom obtained the strands as part of diplomatic exchanges, treaty ratification, and mortuary gifts. Others, however, actively sought to purchase wampum and managed to do so when owners would sell off privately owned strands to obtain cash in a changing economy.

But much wampum was not privately owned. This "national" or "tribal" wampum was held collectively by a nation but was often sold to dealers by unauthorized persons. This was the case with the belts mentioned above that were sold without authorization by Chief Thomas Webster. In 1899 a suit was filed against collector John Boyd Thatcher for the return of the four belts by the Onondaga Nation and the state of New York. The ruling judge stated that the belts could not be returned because of their being "curiosities and relics of time and condition and confederation which has ceased to exist" (Hill 1996: 85). In 1909 a law was passed that declared the state of New York to be the "wampum keeper" with rights to "any wampum once in the possession of any Iroquois, past, present, or future" (85). Wampum thus began to be donated to the New York State Museum, including the four belts under question, in 1927. In 1970 the Onondaga people demanded that their belts be returned, but they were contested by a group of anthropologists (Second Convocation of Indian Scholars 1974: 190). It was not until 21 October 1989 that the belts were returned to Onondaga, following an important repatriation of eleven wampum belts from the Museum of the American Indian to the Six Nations Council of Chiefs in Grand River, Ontario, on 8 May 1988.

The story of these eleven belts is fascinating but confusing if all of the various threads are followed. The history of the alienation and repatriation of these belts reveals a complex story of private gain, cultural misunderstanding through cultural loss and marketplace pressure, museum shenanigans, tribal inertia, cultural renovation, and indigenous organizing to achieve repatriation. Key players in the return of the eleven national belts included a Canadian government official, an anthropologist, and a lawyer, as well as non–Six Nations members of the Union of Ontario Indians, who made a renewed claim for the return of the belts in 1977 (Fenton 1989: 393, 398–401).

The national belts were sold as if they were private belts around 1893, when John Skanawati Buck died after caring for the belts for more than fifty years. His heirs incorrectly claimed the belts—Buck was the wampum keeper, not the owner—as part of Buck's estate, which was contested by the Council of Chiefs as early as 1893 and again in 1894, when they succeeded in recovering some other belts that had been illegally sold (Fenton 1989: 403–4). The eleven belts were eventually purchased by a Chicago dealer who then sold them in 1910 to George Heye, arguably the most obsessive and successful private collector of American Indian objects ever. (Heye's collection became the basis of the Museum of the American Indian in New York City, which has now moved to the Smithsonian National Museum of the American Indian, in Washington DC.)

Heye exhibited the belts at the University Museum of the University of Pennsylvania, where they were viewed by anthropologist Frank G. Speck, who conveyed what he had seen to Edward Sapir, then head of the Anthropological Survey of Canada. Sapir knew that these were the missing Six Nations belts that had been illegally sold, and he tried to get the belts returned to the Six Nations by writing to the deputy superintendent general of Indian affairs in Ottawa, Duncan Cameron Scott. Scott then wrote several letters to George Heye, who denied that they had been stolen. Scott pressed the matter, asking for help from the council chiefs, who at that time would do no more than assert that the belts were collective, national property that could be positively identified. Scott needed them to take a stronger stand, but they declined to state who had sold the belts in the first place, information that the attorney general of Canada would need to press a claim against Heye for possession of illegally acquired objects (Fenton 1989: 406–7).

The eleven belts thus remained in the New York museum for another seventy years, until an attorney for the Union of Ontario Indians asked the Museum of the American Indian for detailed acquisition information about the belts. The museum said that it did not have the time or staff to complete the inquiry, but an anthropologist who had long worked with the Iroquois, William N. Fenton, volunteered to carry out the research to trace the various strands. The results of this research convinced the museum board of trustees that the wampum belts should be returned, which was done in an elaborate and moving ceremony in 1988 (Fenton 1989: 393–96).

REPATRIATING THE STOLEN WAR GODS TO THE ZUNIS

I want our fathers back. As the elder brother Bow Priest, I support the statement of the Bear Clan leader about the need for our War Gods to return to Zuni country. I have gone to many places outside of our Zuni land to recover War Gods. I have gone to Wisconsin, to New York, to San Francisco, to Tucson, Arizona, and to Santa Fe many times. We want our fathers to be returned to our land. I will go after them if I need to, and I am willing to meet and talk with anybody about the return of the Zuni War Gods to our Zuni country. For the good of the people I want our fathers back. — Perry Tsadiasi (Zuni), Elder Brother Bow Priest, 1991

At the winter solstice each year, and when a new bow priest (also called a war chief) is initiated, leaders of the of the Deer Clan of the Zuni people of New Mexico carve and paint an image of the Elder Twin War God, Uyeyewi (Merrill, Ladd, and Ferguson 1993: 523). Meanwhile, leaders of the Bear Clan carve Uyeyewi's younger brother, Ma'a'sewi, who, like his brother, is endowed with living powers that can be used to ensure the safety, health, and success of the tribe by bringing rain or defending the Zunis against enemies and other trials (Merrill and Ahlborn 1997: 181–82). Ethnologist Frank Hamilton Cushing recorded several stories about the actions of the Twins, or Ahayu:da, one of which involves a poor maiden whose brothers have died and whose parents are too old and poor to procure meat. The maiden decides that she will hunt rabbits rather than marry a man who might provide her family with meat, and she sets out with rabbit sticks and a stone axe. After capturing many rabbits, the young woman loses her way and has to seek shelter in a cave, where she feasts on roasted meat and corn cakes her mother has sent with her.

After her meal, the girl hears what she thinks at first is a cry of distress, but which turns out to be one of the Cannibal Demons who has seen her cave fire and wants some of her rabbits. He is too big to insert himself through the small cave entrance but so frightens the maiden with his threats that she throws out to him all her rabbits, her deerskin overshoes, her moccasins, and eventually all the rest of her clothing. Finally, wishing to enter the cave so that he may devour the maiden, the Demon begins insistently pounding the opening with his axe. The sound reaches the two War Gods, who are sitting in their home and who know what has transpired that night with the maiden and her rabbits. Taking up their weapons, they fly to the cave.

> Just as the Demon was about to enter the cavern, and the maiden had fainted at seeing his huge face and gray shock of hair and staring eyes, his yellow, protruding tusks, and his horny, taloned hand, they came upon the old beast, and, each one hitting him a welt with his war-club, they "ended his daylight," and then hauled him forth into the open space. They opened his huge paunch and withdrew from it the maiden's garments, and even the rabbits which had been slain. The rabbits they cast away amongst the soap-weed plants that grew on the slope at the foot of the cliff. The garments they spread out on the snow, and by their knowledge cleansed and made them perfect, even more perfect than they had been before. Then, flinging the huge body of the giant Demon down into the depths of the cañon, they turned them about and, calling out gentle words to the maiden, entered and restored her; and she, seeing in them not their usual ugly persons, but handsome youths (as like to one another as are two deer born of the same mother), was greatly comforted; and bending low, and breathing upon their hands, thanked them over and over for the rescue they had brought her. (Cushing 1979: 398)

The War Gods protected the maiden that night as she slept in the cave wrapped in the garments they had cleaned with their knowledge, and in the morning they instructed her in many things and advised her to marry when she returned to the village. They slew many rabbits for her in the morning and guarded her through the snowy valley back to her home, telling the maiden their names just before leaving her at the entrance to her village. As she entered the village, people looked in wonder at the Maiden Huntress of K'yawana Tehua-tsana, who has procured more rabbits than any other hunter. Upon entering her parents' house, the maiden tells them how much danger she passed through as she took on the role of a man: "But two wondrous youths have taught me that a woman may be a huntress and yet never leave her own fireside. Behold! I will marry, when some good youth comes to me, and he will hunt rabbits and deer for me, for my parents and my children" (Cushing 1979: 400).

The Ahayu:da are thus far more than "idols" or "carvings"; they are protectors and instructors and transformers for both men and women. They helped the Zunis find their final home during the period of migration and continue to be living beings without whose existence the Zunis cannot be Zunis. The two new gods serve for one year, after which they are placed in hidden shrines to decay of natural processes and thus to return their natural powers to the earth, the whole earth on which we all live (Merenstein 1993: 590–91). The War Gods' powers are regenerated by the creation of new images each year.

One of the least discussed and most misunderstood aspects of the repatriation movement is that the purpose of returning sacred remains and property to their rightful caretakers is not just because they are the "property" of a particular person, family, group, or tribe, but because in many cases unless they are returned the world cannot be healthy, sane, beautiful, nurturing, or "right" for any of us. When Mr. Tsadiasi says he wants the Zuni fathers back "for the good of the people," he thus means all people, not just the Zunis of New Mexico. As is consonant with the reciprocity inherent in Zuni cosmology, the Bow Priests and clan leaders must instruct each new set of images so that their powers might work for the protection of the Zunis. Uninstructed, their powers can be deadly. The destructive powers these twin War Gods possess—which can be manifested in earthquakes, floods, and tornados—must be controlled through the proper prayers and rituals performed by knowledgeable Zuni priests within their proper shrines (Hustito 1991: 12; Merrill, Ladd, and Ferguson 1993: 525; 530).

On these universal humanitarian grounds, as well as on the grounds of self-determination, human rights, and sovereignty, Zuni religious leaders decided in 1978 that all the Ahayu:da who had been removed from their territory had to be returned to their home (Ferguson 1991: 13). It was estimated in the 1990s that at least eighty Ahayu:da had been taken to museums. By 1993, sixty-five War Gods had been located and repatriated to the Zunis from places as geographically diverse as the

Denver Art Museum and the Denver Museum of Natural History, the Tulsa Zoological Society, Beloit College in Wisconsin, the Milwaukee Public Museum, the Museum of the American Indian in New York City, and the Winnipeg Art Gallery in Canada (Ferguson 1991: 13). To regain their property, the Zunis had to negotiate separately with more than thirty private collectors and institutions, a grueling, time-consuming, and heartrending task.

In 1987 the Smithsonian returned four wooden carvings that had been taken from Zunis between 1879 and 1884 by the Smithsonian expedition organized by John Wesley Powell, the founder and director of the Bureau of American Ethnology (Green 1990: 370–71). Two of these were statues of the archangels Saint Michael and Saint Gabriel, which had been taken from the Catholic mission church. The other two images were Ahayu:da, which, after their theft, were kept in the private collections of James Stevenson and Frank Hamilton Cushing in their respective homes on the East Coast (Merrill, Ladd, and Ferguson 1993; Merrill and Ahlborn 1997: 191). Although Cushing, especially, worked to protect the rights of the Zunis and Zuni territory against outside encroachment, the fact that he still viewed them as a vanishing people whose patrimony needed to be "salvaged," as world patrimony fueled his inability to treat their objects—and thus the Zuni people themselves—with the full respect they deserved as his gracious hosts for over four years.

The two examples of wampum and the Zuni War Gods underscore the fact that the repatriation movement existed long before the state and federal laws of the 1980s and 1990s that brought these long-standing concerns of Native Americans to the broader American consciousness. In the remainder of this chapter we look at some brief examples of other kinds of practices and legislation that would serve as a basis for the 1990 NAGPRA.

U.S. State Statutes

As June Camille Bush Raines points out, every state has laws against grave robbing and tampering with corpses. Yet despite the fact that such actions violate the treaty rights of sovereign nations, scientists have been allowed to disinter the bodies and grave goods of Native Americans (Raines 1992: 640). Only one federal law was passed in the 1980s that addressed repatriation; the National Museum of the American Indian

Act is discussed below. However, by the end of the 1980s, some new state laws had been passed regarding graves protection and reburial, and by the end of the 1990s, thirty-eight states had graves-protection laws (Thoms 1999: 101).

As discussed in chapter 2, the 1966 National Historic Preservation Act (NHPA) provided a means by which federal programs could be delegated to state implementation by requiring that each state set up a State Historic Preservation Office (SHPO; pronounced "shippo"). The NHPA assigned responsibilities to the SHPOs, including the nomination of eligible properties to the National Register, preparing statewide historic preservation plans, and assisting local governments in developing historic preservation programs (Collins 1992: 97–98). Although the federal government provides some grant money to carry out historic preservation, the state must raise matching funds and must enforce national programs and national standards at the local level (98).

The intersection of federal, state, and tribal regulations has made conducting archaeology a complex task, with regulations often at odds with each other. The following is a brief sampling of a few states' policies and actions regarding Native American human remains and cultural properties. It is important to note that while most states mandate preservation of "archaeological resources," very few address repatriation. Most states have statutes that prohibit opening graves and removing or abusing dead bodies, but when the remains are completely decomposed and residing in unmarked graves the laws are often unclear. Many states simply give little consideration to Native American cultural, spiritual, and emotional concerns (Price 1991: 46, 49).

CALIFORNIA

According to H. Marcus Price III, who has compiled one of the most thorough accounts of state and federal burial and grave goods laws, California has one of the most "sweeping and severe" burial laws of any state in the nation, legislation that applies to both public and private property (Price 1991: 50). When human remains are discovered outside of a cemetery, the county coroner is notified, who then notifies the Native American Heritage Commission (NAHC, a state agency) if the remains are of Native American origin. If the NAHC cannot locate any likely living descendants or if the descendants fail to make a recommendation, the remains must be reburied by the landowner. Violation of this law is a felony punishable by imprisonment. In addition, it is illegal under most circumstances to possess Native American artifacts or human remains taken from a grave on or after 1 January 1984 (Price 1991: 50).

There has been a great deal of resistance to the law. In 1981 when the NAHC asked that two collections of Indian burial materials be reinterred, a group of people opposed to burying the artifacts formed the Committee for the Preservation of Archaeological Collections. Although 840 human remains were reburied, the CPAC was successful in stopping the burial of the remainder of the materials (Hill 1996: 88).

However, much voluntary repatriation has also been carried out. In June of 1989 Stanford University returned 550 remains to the Ohlone-Costanoan tribe (after conducting scientific analysis) and passed a resolution to protect the fifty archaeological sites known to be on the Stanford campus (Hill 1996: 88; Price 1991: 50).

COLORADO

Colorado's first antiquities act was passed in 1967 (CRS 131–12), which reserves title to historical, prehistorical, and archaeological resources found on state-owned lands to the state. The state Historic Preservation Act was revised in 1973, and then again in 1990 (the latter revision adding a section that protects unmarked human graves and stipulating procedures to follow in the case of inadvertent discovery) (Collins 1992: 108). The act does not apply to private lands, which, in some parts of the state, contain a great many Native American ancestral sites and human remains. The presence of the federal government is quite strong in Colorado, which has two major Indian reservations and a great many areas designated as public lands, and where the creation of Mesa Verde National Park in 1906 (the same year that the federal Antiquities Act was passed) brought the National Park Service squarely into activities involving Native American "archaeological resources" within Colorado state boundaries (Matlock and Duke 1992: 187). The federal government has created, in the words of Matlock and Duke (188), a veritable "cultural-resource-management-industry" where the private sector has taken a leading role in fulfilling the mandates of state and federal laws to "mitigate" damage to "archaeological resources."

As State Archaeologist Susan Collins points out (1992: 100), a great deal of mistrust of the federal government exists in Colorado, as it does in many other western states, for a variety of reasons. From the time of the Wetherill brothers, who "discovered" the cliff dwellings at Mesa Verde in the 1880s, a strong amateur archaeological community has existed in Colorado. Federal archaeologists working for the Forest Service, the National Park Service, the Bureau of Land Management, and the Bureau of Reclamation, as well as academic anthropologists, often express debts of gratitude to conscientious professionals within the amateur ranks who work to protect archaeological sites. (For detailed discussions of the role of amateur archaeology in Colorado, see Ooton (1992) and Duke and Matlock (1999).

In the mid-1970s Colorado established the Commission of Indian Affairs (*www.state.co.us/gov_dir/ltgov/indian*) to work as a liaison between the state of Colorado and the two Indian nations located within its boundaries, the Southern Ute Tribe and the Ute Mountain Ute Tribe. The commission works with these tribes in areas of economic development, natural resources, education, and human services and is contacted when unmarked human graves located on state, local, and private lands are determined by the state archaeologist to be Native American (Schamel, Schaefer, and Neumann 1997). The commission therefore serves as a liaison between the Colorado Historical Society (CHS) and the tribes, as well as between the federal government and the CHS (Ken Charles, personal communication). For an excellent overview of state and federal laws as they apply to Colorado, see Lipe, Varien, and Wilshusen (1999).

KANSAS

In the 1980s the Native American Rights Fund (NARF) took on legal representation of "the Indian victims of the grave desecration in Kansas and the massive grave expropriations in Nebraska" (Echo-Hawk 1988: 1; see also Echo-Hawk and Echo-Hawk 1994). In an article written for NARF concerning the treatment of Native Americans and their dead in Kansas and Nebraska, Walter R. Echo-Hawk provides a chilling report of what he calls "examples of brutal ethnocentrism which originated in the last century, and which continue to haunt Native people":

> In Kansas, a farmer dug up an entire Indian cemetery located on his land and has put all 146 dead bodies on public display as a roadside "tourist attraction." Despite the fact that the State Legislature has enacted over 70 statutes to comprehensively regulate and protect burial grounds of every imaginable description, the repugnant commercial exploitation of the Indian burial ground is permitted to

exist by virtue of an alleged "loophole" in state law. In Nebraska, after the aboriginal Pawnee Nation was removed to a distant state by the federal government, private parties and state archaeologists swept into Pawnee cemeteries and removed hundreds of bodies and thousands of burial goods from historic graves. When asked to return these dead to the Pawnee government for a decent burial, the all-white Historical Society first claimed that the bodies were "owned" by it, citing federal regulations later admitted to be "non-existent," then loudly decried what it termed an Indian "raid" on museum "property" (Echo-Hawk 1988: 1).

The descendants of the 146 individuals put on display—northern Caddoan Indians who are the original inhabitants of Kansas—hired NARF to make it possible that their ancestors could be buried rather than displayed to tourists (Echo-Hawk 1988: 4; Native American Rights Fund n.d.). While NARF worked to negotiate with state and local officials, including the landowner, state legislation was sought in Kansas and in thirteen other states regarding reburial rights.

In 1986 Haskell Indian Junior College held a symposium on reburial that, like the NARF litigation, contributed to the passing of H.B. 2144, the Kansas Unmarked Burial Sites Preservation Act, which protects human remains and artifacts found on both private and public lands. The law prohibits individuals (without a permit) from disturbing unmarked burial sites, possessing any human remains or funerary objects, or displaying or engaging in commerce with these materials. Penalties range from $100 for failure to report a violation to $100,000 for the violation itself (Price 1991: 66–67).

NEBRASKA
Pawnees

In March of 1988, Lawrence Goodfox Jr., chairman of the Pawnee Tribe of Oklahoma, asked the Nebraska State Historical Society (NSHS) to return the remains of hundreds of deceased Pawnee individuals and their burial offerings stored in the NSHS museum. The executive director of the NSHS refused, on the ground of protecting scientific knowledge—"a bone is like a book . . . and I don't believe in burning books"—and on the ground of cultural authenticity when he questioned whether today's Pawnees still abide by traditional mortuary practices (Peregoy 1999: 230). To Hanson this question had relevance because the Pawnees were claiming that without the correct burial practices and offerings the spirits of their dead would wander without peace. This question, of course, is as irrelevant to the Pawnees as it is to other peoples who are held to "traditional" standards to which they may no longer adhere because of the very colonialist practices that alienated the remains of their ancestors in the first place. The Pawnees also pointed out, as did the Zunis in regard to their War Gods, that until Pawnee remains are repatriated and reburied, not only are the living Pawnees in jeopardy of their lives, but so are those in museums who handle the offerings and remains.

With the assistance of NARF, the Pawnees of Oklahoma (whose relatives once lived in Nebraska, which is how the NSHS acquired their remains) joined forces with other Nebraska tribes to get Native American burial and repatriation legislation passed. The battle in the Nebraska Legislature was a difficult, if exciting, one, based on federal Indian law, constitutional law, previous Nebraska state law, and United States common law, which allows no alien ownership rights to dead bodies (see Peregoy 1999: 232–36 for details). The Pawnees were persistent in their efforts as they dealt with the federal government and with all three branches of Nebraska state government. "The courageous vision of enlightened Nebraska lawmakers firmly committed to the principles of fairness, equality, and human dignity won the day for a traditionally oppressed minority group, many of whom could not even vote for the lawmakers who carried the banner of justice on their behalf" (231).

In 1989, the Nebraska Unmarked Human Burial Sites and Skeletal Remains Protection Act (LB 340) was passed. This law was "the first in the country to require public museums to return all tribally identifiable skeletal remains and burial offerings to Indian tribes that requested them for reburial" (Peregoy 1999: 231). The law became the model not only for similar legislation passed in several other states (e.g., Arizona and Hawaii) but for the federal National Museum of the American Indian Act (1989) and the Native American Graves Protection and Repatriation Act (1990), both of which are discussed below.

On 11 September 1990, the remains and funerary offerings of 403 deceased Pawnee ancestors were reburied in the municipal cemetery at Genoa, Nebraska, the site of the last town—Wild Licorice Creek—inhabited by the Pawnees before they were forced to move from their Nebraska homeland to Oklahoma (Echo-Hawk and Echo-Hawk 1993, 1994; Native American Rights Fund 1990).

Before LB 340 was passed, and before NAGPRA became federal law, the Omahas of Nebraska worked hard for the repatriation of Umon'hon'ti, the "Real Omaha," the "Venerable Man," also known as the "Sacred Pole"; for Umon'hon'ti's companion, Tethon'ha, the Sacred White Buffalo Hide; and for two sacred catlinite pipes associated with the pole and hide. The remarkable stories of their repatriation from the Peabody Museum of Harvard University is told by anthropologist Robin Ridington and Omaha tribal historian Dennis Hastings in *Blessing for a Long Time* (1997). These stories are instructive in their weaving together of nineteenth-century history, private museum policies, anthropological advocacy for Native American rights, and state law that connects and contributes to federal law.

The sacred person Umon'hon'ti traveled from Macy, Nebraska, to the Harvard Peabody Museum via Omaha-Ponca anthropologist Francis La Flesche, who in 1888 convinced the Sacred Pole's keeper, Yellow Smoke, to send Venerable Man "to some eastern city where he could dwell in a great brick house instead of a ragged tent" (Ridington and Hastings 1997: xvii–xix, 24).[1] Ridington, a Harvard graduate who had first become aware of the pole in 1962, arranged for an Omaha delegation to visit the Peabody on 27 June 1988, when the Sacred Pole was touched for the first time in one hundred years by Omaha persons (24–35). By 1988 the Omahas were involved in two important projects: negotiations with the Peabody for the return of Umon'hon'ti and the struggles of the Pawnees to challenge the Nebraska State Historical Society's opposition to legislation that would repatriate human remains and burial goods. By 1989 the Sacred Pole was returned to the Omahas, and since 12 August 1990 it has been in the care of the University of Nebraska at Lincoln. On 20 September 1990, the Peabody returned an additional 280 sacred objects (193), and on 3 August 1991, the Sacred White Buffalo Hide and its pipe were returned to the Omahas from the National Museum of the American Indian (229).

OTHER NOTABLE STATE ACTIONS IN THE 1980S

In March of 1985 the Tunica-Biloxi tribe of Louisiana claimed title to a private collection of ancestral remains totaling 2.5 tons after the state of Louisiana ruled that these eighteenth-century artifacts belong to the tribe and not to the landowner. The remains were reburied in 1987, and the tribe began construction of a museum to house the remaining objects (Hill 1996: 88).

In 1989 the University of Minnesota complied with a 1981 state law requiring repatriation by agreeing to return the remains of nearly a thousand Indians.

In 1988 the University of Vermont said that it would repatriate Abenaki ancestral remains if the tribe purchased a site in which the remains could rest.

A REPATRIATION CHRONOLOGY FOR THE 1980S

Although I am providing only the briefest overview, it is clear that many repatriation-related activities, discussions, and legislation took place in the 1980s at federal, state, tribal, and private levels, from auction houses to Native American rights groups to universities and museums. I summarize a few of the major events below, relying heavily on an excellent chronology prepared by Richard Hill Sr. regarding "Removal and Repatriation" that is published in the *Native American Repatriation Guide* (1996) prepared by the American Indian Ritual Object Repatriation Foundation:

1978 (Aug.) Four carved sacred Hopi Taalawtumsi figures are stolen from Second Mesa and sold for $1,600 to a collector who chopped them up and burned them sometime in 1980–81 rather than be caught with them. Although it is known who stole the figures, no one was charged with any crime after a thirteen-year investigation. As repatriation becomes a "hot" issue from the mid-1970s onward, the market for Native American "antiquities" grows hotter as well, with a marked increase in thefts and illegal sales.

1980 Three stolen Hopi masks are sold to collectors by a Chicago art dealer who pleads guilty but receives only a fine of $1,000. The masks are donated to the Art Institute of Chicago by the collectors, who receive inflated tax deductions for them.

1981 A statement regarding ethical standards for the treatment of Native American collections is published by the American Association of Museums.

1982 The National Park Service produces a document entitled "Guidelines for the Disposition of Archaeological and Historical Human Remains" that suggests that Native Americans should be consulted regarding sensitive issues surrounding scientific, cultural, and religious values.

1983 Five ritual objects are stolen from the Museum of the American Indian by known persons who are nonetheless never indicted.

1984 A comprehensive bibliography on repatriation issues is published by the National Museum of American History.

1984 The Smithsonian returns five Modoc remains to their living descendants.

1984 The Zunis regain title to their ancient sacred site, Kolhu/wala:wa, where deceased Zunis reside. It is not until 1990 that Zunis gain the right to cross private land to reach Zuni Heaven (Bad Wound 1999h: A6).

1985 Michael Bush, executive director of the American Indian Community House in New York City, publishes a letter in the *New York Times* (24 March) calling for the Smithsonian to either give Indians access to their cultural patrimony or return the items to them.

1985 The Smithsonian provides 225 tribes with an inventory of the Indian remains in their collection with details regarding methods of storage and public access.

1986 The National Museum of Natural History (Smithsonian) establishes an outreach program for Indian communities to encourage research and program design regarding Native American peoples.

1986 Senator John Melchor of Montana introduces S.2952 to create a Native American Claims Commission Act to provide a forum for the airing of disputes between Indians and museums regarding human remains and sacred objects. This "Bones Bill" is ultimately defeated "due to strong opposition from museums."

1986 The Navajo Nation establishes the first tribal preservation program. By 1999 there are nineteen Tribal Historic Preservation Offices established throughout the United States (Downer 1999: 14, 19).

1986 (26 September) The National Congress of American Indians adopts a resolution during its annual convention that "rejects the federal laws which define Indian and Native burial sites, human remains and grave goods as 'archaeological resources' and which permit the continued curation, storage, and display of these sacred materials in museums, universities and other institutions." Further, "Federal laws must be changed to reflect Indian and Native religious and cultural rights to determine the treatment and disposition of these materials."

1986 (December) The *Anthropology Newsletter* creates a discussion surrounding the "archaeologist's dilemma"—whether to support science and be forever depicted as "ghoulish exploiters," or to support Native American interests and be seen as pandering to Indians at the expense of valuable scientific knowledge.

1987 (February) A real estate developer in New Mexico agrees to rebury five Ancestral Pueblo Indian remains and thousands of associated objects at the request of Sandia Pueblo.

1987 Two of the War Gods removed from Zuni Pueblo by anthropologists James Stevenson and Frank Hamilton Cushing are returned by the Smithsonian to the tribe.

1987 (July) The Larsen Bay Tribal Council from Kodiak Island, Alaska, sends a resolution to the National Museum of Anthropology (Smithsonian) calling for the return of all Uyak site ancestral human remains and the materials associated with them. These remains were collected by the "skull doctor" discussed in chapter 1, Aleš Hrdlička, in the 1930s (see Bray and Killion 1994).

1987 (August) The National Congress of American Indians holds meetings so that Indians can comment on the policy proposed by the United States Forest Service to protect Indian burial sites and to rebury remains from federal lands east of the Mississippi.

1988 The American Association of Museums publishes a "Policy Regarding the Repatriation of Native American Ceremonial Objects and Human Remains."

1988 The Mohawk Nation requests that an Iroquois medicine mask be removed from an exhibition at the Glenbow Museum, which is then ordered by a court to comply.

1988 (8 May) The eleven sacred wampum belts discussed above are returned from the Heye Foundation museum (which became the National Museum of the American Indian in 1989) to the Six Nations Council of Chiefs.

1988 (September) An auctioneer in Baltimore returns three sacred headdresses to the Blackfeet Nation.

1988 The Pawnee Tribe of Oklahoma begins formal actions to repatriate all Pawnee human remains and funerary items.

1989 The National Congress of American Indians and the Heard Museum of Phoenix organize a "Dialogue on Museum and Native American Relations" with official support from Senator John Mc-

Cain (R–AZ). Representatives from museum, scientific, and Native American communities attend.

1989 The Field Museum of Chicago adopts a repatriation policy and begins returning remains to tribes. (In 1972 the museum issued a "Policy Statement Concerning Acquisition of Antiquities" that focused on the responsibility of the museum to stay clear of the illicit international trade in antiquities.)

1989 The Commission on Native American Remains is formed by the American Anthropological Association, which includes Native American anthropologists in its composition. The commission issues a report that opposes federal legislation regarding repatriation because of the possibility of reducing Native American diversity to stereotypes and removing solutions from the local arena.

1989 The Navajo Nation Departments of Historic Preservation and Archaeology cosponsor a groundbreaking conference, "Preservation on the Reservation," to discuss preservation practices on Indian lands (Downer 1999; McKeown 1999). This conference, and the publication it produced by the same title, "would foreshadow events of the coming decade: the applicability of preservation law to tribal culture and how Native Americans and archaeologists could work together given the antagonisms of the time" (McKeown 1999: 10).

1989 (May) The Blackfeet Tribe in Montana conducts a reburial ceremony for objects returned to the tribe by the Smithsonian in 1988.

1989 Six bills are submitted to the U.S. Congress concerning repatriation.

1989 The Smithsonian Institution publishes a statement answering questions regarding their Native American collections and holding fast to the idea that unless descendants requested the remains of named individuals, human remains would stay in their collection for scientific and medical research.

1989 (28 November) The National Museum of the American Indian Act is passed, which requires the return of Native American human remains and funerary objects from the Smithsonian and the creation of a national advisory committee. The act also calls for an appropriation of $1 million for 1991 to carry out the required inventory.

National Museum of the American Indian Act

As indicated in the list above, it is clear that claims for the return of Native American artifacts and human remains were being made to the Smithsonian for many years before actual legislation was passed that established federal guidelines. But Public Law 101–185 did more than enact repatriation guidelines. The act created a new museum, the National Museum of the American Indian, by transferring ownership of the more than one million objects and 86,000 photographic prints and negatives, in the Museum of the American Indian, located in New York City, to the Smithsonian (Bray, Rand, and Killion 1996: 47). When it was determined that the massive Heye collection that comprised the Museum of the American Indian needed a larger facility and a better locale, a tug of war ensued between various parties, including the American Museum of National History, Ross Perot, and the Smithsonian. The Heye collection was amassed by a wealthy banker, George Gustav Heye (1874–1957) who traveled extensively throughout the United States and Europe, searching for Native American objects for his private collection. This collection turned into a museum that opened to the public on a limited basis in 1922 and was itself the subject of many claims and controversies over the years (Raines 1992: 651).

Growing International Concern for Repatriation

Although it is beyond the scope of this book to discuss in detail hemispherical and global indigenous movements, I must at least mention that Native American activism was also taking place south of the Rio Grande and into South America in the 1970s and 1980s, much of it oriented toward human rights and sovereignty. Native peoples of the Americas have resisted genocide, dispossession, and ethnic erosion since the beginnings of European contact, in ways both violent and nonviolent.[2]

Cultural revitalization movements such as the *taki onkoy* ("sickness dancing") that took place in the 1560s in the Andes sought to cleanse and heal Native cultures of Spanish customs and religion and the overall sickness that had been injected into their world. Rebellions took place on two continents from the fifteenth to the twentieth centuries as indigenous peoples refused to accept slavery, land theft, and forced assimilation. In the 1920s a movement called "indigenism" grew in Mexico and the Andes formed by primarily non-Indian supporters of what was usually an idealistic version of indigenous sociocultural and political life. This movement culminated in 1940 in Patzcuaro, Mexico, with the formation of the Inter-American Indian Institute, where nineteen of the Indian delegations signed a treaty agreement to meet every four years (Wilmer 1993: 211). In 1964 Shuar and Achuar Native peoples formed the Shuar Federation, an organization that coalesced regional forces to resist colonization, cattle raising, and other encroachments on tropical forest territories in eastern Ecuador. The Shuar Federation is still active today, offering people in its area a bilingual radio station, their own cultural and language studies publications, legal services, and transportation by ground or air (Wearne 1996: 167).

In 1971 the World Council of Churches, responding to a growing liberation theology movement, organized a conference in Barbados on the "Liberation of the Indian," which was attended by anthropologists, governmental representatives, and missionaries. The council issued the "Declaration of Barbados" calling for action to reverse the global trends of indigenous dispossession and cultural degradation and emphasizing the importance of recognizing "that the liberation of the indigenous populations must be accomplished or it is not liberation" (Wearne 1996: 166; Wilmer 1993: 212). Indigenous peoples already knew this, however, as illustrated by the many actions that predated the Declaration of Barbados. By the 1970s many major indigenous organizations had emerged in the Americas, many of them issuing public declarations or manifestos to make their positions clear. In 1973 the Manifesto of Tiwanaku was drawn up by four indigenous organizations and presented in La Paz, Bolivia. The manifesto reasserted Indian identity following a 1950s revolutionary movement that tried to re-identify Indians as "peasants." In 1974 the Dene people of Canada issued a declaration stating that "the government of Canada is not the government of the Dene," and in 1979 the Six Nations Iroquois Confederacy issued the Declaration of the Haudenosaunee that announced itself as "among the most ancient continuously operating governments in the world" (Wearne 1996: 165–66). From 8 to 16 June 1974, representatives from 97 Indian tribes and nations from both North and South America met on the Standing Rock Sioux Reservation to form the International Indian Treaty Council (IITC). By the end of this first meeting, the IITC had issued a

"Declaration of Continuing Independence," a portion of which follows: "The United States of America has continually violated the independent Native Peoples of this continent by Executive Action, Legislative fiat and Judicial decision. By its actions, the U.S. has denied all Native people their International treaty rights, Treaty Lands and basic human rights of freedom and sovereignty. . . . In the course of these human events, we call upon the people of the world to support this struggle for our sovereign rights and our treaty rights. We pledge our assistance to all other sovereign people who seek their own independence" (International Indian Treaty Council 1974: 1–2).

By the 1970s what Phillip Wearne calls "the 'pyramid' building of indigenous organizational structures had taken off, particularly in South America" (Wearne 1996: 170). For example, the Shuar Federation is also a member of CONFENIAE, the Confederation of Indigenous Nationalities of Amazonian Ecuador, which in turn is part of CONAIE, the Confederation of Indigenous Nationalities of Ecuador. CONFENIAE is also part of COICA, the Coordinating Body of Indigenous Peoples of the Amazon Region, which includes indigenous groups from most South American nations that have Amazonian territory and which is the largest indigenous organization in the Americas.

At the international level, where do these indigenous organizations fit, including those of North America, Central America, and Canada? Although the speaker of the Council of the Iroquois Confederacy, Deskaheh, visited the new League of Nations in 1921 to report a dispute between the league and the Canadian government, indigenous peoples generally did not enter the United Nations again for nearly fifty more years (Tauli-Corpuz 1999: 4; Wilmer 1993: 211). Various instruments were forged to address indigenous rights, but only very slowly. Although the Universal Declaration of Human Rights (UDHR) was issued by the General Assembly of the United Nations in 1948, it was oriented toward the protection of individuals' rights from state violation, not toward collective cultural rights (see Morsink 1999).[3] Nonetheless, it set the stage for the creation of the hundreds of human rights documents that emerged in the second half of the twentieth century.

The only international binding convention that addresses indigenous rights is said to be the International Labor Organization (ILO) Convention No. 107, issued in 1957, "Concerning the Protection and Integration of Indigenous and Other Tribal and Semi-Tribal Populations in Independent Countries" (Wilmer 1993: 212). While this convention focused on the importance of paying attention to the rights of indigenous populations, especially as concerns their relationship to their lands, it also stated that national governments had the responsibility to progressively integrate indigenous populations "into the life of their respective countries." An improved version of this convention was thus issued in 1989 as the ILO "Convention Concerning Indigenous and Tribal Peoples in Independent Countries," No. 169, which not only eliminates the integrationist language, but provides penalties for unauthorized intrusion upon or use of indigenous lands. The convention recognizes resource rights and the importance of "self-identification as indigenous or tribal" as a fundamental criterion for consideration under the convention (Wilmer 1993: 179–80; 215).

In 1971 the United Nations Economic and Social Council (ECOSOC) called for a "Study of the Problem of Discrimination against Indigenous Populations." This study, finally completed in 1986, forwarded 332 recommendations for addressing indigenous peoples' grievances in global and national arenas (Wilmer 1993: 184). The work on this document was accompanied by the formation in 1982 of the UN Working Group on Indigenous Populations (WGIP) and by the formation of the World Council of Indigenous Peoples (WCIP) in the 1980s (Petersen 1999: 8–9).[4] The work of the WGIP and the results of the 1986 study led to discussions surrounding the creation of a permanent forum for indigenous peoples, so that they would have representation in the UN (for details, see the International Work Group for Indigenous Affairs 1999), and surrounding the creation of a Declaration of the Rights of Indigenous Peoples and the Proposed Inter-American Declaration on the Rights of Indigenous Peoples. It is within these documents that provisions regarding the protection of cultural property, human remains, and repatriation are included, but they did not emerge beyond provisional draft forms until the mid-1990s.

As the 1992 quincentennial recognition of five hundred years since Columbus's "discovery" of America approached, indigenous organizations in the Americas planned a variety of expressions of resistance and oppositional histories. One continental, pan-indigenous event organized by CONAIE, ONIC (the Organization of Indian Nationals of Colombia), and SAIIC (the South and Meso American Indian Rights Center, based in San Francisco) was the "500 Years of Indian Resistance" gathering held in Quito, Ecuador. From 17 to 20 July 1990, 120 Indian nations and organizations met to create a manifesto called the "Declaration of Quito" in which the quincentennial celebration is rejected, the continued victimization and dispossession of Indian peoples is denounced, and "respect for our right to life, to land, to free organization and expression of our culture" is demanded (South and Meso American Indian Information Center 1990: 21). Although cultural property, repatriation, and museums are not specifically discussed, points 3 and 4 lay the groundwork for their serious consideration:

3. [We] affirm our decision to defend our culture, education, and religion as fundamental to our identity as Peoples, reclaiming and maintaining our own forms of spiritual life and communal coexistence, in an intimate relationship with our Mother Earth.

4. We reject the manipulation of organizations which are linked to the dominant sectors of society and have no indigenous representation, who usurp our name for (their own) imperialist interests. At the same time, we affirm our choice to strengthen our own organizations, without excluding or isolating ourselves from other popular struggles (21).

Various international conventions, recommendations, and declarations were issued following the devastation of World War II to control the illicit transport of cultural property. The most important of these, mentioned in chapter 1, was the 1970 United Nations Educational, Scientific and Cultural Organization (UNESCO) Convention on the Means of Prohibiting and Preventing the Illicit Import, Export and Transfer of Ownership of Cultural Property, which had a significant impact on museums, requiring them to create policies regarding what they would and would not acquire. The parallel developments of these cultural property statements and the international indigenous movement for human rights and cultural autonomy eventually combined into a global international indigenous repatriation movement, the national versions of which can be seen in the growing number of state and federal laws concerning burial and cultural property protection.

What becomes clear, however, in reading through the accounts of museums' changes in attitude regarding the objects in their care is that it took much longer for sentiment to turn positive toward repatriating human remains than it did for the return of artifacts. Human remains determined to be thousands of years old were viewed as "problematical" as regards their direct relationship to any living human groups and their loss tantamount to a scientific research tragedy (Raines 1992: 645). The Smithsonian's Larsen Bay repatriation process was especially emblematic of this reluctance to give up potential scientific knowledge because of the fact that the most famous physical anthropologist of his time, Aleš Hrdlička, was deeply involved with the collection of the skeletal materials from the Uyak site on Kodiak Island. Hrdlička was an enthusiastic collector of human remains, employing equally enthusiastic locals who obtained not only Native American skeletons for the Czech scientist but also those of deceased Chinese fish cannery employees (Loring and Prokopec 1994: 32).

It is very difficult in a little book like this to give the issues their due, and to spend time talking about the actions and motivations of nineteenth-century European scientists takes away from the real issue at hand, which is the ways the world-view and attitudes they institutionalized within the scientific community and museum world have been addressed, contested, resisted, and revised (see Hill 1996: 90; Killion and Bray 1994: 3–4). Nevertheless, the idea that scientific truth is timeless, apolitical, and somewhat sacred is what makes it difficult to discuss these matters without entering into a polemic that treats science as a monolithic, self-serving monster and Native American claims for justice as little more than fanatical fundamentalism at odds with the universal quest for truth. I have perhaps oversimplified the issue, but it is worthwhile to introduce an important insight here. If Americans have been won over somewhat to the idea of cultural property repatriation, it is because of their affinity to the idea of "property." Alienated "property" should revert to "rightful owners." This idea has little to do with spirit, other than the fetish of the commodity. But when the "property" is bones rather than artifacts, and these bones cannot be directly traced to any "one" in particular, what then? On what basis can a claim be made that is comprehensible to a world-view that divides phenomena in an idiosyncratic way, where spirit and flesh are not only divided but at odds with one another?

The creation of the Museum of the American Indian and of the concomitant set of regulations surrounding the handling, representation, and repatriation of Native American human remains and cultural objects has been a process in which the struggle to cross various divides has been emotional and instructive, painful and redemptive. As the premiere

113

national institution for scientific practice, national mythmaking, and historical precedent, the Smithsonian's National Museum of the American Indian and its associated regulations for conferring with Native Americans regarding the repatriation of museum holdings set the tone and the model for the federal legislation that came one year later.

Part 2: Interpretation, Compliance, and Problems of NAGPRA

4

NAGPRA and Repatriation Efforts in the 1990s

> The major policy achievement and the hardest-fought battle in the development of the repatriation laws has been the humanization of Native Peoples—the legal recognition that we, too, have the human right to get buried and stay buried, to recover our people and property from those who want to own them, to worship in the manner and with the objects of our choosing. —Suzan Shown Harjo, 1995

After the Kansas and Nebraska burial laws and the subsequent National Museum of the American Indian Act (Public Law 101-185) were passed, a coalition was formed of representatives from the National Congress of American Indians, the Native American Rights Fund, the Association for American Indian Affairs, and the National American Indian Council "to lobby for the passage of Federal legislation to repatriate Indian dead for proper reburial and to protect against this activity in the future" (Ducheneaux 1990). A briefing document issued on 16 February 1990 by the coalition that asked for support of additional federal burial legislation framed the argument in terms that by now should be familiar to the reader:

Indian dead bodies are viewed as specimens or trophies and not as people by American society. This attitude has resulted in mass desecration of Indian graves and remains throughout the country. This increasing problem has reached crisis proportions in many victimized Indian communities. No right thinking person would desecrate a white man's grave, but too many people do not think twice about desecrating an Indian grave in the name of science, profit, or entertainment.

In the mid-1860's it was official U.S. policy to procure Indian heads. Subsequent federal antiquity or archaeological protection laws converted Indian graves and dead bodies located on public lands into "federal property." Today, over 18,000 Native remains are warehoused in the Smithsonian alone. Untold thousands are held by other federal agencies. Last session, P.L. 101-185 was passed, which requires the

Smithsonian to return remains and funerary objects to proper Tribes. While the new law signals an historic change in federal policy, it does not cover other federal agencies and museums or non-federal museums which receive federal funds.

There are three basic issues that Indian people are deeply concerned about. First, is the return of dead bodies and funerary objects held by museums or similar institutions to proper Native heirs or governments. Second, prospective despoliation of Indian burials on public lands must be stopped. Third, important tribal religious material that was improperly acquired by museums without good legal title must be returned (Native American Rights Fund et al. 1990).

This lobbying effort resulted in various proposed bills in the House and Senate (S.R. 1021, Native American Grave and Burial Protection Act; S.R. 1980, Native American Repatriation of Cultural Patrimony Act; and H.R. 1646, Native American Grave and Burial Protection Act). On 16 November 1990, the Native American Graves Protection and Repatriation Act (NAGPRA) was passed by the 101st Congress of the United States and signed into law by President George Bush. Public Law 101–601 addresses "the rights of lineal descendants and members of Indian Tribes and Native Hawaiian organizations to certain Native American human remains and cultural items with which they are affiliated" (U.S. Department of Interior 1995). Unlike the largely ineffectual American Indian Religious Freedom Act, NAGPRA provides a more solid legal means to implement just practices as regards the treatment and disposition of Native American (including Indian, Native Alaskan, and Native Hawaiian[1]) human remains, burial offerings, religious artifacts, and objects of cultural patrimony found on federal or tribal lands. NAGPRA establishes the conditions and procedures for excavating or removing these remains and objects—including, as a key condition, consent of the appropriate Native American tribe or organization—and it calls for criminal penalties for the sale, purchase, or transport of human remains or cultural property without a legal right of possession.

Summaries and Inventories

A central element of the law directs federal agencies and any institutions that have received federal assistance to publish an inventory of their

Native American holdings in the *Federal Register* so that the repatriation of these materials and human remains can take place upon request. This aspect of the law has two main requirements. The first is to prepare a "summary for unassociated funerary objects, sacred objects, and cultural patrimony," as discussed in Section 6 of the law (see the appendix for the complete text of the law). This summary is in lieu of an object-by-object inventory and must be followed by consultation with representatives of Native Hawaiian organizations, tribal governments, and traditional religious leaders, who, "upon request . . . shall have access to records, catalogues, relevant studies or other pertinent data for the limited purposes of determining the geographic origin, cultural affiliation, and basic facts surrounding acquisition and accession of Native American objects subject to this section" (U.S. Department of Interior 1995). The second requirement (Section 5 of the law) is to prepare an "inventory for human remains and associated funerary objects." This inventory must "identify the geographical and cultural affiliation of such item" held by the museum or agency, with designation of such based "to the extent possible . . . on information possessed by such museum or Federal agency." Further, the inventories "must be completed in consultation with tribal government and Native Hawaiian organization officials and traditional religious leaders" no later than 16 November 1995 (U.S. Department of Interior 1995). Tribes can make claims following the publication of inventories in the *Federal Register*. As of 10 March 2000, 736 inventories had been submitted to Washington (U.S. Department of Interior 2000). The first museum to submit an inventory under NAGPRA was the Joshua Tree National Monument (Campbell Collection), Twentynine Palms, California (18 June 1992). The Joshua Tree inventory is listed as completed, but many of the rest are not. Because any institution that has ever received federal money is required to submit an inventory, the variety of respondents and the scope of the project are enormous: From cultural resource offices to city museums to universities to public libraries to art centers to zoos—more than seven hundred organizations and still counting—and this does not cover private and state organizations that have never received federal grant monies or the many individuals who have their own private collections of "antiquities."

The NAGPRA Review Committee

Section 8 of NAGPRA mandates the secretary of the interior to establish a committee to "monitor and review" the inventory and identification process. The NAGPRA Review Committee is required by the law to be composed of seven members, three of whom are appointed based on nominations from Indian tribes (at least two of whom are to be "traditional Indian religious leaders"); three of whom are appointed from nominations from national museum and scientific organizations; and one who is appointed by the secretary "from a list of persons developed and consented to by all of the [other six] members," excluding federal officers or employees (U.S. Public Law 101–601, 1990).

By October 2001, the committee had met a total of twenty-two times across the United States, from Fort Lauderdale to Rapid City to Honolulu to Anchorage. Each meeting is announced publicly, and the agenda is distributed well in advance. At the first meeting, held in Washington DC from 29 April to 1 May 1992, only 11 persons attended apart from 6 members of the Review Committee and 5 representatives of the National Park Service (NPS). At the eighteenth meeting, held from 18 to 20 November in Salt Lake City, 113 persons were in attendance to hear the discussions and ask questions of the 7 Review Committee members and 5 NPS representatives. The transcripts of these public forums, which are readily available online,[2] are important sources of information regarding the painful and important complexities of repatriation. The meeting topics range from implementation updates to conflicts between tribes and institutions to conflicts between one tribe and another. But the committee by no means merely provides information or attempts to mediate disputes; it also engages in dialogue concerning the most problematic and difficult aspects of the repatriation process. Questions and issues emerge concerning the definitions of culture, the ways that one "identifies" a culture, the utility or harm of DNA testing, the psychic pain suffered by Native peoples that continues despite the repatriation process, and many other concerns. I return to some of these issues in chapter 5.

Consultation

The law requires that institutions produce their inventories—lists and descriptions of their holdings, along with a surmise regarding to whom the human remains or cultural objects most likely belong—on the basis of consultation with Native peoples thought to have ancestral ties to the territories from which the human remains and objects were taken. The Review Committee does not travel to each institution; instead, representatives of tribes must travel often great distances to look at the collections of an institution that is preparing its inventory. The tribal representatives should receive a summary of the institution's collection before they arrive to look over the materials and remains so that the much more detailed inventory can be prepared based on the consultants' expertise. Sometimes representatives of institutions such as the U.S. Forest Service visit tribal offices with inventories and photographs in hand to facilitate the process, but usually it is the tribal representatives who must travel so that they can see the condition of the possible remains of their ancestor and make more detailed identification of the associated objects.

To give the reader a better sense of what the consultation process can be like, I describe it below as it unfolded at the small college where I teach anthropology. Perhaps this account will also help the reader understand why someone like me is writing a book like this.[3]

Federal Law Meets a State College

Fort Lewis College is located in Durango, Colorado, near and among the largest concentrations of Native peoples in North America. There is ample opportunity for students to visit many of the contemporary and ancient communities that they study in classes or that may be the home villages and towns of their friends. Mesa Verde National Park and other archaeological centers are just short drives away from campus. This well-romanticized ambience means that more students than is common for a college of 4,000 decide to major in anthropology (144 in 1995–96), with the numbers growing every year. As a result, the Department of Anthropology employs seven full-time anthropologists (six in 1995–96), three of whom teach archaeology, the most popular subject matter. Archaeological excavations have been conducted by the department since the 1960s, either at the site donated to the college or at nearby sites that are threatened with destruction unless they are "mitigated." A state-of-the-art field school, centered on ancestral Puebloan prehistory, has been conducted nearly each summer at one of these sites.[4] As a result of this work and of various other donations and acquisitions, a collection of artifacts and human remains has accumulated over the years, a not-uncommon circumstance for any college conducting field schools and cultural resource management (CRM) work.

What is unusual about this college is that in any one year about 10 percent of its student body is made up of individuals enrolled in anywhere from thirty-two to more than fifty North American Indian tribes. The irony of this, to those who know the history, is that the original Fort Lewis was a United States Army post established to protect white settlers from Indian attacks. When the post was abandoned in 1891, it was transformed into a federal Indian boarding school to which primarily Ute children were sent, following the then-common national ideology and practice of assimilation. The Indian school was closed in 1911, and the land was eventually deeded to the state of Colorado with the stipulation that Native Americans receive tuition free of charge. College courses were first offered in 1925, and the first four-year B.A. degree was awarded in 1964.

Teaching anthropology at Fort Lewis is thus a bit different matter than it is at most other institutions, not only because Native American students are often sitting in the classroom, but because many of the other students have expectations that they will learn something about "Southwest Indians," no matter what the subject matter on hand might be. The anomaly of being a school that has a sizeable percentage of Indian students but is not an Indian college per se can create tensions and confusion for students and faculty alike. To address this and other matters, the college has set up "diversity" seminars and workshops in which participants are educated about matters of race, gender, and ethnicity (the standard trio) and examine their own "positionality."[5]

When one works as an anthropologist in the Southwest, however, one's position is doubly suspect due to the peculiar place anthropology holds in the history of white-Indian relations in the United States. Although all of us in the Department of Anthropology have had extensive dealings with Native American people at every conceivable level of interaction, we nevertheless viewed the NAGPRA meetings as an opportunity to clear up any doubts or suspicions the consultants might have about our "position," especially as few of them had ever had personal contact with us. We also wanted to demonstrate that we regularly observe the late Native American anthropologist Alfonso Ortiz's admonition that we "consider ourselves students *with* as well as *of*" the peoples whose objects and human remains we curate and whose cultures and lives we discuss in our classrooms (Ortiz 1972: xx). I discuss these consultation sessions after briefly describing how we were introduced to the obligation of complying with NAGPRA.

NAGPRA COMPLIANCE AT FORT LEWIS COLLEGE

The 1990 NAGPRA did not become a major part of our department's work load until September of 1994, when the vice president for academic affairs forwarded to me a form letter he had received in August from the Washington office of the National Park Service. In this communiqué we were told that our institution's collection summary of unassociated American Indian funerary objects, sacred objects, and objects of cultural patrimony was due on 15 November 1993 (a date that had long since passed). We also learned that the deadline for our inventory of Native American human remains and associated funerary objects was 16 November 1995, a little more than a year away. This inventory, of course, was to be completed in consultation with all relevant American Indian tribes, which in the Southwest can mean as many as twenty-five to thirty, depending on the precise region. Those of us in the Department of Anthropology had heard of NAGPRA but thought that the law did not apply to our department because we had never received any federal funds for archaeological field projects. We soon realized, however, that because other departments at the college had received funding from the National Science Foundation and other federal sources, those of us in the anthropology department were indeed to bear the very expensive and time-consuming burden of federal compliance.

As a cultural anthropologist whose field research has been primarily in the Andes, I could not believe that I was really expected to deal with something as monumental and even alien as this. I initially thought about it as something for the archaeologists and physical anthropologists and museum people to worry about. In fact, my first inclination as department chair upon hearing about this mandatory extra job was to pass the buck to the archaeologists: "You created this mess," I said in the mirror, rehearsing my diatribe, "you and your colonialist practices of digging things up and not putting them back where they belong." But as I thought about it further—which I had to do, as these people, after all, are my friends—I realized that this process would require the entire so-called four-field approach, one that weaves together ethnology, archaeology, linguistic anthropology, and biological anthropology to assess those corresponding aspects of cultural affiliation. Would that my department, or the field as a whole, had this mythical but soon-to-be-constructed-by-the-seat-of-our-pants Renaissance breadth. I resolved to be more honest in class lectures about anthropological holism, and I daydreamed that we could subcontract a quintessential four-fielder to be on staff, just to take over the job of NAGPRA.

As the days of Franz Boas have long passed, however,[6] I decided what we really needed was help in the form of a National Park Service NAGPRA grant. I learned from some very sympathetic NPS personnel in Washington that these grants were very competitive, but possible. My colleague Philip Duke, who served for a time as the college's NAGPRA coordinator, wrote much of the narrative and figured out the budget, while I worked on coming up with a concept compelling enough to convince the Park Service that we were going to use the funds for more than just cataloguing purposes (which they rightly claimed we should have already done) or just to pay for tribal representatives' travel, lodging, and consultant fees.

The direction I took actually resulted from my participation in a grievance issue on behalf of the Hopi Office of Cultural Preservation and Protection in response to their learning that courses on Hopi prophecy were being taught in the college's para-academic Extended Studies program. The conflict, which was eventually resolved (see Fine 1994), raised the issue of whether any academic unit (para- or otherwise) had the "right" to teach matters that are increasingly considered to be the cultural property of Native peoples. What therefore might have started out as an "angle" to receive desperately needed grant monies became an opportunity to open our program to the exciting possibility of enhancing the integrated, practical, and ethical potential of anthropology education at our college.

We ultimately designed a project to facilitate and enhance communication between Fort Lewis College and regional Native peoples concerning not only our "archaeological holdings" (a crude way of referring to something much more sacred and profound) but what we teach about American Indian cultural and historical traditions. Within the proposed project we offered all regional tribes the opportunity to make comments on what we teach and how and to give advice concerning the appropriateness of what we do with respect to their traditions and history. We sent our proposal to twenty-five tribes and received ten letters of support that we included with our submission to Washington. In August of 1995 we received the news that our project, entitled "Cultural Property, Cultural Privacy, and Repatriation: A Long-Term, Collaborative Dialogue," had been funded.[7]

The challenges were great, as they involved hosting people who might very well be hostile not only to the ways in which we had conducted our consultation process and had treated the artifacts and human remains all these years, but perhaps to each other's claims as well.

THE CONSULTATION SESSIONS

As discussed above, NAGPRA is not just about repatriating existing holdings; it also includes procedures for dealing with future "inadvertent discoveries" of human remains and related artifacts, and it explicitly prohibits the unauthorized trafficking in Native American cultural items and human remains (see Raines 1992 for more background and commentary). Because of this, consultations that open ongoing lines of communication are very desirable and contain the key both to NAGPRA's success and to its legitimacy. And the anthropologists at Fort Lewis were concerned with far more than the legitimacy of a federal law: we wanted to demonstrate our own legitimacy and sincerity. The responsibility of inviting these particular guests to "our" terrain made us very nervous, as it entailed a reversal of the usual act of ethnographic scrutiny. This time we were to be judged and observed by people who would be there for only a brief stay and thus not get a full picture of our views, attitudes, practices, and good intentions. As a cultural anthropologist, I was acutely aware of the ways that being observed can create defensiveness and resentment, as guests can always exert power over hosts who can be judged as stingy or insincere. But this was not the usual host/guest situation: it was two sets of meetings mandated for both hosts and guests by a more powerful outsider, the federal government, which made any sense of clear "sides" in the issue quite murky.

The four of us most heavily involved in this process have never really talked much among ourselves about this nervousness, or why some of us had the jitters more than others, but my sense is that we knew that more was at stake than our individual reputations. We knew we were being dealt with as a *collective*—the Fort Lewis College anthropologists—and that who went to graduate school where and had what status as a scholar, who did fieldwork where, who was an archaeologist and who was not, and who was hired when and for what reasons did not matter at all. I was acutely aware that we represented not only the discipline as a whole but the college as an important institutional arm of the state of Colorado. Being "white" or "Anglo" mattered much less than two other issues: how we were collectively *doing* North American anthropology at Fort Lewis College and how we were teaching about Native American histories, cultures, and individuals. And although the Department of Anthropology had been visited over the years by administrators, legislators, and prominent colleagues, the visits from the tribal consultants mattered the most in helping us think about our overall educational "mission."

TRIBAL CONSULTANTS' CONCERNS

On 25 January 1996, twenty-three individuals sat down to talk about and listen to matters related to NAGPRA and well beyond it. Six of us were from the college: three archaeologists and myself, plus the archivist of the Center of Southwest Studies and a Navajo student who had been doing professional archaeology for the Navajo Nation. The rest of the participants came from the Pueblo of Acoma, Zuni Pueblo, Nambe Pueblo, the Hopi Tribe, the Ute Mountain Ute Tribe, Taos Pueblo, the Jicarilla Apache Tribe, the Southern Ute Indian Tribe, and the Navajo Nation. Acoma Pueblo had three representatives, the Hopis brought five, and two came from Nambe Pueblo, but the rest of the tribes sent only one representative each. The group was smaller at the session held on 29 February 1995. The same representatives from the college were present, plus two consultants from the Uintah and Ouray Ute Indian tribe, three from Pojoaque Pueblo, two from Tesuque Pueblo, two from Santa Clara Pueblo, and one from Zia Pueblo. A Fort Lewis College student from Tesuque Pueblo also attended.[8]

The sessions were held on campus, in the Center of Southwest Studies and in the laboratory of the Department of Anthropology. It was agreed that the parties would feel more comfortable if tape recorders were not used, as they had not been at three previous NAGPRA consultations held at Mesa Verde National Park. Instead, I took detailed notes, which limited my ability to participate in the conversation or to write when I was conversing. In the typed transcripts of my handwritten notes there are, therefore, two noticeable absences. There are few extended direct quotes from any of the participants, although I recorded the gist of most exchanges rather thoroughly; and there is also almost no record of anything I said. I reworked my initial notes into two sets of minutes that were distributed to all relevant tribes in the Southwest, including those who could not attend either consultation session. The discussion below is based on a synthesis of the minutes, reorganized according to some crosscutting themes. When I use quotation marks in this section of the chapter it is never to express irony but merely to mark the phrases and words that were directly quoted by participants.

The sessions began in the morning on the top floor of the college library, in the Center of Southwest Studies study room, which also serves as a museum. The participants chatted with each other over coffee and muffins before the sessions, joking about the weather and about NAGPRA and going through their packets of information. The center has high walls that are covered with collections of southwestern art and artifacts, primarily Native American rugs and baskets. Some people milled about the room, looking at the large map of the Southwest made from tiles on one wall or at the contents of the Zuni fetish cases. Although the fetishes that are displayed are said to have been made for a tourist art market, there was a hushed and somewhat tense feeling as we sat among all the objects that carry so many layers of meaning, power, and perhaps danger. Some Native American objects, such as the collection of "tourist" kachinas, were behind glass in another room next to cavalry rifles, old state flags, artifacts from the mining industry, and other western paraphernalia.

After a prayer was offered, introductions were made, the agenda was reviewed, and the goals were laid out, each group from the two sessions walked across campus to the main administration building to review Native American objects arrayed in a case in the lobby in order that recommendations be made concerning the appropriateness of having those particular items on display. Although reviewing an institution's display items is not technically part of the required NAGPRA process, at both Mesa Verde National Park (where I attended two sessions) and at the college, tribal representatives took the opportunity to comment on not only the objects displayed (requesting, in some cases, that they be removed) but on the language of the exhibit texts.

From the administration building the groups walked past the Native American Center and could easily see the snowy peak of Hesperus Mountain beyond it, one of the four sacred boundary markers of the Navajo cosmos. We then entered the bland, barracks-like building in which the anthropology department is located and sat at black and green lab tables to discuss the curation and repatriation of human remains. Although the tribes had been sent preliminary summary lists of our holdings, they wanted to hear from us what we had in the storerooms and how, in particular, we acquired them. Some people also wanted to know details about how the skeletal materials were analyzed and then stored. Because Fort Lewis has no physical anthropology specialist on staff, the work on human remains was carried out by an archaeologist who teaches a biological anthropology course and has had only minimal training in skeletal analysis. She had therefore driven most of the skeletal remains three hours south to Albuquerque to be examined by a forensic expert at the University of New Mexico and then had driven them back to be returned to safe storage. Some irritation was expressed by a representative of Acoma Pueblo when the specialist could not answer detailed questions relating physical and anatomical features to anything more than sex and age. This elicited a discussion from the group concerning the degree of destruction that might be expected when more than age, height, and sex are examined, and some consultants expressed their opinions regarding what they felt would be the proper handling of human remains.

It is difficult to describe the feeling in the room as we talked about the human remains, knowing they were just a few feet away, crammed onto steel shelves in the adjacent storeroom. I realized that I had never seen them myself, partly because my work does not require me to, but also perhaps because I had always wanted to pretend they were not there. Until about 1985, some of the remains were used in a teaching collection. On those days, the lab door windows would be covered with paper, so that no one could see inside. The idea was not to hide the activity because it was thought to be questionable in general, but to protect any Native students who might inadvertently look through the window and be taken ill at the sight of the remains of the dead. At this time another anthropologist on staff taught the course, and the chair at that time made the decision to remove all human bones from the teaching collection and to replace them with plastic casts, none of which were made from Native American skeletons.

Although the bones and skulls were placed under lock and key, there were Native American students and faculty who said they could feel the presence of these remains and that they exerted a sad, evil feeling that was detrimental to the best interest of all Native Americans on campus. Some of the remains were removed to a storage facility located off campus, but many of them remained in sealed plastic containers in the storeroom that the consultants now faced. During the January meeting, a discussion took place in which it was decided that cardboard boxes would be better for storage than plastic, as they would allow oxygen to enter and natural processes of decomposition to take place. An archaeologist asked if anyone wanted to enter the storerooms and inspect the collection. Most people declined, but a few elders went in and dusted the boxes, and the archaeologist, with corn pollen to bless the remains and to protect all of those who put themselves in danger by working with or near them.

Perhaps sadder and more frustrating were the discussions that took place during both sessions concerning how reinterment might take place once the cultural affiliations of materials and human remains were established. We all felt acutely the bitter fact that, despite the provisions for repatriation that NAGPRA mandated, it provided no protected land near the places from which the skeletons had been disinterred. To obtain this land, in most cases one would have to deal with the states and private landowners. This discussion also illuminated the great many differences between tribes in terms of cultural values concerning death and burial, differences that obviate any solutions based on, for instance, common burial grounds located at a distance from where the individual died. And the fact that bags full of skeletal material had sometimes been delivered anonymously to the "doorstep" of the college further complicated the issue.

Apart from the issues mentioned above, most of the discussion during the two sessions centered around the broader concerns entailed by the NAGPRA process and, specifically, the document that was to be written jointly by interested tribal representatives and our faculty and students. The purpose of this document, as it was discussed among the groups, was to provide some clarity regarding Fort Lewis College's policies and practices as they concern the treatment of Native American human remains, objects, and cultural knowledge. For the college, the ostensible purpose of such a document is to keep us mindful of important cultural property, intellectual property, representation, curation, and ethical issues. It also gives the college a tangible, ongoing link to the tribes; the document is to remain incomplete because issues will constantly be added and reformulated.

During the morning of the second session a consultant from one of the Eight Northern Pueblos said that she hoped consultation—and the longer-term dialogue and collaboration that the Fort Lewis project proposed—would in fact be "meaningful" and mutual. She made it clear that collaboration must be "even," and that no final products should be rushed or produced on the basis of only minimal discussion. She said that they did not come as "performers" in a show over which they had little control, but as "equal participants."[9] It was decided that the document under discussion should in no circumstances be rushed or imposed upon the tribes in the interest of fulfilling a federal deadline. Instead, Fort Lewis should draft the document and send it out for review, in a process that has now extended several years, because of the importance of getting as many views as possible from each tribe.

In this vein, several representatives reminded us that despite how the law is worded, the relevant parties for consultation are clans and religious societies, not entire tribes per se. Moreover, several representatives wanted it made clear that although they were acting as liaisons to their tribes, the opinions expressed were their own. They wanted it understood that just as there is no such thing as a monolithic "Indian" perspective on most matters, that neither could there be a singular "tribal" perspective. As some of them have explained the matter, one significant reason that the process is so arduous and time-consuming is that they have to return to their communities and make reports to several different groups of people, sometimes more than once, as they enact their own consultations at home. It is therefore important that the document stress the individualism and diversity found in Native American communities and in urban areas where Native Americans also live.

Socioeconomic and structural diversity must also be taken into consideration. One issue that was raised repeatedly was that tribes are disproportionately prepared to deal with the whole NAGPRA process. Although some tribes have lawyers and archaeologists on their payroll and can afford to send cultural resource officers to national meetings, others barely have any funding or staff. There was some justified anxiety that the poorer, less prepared tribes—in terms of cultural resource management and NAGPRA issues—might be rushed, unable to make the claims to which they are entitled within some allotted amount of time. While it is clear that many tribes with more resources are quite willing to help those with fewer, the ability of the law to exacerbate the very real differences between tribes in terms of access to knowledge and resources was not lost on anyone. Along these lines, the deadlines given by the federal government were described as unreasonable and as providing a hardship for many people. There is a strongly grounded perception that although the deadlines are critical in getting museums to take the law seriously and to respond in a "real way" to repatriation, many museums have been dragging their feet. These "so-called scientists," as one consultant called them, may just be going through the motions of NAGPRA compliance and in a manner that reveals great resistance to change and that requires the tribes to do most of the work. The deadlines may also result in some tribes "missing the boat" because they have not been able to marshal the resources they need.

Political differences between tribes also played a role in the discussions. One consultant asked directly if "politics"—by which he meant the Navajo-Hopi dispute over the Joint Use Area—should be involved in the NAGPRA consultations. This bitter dispute is far too intricate a matter to undertake here, but it involves simultaneous claims to original residency and emergence from a large section of land in north central Arizona, located adjacent to the Hopi mesas and within the broad zone encompassed by the Navajo Nation. Archaeology and other forms of science have been employed to support what are essentially deep religious claims, which has placed anthropologists in some very conflicted and contentious situations.[10]

While the Navajo and Hopi representatives did not exchange words during the Fort Lewis consultation sessions, and we were not pulled directly into any disputes, it was apparent that there were subtexts to many discussions that reflected this broader, long-standing conflict. To some Hopi, the Navajo belief that its people are descended from the prehistoric Anasazi (a Navajo term for what the Pueblos consider to be Ancestral Pueblo prehistoric society) is a type of cultural thievery that cannot be tolerated ("Repatriation Standoff" 1996: 12). The large, well-organized Navajo Nation Archaeology Department is also seen as a threat to Hopi sovereignty, and the fact that several of its highest-level positions are held by non-Indians further complicates the situation. Some consultants openly expressed their discomfort that the Navajos had been invited to these consultations at all, because they felt that the material remains in the possession of places like Mesa Verde and Fort Lewis College could only be those of Pueblo ancestors and that any Navajo claims to them could be only political and not religious.

Other consultants expressed their disappointment with all the Navajo-Hopi realpolitik and said that the process should be focused on a pan-Indian religious and cultural concern with getting their collective ancestors "back in the ground where they belong." An unexpected aspect of this issue emerged during the first consultation meeting in January, when the group split up after lunch into private Pueblo and non-Pueblo groups. This idea was mine, as I had seen this procedure at Mesa Verde and thought that somehow it was required at all consultation sessions. Most of the Pueblo representatives supported this idea because it gave them the opportunity to discuss issues of concern to them as peoples with related cultures and history. From the perspective of the Southern Ute representative, however, this was just another tactic to separate the "nomadic" from the "civilized" Indians, thereby imposing "Anglo" (non-Indian) categories once again into the "Indian way of doing things." Apologies were offered by myself and by the Hopi and Acoma representatives, but the objection was made strongly enough to this divisive practice that it was not repeated in the second consultation session.

As most of the consultants who visited the Durango campus came from tribes located in Arizona, Utah, and New Mexico, the Southern Ute representative raised another important issue, which was that the state laws they would have to deal with in Colorado would reflect a history of Indian-white relations somewhat different from those in other states. The attempts at "ethnic cleansing" of all Native peoples that took place in Colorado during the late nineteenth and early twentieth centuries was something this gentleman felt colored the policies of the state of Colorado and perhaps the state's reluctance to provide much in the way of land and protection for reburial. In other words, the fact that this federal process, in real terms, is conducted within individual state jurisdictions and vis-à-vis different sets of challenges to tribal sovereignty (see Russell 1995 for a discussion of this issue in Texas) means that state laws and histories must be taken into account during consultation and repatriation (see chapter 3 for a brief discussion of a few state statutes and policies, particularly those of Colorado).

Tribal consultants strongly recommended during the first consultation session that anthropology take "more responsibility" in the NAGPRA process for the "mess it has created" by conducting field schools each year that produce a great deal of artifacts and human remains in need of analysis.[11] Furthermore, discussion of these matters should take place at the national level, in forums such as the American Anthropological Association (AAA) and Society for American Archaeology (SAA) meetings. A Hopi representative offered his opinion that departments of anthropology in general should teach more courses on ethics, intellectual property rights, religious freedom, sovereignty, cultural property and repatriation, and other "national" issues such as NAGPRA. There was also general agreement that Native peoples' knowledge should be solicited more often when curricular materials dealing with Native peoples were taught and archaeological and ethnographic programs planned. This knowledge should not be of a sacred or religious nature, however, but of a practical nature, such as that concerning agriculture or architecture.

One of the Hopi representatives expressed his view that it is far more appropriate for non-Indians to be interested in the ways Hopi people are masters at growing corn with very little rainfall than it is to pursue the esoteric matters of prophecy. And although religion and agriculture cannot be thoroughly separated, it is possible, in his view, to learn enough religious concepts to allow the agricultural techniques to make sense.

In a related vein, one consultant suggested that anthropologists act as "partners" with Native Americans on these complex issues and take responsibility for our end of things. We should find ways, even when federal funds run out, to have more meetings, bring more Native opinions to our campuses, and keep Native peoples included in our acts of representing and teaching their culture and history. We ended these consultation sessions with an expressed desire to obtain funding for more sessions and to get the proposed document underway.

Civil Penalties for Noncompliance

If Fort Lewis College or any other federally funded museum had not gone through its repatriation process and published its inventory, what might have happened? Section 5(c) of the original statute provides an extension of time for a museum to complete its inventory. The institution must make an appeal to the secretary of the interior indicating that a "good faith" effort is being made to comply with inventory completion. Because the 1990 law is not more specific than this, however, institutions must consult the regulations published in the *Federal Register*, which provide what is known as a "Final Rule" establishing "definitions and procedures" for carrying out the law systematically.[12] According to the 1995 Final Rule, a "good faith effort" entails at least the following:

a) initiation of active consultation;

b) documentation regarding the collections; and

c) the development of a written plan to carry out the inventory process.

This plan must include a definition of the steps required; the position titles of the persons responsible for each step; a schedule for carrying out the plan; and a proposal to obtain the requisite funding (U.S. Department of the Interior 1995, Sec. 10.9[f]).

On 13 January 1997 more specific interim civil penalties were published in the *Federal Register* based on 0.25 percent of the museum's annual budget, or $5,000—whichever is less—plus damages suffered by an aggrieved party and the importance of the cultural items to the performance of traditional practices. An additional penalty of $100 per day may be assessed if the museum continues to violate the law. The administrative procedures for litigation are patterned after the Archaeological Resources Protection Act (ARPA) (U.S. Department of the Interior 1997).

Criminal Penalties

Like ARPA, NAGPRA prohibits illegal trafficking in cultural property and human remains. Offenders may find themselves going to prison for one to five years and/or paying fines ranging from $100,000 to $250,000 (De Meo 1994: 48). Although the first offense is considered a misdemeanor, subsequent violations are treated as felonies. In the opinion of some, however, these penalties are not severe enough to deter traffickers, for whom the much greater profits they stand to gain outweigh the possible penalties incurred. Because illegal trafficking is defined as a "general intent" crime under NAGPRA, it must be proven that cultural items as specifically defined under NAGPRA were removed from federal or private land without tribal consent or without an ARPA permit after 16

November 1990. Human remains are given greater protection, however, as it is prohibited to sell all human remains that have been wrongfully obtained, regardless of when or where the removal took place, including from state or private lands. As De Meo explains, "human remains are contraband to all wrongful possessors. NAGPRA is the first law to extend significant protection to human remains located on private and state lands without a requirement that the remains be involved in interstate commerce, as required by ARPA" (49).

In 1996 a jury convicted Richard Nelson Corrow for violating NAGPRA by trying to sell twenty-two Navajo Yei Bi Chei masks on the illegal art market and for illegal possession of items made with feathers of protected bird species ("Guilty Verdict" 1996; NAGPRA Review Committee, meeting 12, Myrtle Beach, 1996; Saltzstein 1996a, 1996b). Corrow, a resident of Scottsdale, Arizona, was sentenced to five years' probation and one hundred hours of community service to the Navajo Nation. (Because he had already spent $10,000 for the masks and was unable to pay, he was not given any monetary fines.) He was further restricted from carrying firearms ("Guilty Verdict" 1996). Although Corrow and his attorney appealed the ruling on grounds that the concepts of "cultural patrimony" and "cultural items" are "unconstitutionally vague," the Tenth Circuit Court of Appeals upheld the lower court ruling, saying that these terms were not vague, and that Corrow had ample time to verify whether or not he was in illegal possession of tribal property. The Supreme Court declined to review Corrow's appeal request altogether ("Navajo Mask Case" 1998).

On 26 September 1996, a special ceremony was held in Albuquerque, New Mexico, to welcome home the Nightway Yei Jish that had been illegally sold and to return them to the Navajo Nation. In turn, the Nation returned the sacred masks to descendants of the original owner, Mr. Hastiin Hataalii Walker. According to the ceremonial singer who performed the hour-long repatriation ceremony, Mr. Alfred Yazzie: "It was common knowledge at one time that the Nightway ceremony was not to be done outside the boundaries of the Four Sacred Mountains of the Four Directions. . . . The Nightway Yei Jish are alive and not to be carried here and there once it leaves the chanter's home" (Taliman 1996: C2).

The then-president of the Navajo Nation, Mr. Albert Hale, summed up the reason why the crime was such a serious one:

The Yei Bi Chei items should never have been taken from Dinetah, Navajo land, in the first place. . . . To the Navajo people, this taking equates to the kidnapping and captivity of the pope. The caretaker of sacred items can only be those who are blessed with them through proper ceremony. . . . The policy of my administration is to ensure that these sacred religious items, regardless of where they may be found, are returned to their rightful owners, the Navajo people. . . . The religion of the Navajo people deserves the same respect as any other religion. . . . Sacred items that are now in the hands of people outside—museums, private collectors and universities—must be returned to the Navajo Nation (Taliman 1999: C2).

Later in 1996 two more Arizona men were sentenced for taking part in an illegal sale of Zuni cultural property. One of the men, Don Edwin Stephenson, received a fine of $2,500 and two years' probation. The other man, Rodney Phillip Tidwell, was sentenced to three years' probation and was told to pay a $10,000 fine ("Would-Be Artifact Dealers" 1996). Both the Navajo and Zuni cases, by the way, involved Native Americans who illegally sold the items in the first place. The Navajo woman who sold the sacred masks and dish to Corrow was not prosecuted in return for her cooperation with the federal authorities and the Navajo Nation. The Zuni man who stole items from his family and sold them to Tidwell died of cancer before his case came to trial.

In 1997 a Kanab, Utah, man named Richard Lamb sold a "prehistoric" skull to an undercover National Park Service agent for $200. Lamb was sentenced to five years' probation and two hundred hours of community service. He was also required to pay what it cost the NPS to pursue the matter and rebury the skull, a total of $6,416.

For the discipline of anthropology, a major part of the history of which is rooted in collecting and studying what historian George W. Stocking Jr. (1988) has called the "bones, bodies, and behavior" of American Indians, the passage of any law that has as its goal the dispossession of archaeological storeroom and museum case holdings would have to have considerable impact on not only the practice of the discipline but also on the raison d'être of many of its practitioners. These impacts are being discussed in all corners of disciplinary practice, from the classroom to the conference hall, and no verdicts are in yet. The idea that museum noncompliance is tantamount to the behavior of quick-buck, skull-selling, criminal traffickers strikes a blow at the heart of academia and "respectable" art dealing. More than the laws that have preceded it, NAGPRA is in some respects a great "equalizer," one that observes no distinctions between pothunters and professors, or between Indian and Anglo thieves.

NAGPRA must therefore be seen as more than a set of mandates; rather, it must be seen as a dense trope that is in the process of being encoded into our practices and discourses concerning the speaking, teaching, writing about, and possessing of culture. These discussions about matters that have unfolded globally and nationally take place in very intimate, immediate, and often poorly funded situations. They often result in new relationships of collegiality building, new understandings emerging painfully in light of old errors, and new humilities forming in the face of old arrogances. They may in some cases stimulate more illegal trafficking, upping the ante and raising the prices, while in other cases they suppress it, as buyers and sellers become more aware of the legal, if not moral, consequences of their actions.

5

NAGPRA as a Cultural and Legal Product

Hopis are a Puebloan people, direct descendants of the Anasazi (an archaeologist's term from the Navajo word meaning "ancestors of the enemy;" Hopis, unsurprisingly, prefer Hisatsinom, meaning simply "ancestors"), who, between 800 and 1300 C.E. built some of the most impressive architectural structures in prehistoric North America. . . . The common refrain of Southwestern archaeologists, "What happened to the Anasazi?" is unequivocally answered by Hopis and other modern Pueblos: "Nothing, we are still here."—Peter M. Whiteley and Vernon Masayesva, 1998

The generations lived on, one after another, and still people kept coming in from the wilderness. Some had been on their migrations so long that they no longer spoke the Hopi language. They spoke the Shoshone language, or Paiute, or the languages of the Hamis people, the Zunis, and the Kawaikas, and they had to relearn Hopi, the language given to them at the sipapuni. The Hopi villages stretched out from Awatovi and Kachinva in the east to Oraibi in the west, and from generation to generation still more villages were made. There were Payupki, Pivanhonkapi, Huckovi, Chimoenvasi, Sowituika, Matovi, Kateshum, Huckyatwi, Kawaika, Chakpahu, Akokavi, Moesiptanga, and many others. And far to the north and south there were villages of other Hopis who had not yet finished their migrations. Some were along the little Colorado River, some along the Rio Grande, some at Wupatki north of the San Francisco peaks, some at the mountain of the north called Tokonave. Beyond the Colorado River to the west, and in the San Juan Valley in the north, and elsewhere in the wilderness there were Hopis who were moving imperceptibly toward the center of things, the land which had been given to the people by Masauwu, Owner of the Upper World.—Harold Courlander, 1971

In Diné oral tradition, the Diné clan system coalesced around people created by the immortal Changing Woman, perhaps the most revered Diné deity. At her home in the western ocean, from different parts of her body, she created four or six couples called the Water People. She sent them ashore to migrate eastward. They reached the San Francisco Peaks at the western end of their predestined homeland, then kept going northeastward by routes in two clearly described corridors. They stopped and settled at a series of places that include what are now archaeological sites that archaeologists say were used before 1300. During their travels, each pair took a name that would designate the clan of their matrilineal descendants. Each clan ancestor pair also linked up with other groups in the various places along the way and absorbed these people as other clans. The ultimate destination of the Water People was the San Juan Basin-Continental Divide. — Klara Kelley and Harris Francis, 1999

NAGPRA is not just about taking careful inventory of Native American cultural property and human remains so that repatriation of them may take place. Perhaps just as important, the law has opened new dialogues concerning the maintenance and further creation of just practices, attitudes, and laws vis-à-vis aboriginal human remains, cultural property, and knowledge. Because of the sensitive nature of what the law addresses, compliance with NAGPRA means dealing with issues and listening to concerns that go beyond the objects in question to the history of power relations in the United States, especially in relation to museums and the disciplines of anthropology, history, and art history (see, e.g., Inouye 1992: 1; Riding In 1992). I discuss some of these issues throughout this book. I believe that opening up the double silence requires a realization that just because some attitudes have changed, some practices have been modified, and some necessary laws have been passed, this does not mean that the current state of affairs, however improved upon the old, does not carry with it old baggage and some of the same old attitudes.

As we saw in chapter 4, the discussions held in consultation sessions have not just been about the creation of inventories per se. Discussions range over a wide range of issues, concerns, irritations, questions, and clarifications, with emotions running the gamut from anger to gracious humor. What the discussions have revealed is that NAGPRA has problems. Some of these problems stem from the history of federal Indian policy upon which the law is based; others come from the fact that the process legislated has never been conducted before. This chapter reviews some of these problems, not to discredit or unnecessarily criticize those trying to carry out the law in good faith, but to contribute to clarity of thought—again, to open up the double silence.

While it will seem that the organization of this chapter runs from the procedural to the conceptual, from the administrative to the political, this impression is somewhat illusory. Procedure is never "merely" procedure but embodies hidden assumptions about the nature of reality, the configuration of power relations, and the limits of dialogue and understanding. It perhaps goes without saying that the issues on which I have chosen to focus are not the only issues or, to some, even the most important ones. As the position from which I write shapes my interpretive powers, I invite the reader to critique, amend, and otherwise continue the interpretive process once this chapter comes to a close.

SOURCES OF INFORMATION

In selecting the issues and problems on which to concentrate in interpreting the broader meaning of the law, I have drawn from a wide variety of sources, both published and unpublished. In addition to reading comments on repatriation by organizations such as the Native American Rights Fund, the American Indian Ritual Object Repatriation Foundation, and the American Museum Association, I follow discussions on NAGPRA that take place in *Indian Country Today* and that are posted on Internet sites such as NativeWeb, kennewick-man, Native American Rights Fund, Society for American Archaeology, and various tribal Web sites. I have also drawn from National Park Service publications, primarily *Common Ground* (formerly *Federal Archaeology*). As is apparent from the many citations the reader has endured throughout this book, I also draw heavily from academic publications ranging from Native American Studies journals such as *Wicazo Sa* to a variety of social scientific texts. In preparing this particular chapter I have drawn from five other important sources.

First, I have listened to and consulted transcripts of discussions held during NAGPRA consultations held at Fort Lewis College, as described in chapter 4, and at Mesa Verde National Park. I attended a consultation session at the park in 1995 on a day when I was asked to answer questions about the section of the cultural affiliation report that I had written for the park regarding evidence in the ethnographic record for American Indian connections to any part of the Mesa Verde area. In addition, I had the chance to speak to several consultants, outside of the context of the meetings proper, who expressed some of their views to me, including some members of the Mesa Verde museum staff.

Second, I have referred to notes I took on a discussion that took place during a session on NAGPRA for the 1997 American Anthropological Association meetings held in San Francisco. I organized this session at the suggestion of the director of the Hopi Cultural Preservation Office, Mr. Leigh (Jenkins) Kuwanwisiwma, who said that more opportunities for dialogue between Indians and anthropologists should take place at a national level. Papers were presented by representatives from the Navajo Nation Archaeology Department, from academic institutions, and from the National Park Service. The discussion that followed, in which members of the audience were involved, was perhaps more instructive than the papers, which largely covered familiar ground.

A third source of information for this chapter comes from reading the available sets of minutes from the NAGPRA Review Committee meetings, which I obtained online at *www.cast.uark.edu/other/nps/nagpra/ rcm.html*. These minutes range from the first meeting held in Washington DC, in 1992, to the most recent, which at the time of this book's publication will be the twenty-third, to be held in Tulsa, Oklahoma, from May to June of 2002. I strongly recommend that the reader go online to consult these transcripts regarding the progression of NAGPRA implementation, dispute resolution, and airing of concerns.

A fourth source of information comes from reading the three volumes of transcripts of talks given and discussions held during the Affiliation Conference on Ancestral Peoples of the Four Corners Region that took place on three separate occasions in 1998 at Fort Lewis College. Funded by the National Park Service, the conference was intended, in the words of its principle organizer, Philip Duke, "to bring together tribal representatives, government agency representatives and members of the academic community to discuss issues concerning the affiliation of archaeological materials and sites that have traditionally been classified as *Anasazi*" (Duke 1999: i).

A fifth source of information comes from the transcripts of the Senate hearings held in 1999 on NAGPRA, where a variety of people were invited to speak their views regarding the successes and failings of the law to this point.

Eleven Elemental Problems with NAGPRA

In this chapter I synthesize the eleven most salient issues as they emerged from these various and varied sources. Because of the immensity of the material, I keep footnotes and citations to a minimum.

1. ADMINISTRATIVE AND PROCEDURAL MATTERS

NAGPRA implementation is such an enormous and expensive undertaking that the inevitable result has been that of delays and backlogs. The federal government is receiving inventory notices faster than they are able to publish them, which delays the ability of tribal offices to respond. Although the National Park Service has awarded millions of dollars in grant monies since the early 1990s to assist tribes and museums in implementing the law, the process is still incomplete, and the funding level is still well below the estimated $10 million per year needed to support tribal repatriation offices. This means that inventory completion has extended beyond the original deadline of 16 November 1995, and repatriation and reburial processes are necessarily significantly delayed as well.

Not all of the delays are due to a shortage of resources, however. There are a few institutions as of this writing that have received a great deal of grant money and inventory extensions but have still not completed the work. During the 1999 Senate Hearings on NAGPRA, the National Congress of American Indians expressed concern that so many extensions had been granted to institutions by the secretary of the interior to complete their inventories that they seemed to be engaging in willful noncompliance (U.S. Senate 1999).

Other procedure-related questions that have emerged in the literature and reports have been how to address the disparities in resources between tribes; what a museum should do if it did not prepare an inventory because it had never received federal money and then it suddenly does receive funding; how to maintain confidentiality during and after the consultation process; and how to deal with illegal trafficking that took place before 1990, which leaves "auction houses and others who have acquired these items before this date, open for the sale of our cultural heritage" (U.S. Senate 1999).

Another label for this set of problems could be "the obvious." Because NAGPRA is a federal law, it applies only to holdings in federally funded institutions. Although this comprises a large set of holding facilities, it by no means covers all of them. Nor does it cover objects and human remains held in institutions outside of the United States. Another obvious problem is that the law only provides for repatriation to federally recognized tribes. This leaves out the claims of thousands of individuals whose tribes were either terminated in the 1950s or were never recognized by the U.S. federal government.

In addition, the law does not consider disparities between tribes that are federally recognized. Some have far more resources than others to support offices of historic preservation, attorneys, staff archaeologists, and trips to Washington DC, to attend consultation hearings and Review Committee meetings. The effectiveness and fairness of the law and its requirements must be considered in light of the fact that "Indian Country" is an extremely diverse domain in political-economic, cultural, and historical terms.

2. COMPLIANCE AND GOOD-FAITH ISSUES

What appears to some to be willful noncompliance is a complaint that has been levied many times in Review Committee meetings against not only some state and private museums but against some federal agencies that do not seem to be taking the law as seriously as others. A separate but related issue, that of the Smithsonian having its own set of guidelines and procedures to follow as a result of the 1989 National Museum of the American Indian (NMAI) Act, presents a problem to tribes that have to deal with two different federal processes. While an attempt is currently being made to bring Smithsonian policies more in sync with those of NAGPRA, one has only to look at the two sets of inventory reports posted on the respective NMNH (National Museum of Natural History) and NPS Web sites to see two very different, if overlapping, scenarios. Finally, there is a deep concern that private individuals and organizations that have not received federal funds should somehow be made subject to NAGPRA-type legislation, although at the present time they are not.

3. LEGAL LANGUAGE PROBLEMS

Understanding and interpreting the concepts on which compliance with the statute hinges is no small feat, and many discussions at Review Committee and cultural affiliation and consultation meetings attempt to sort out the definitions provided in the law. For purposes of this discussion, the reader may wish to consult the appendix, which includes the entire text of the law. Notice that Public Law 101–601 is defined as "An Act" and is divided into fifteen sections. Section 1 merely provides the full title of the act, while Section 2 defines the terms that are used throughout the rest of NAGPRA. It is with Section 3 that we begin to see the outlines of the law as embodied in its main focus, "Ownership," which is itself broken down into five main areas of consideration:

Sec. 3(a): Native American Human Remains and Objects

Sec. 3(b): Unclaimed Native American Human Remains and Objects

Sec. 3(c): Intentional Excavation and Removal of Native American Human Remains and Objects

Sec. 3(d): Inadvertent Discovery of Native American Remains and Objects

Sec. 3(e): Relinquishment

Here we have the main scope of the law, which is designed to establish and return ownership of Native American human remains and objects (otherwise known as *repatriation*) and to establish procedures in the event that Native American human remains and objects are either intentionally or inadvertently discovered or excavated and removed from their burial site. Section 3(e) merely says that nothing in the law prevents any Native American tribe or Native Hawaiian organization from "relinquishing control over any Native American human remains, or title to or control over any funerary object or sacred object."

Of the two main concepts, "human remains" and "objects," it would seem perhaps that the former is the easier to understand. If we return to the definitions provided in Section 2 of NAGPRA, however, we see that "human remains" and "objects" are both classified under "cultural items." This is an interesting and important classification, because it does not separate "nature" (human remains) from "culture" (created objects) but instead considers them both to be within the realm of human cultural meaning and interpretation. This will be forgotten by some scientists who argue for the necessity of maintaining access to biological data through the human remains, and who do not see that human remains are defined differently and occupy a different place in the cosmos for different peoples. It is also important to remember that some of the meaning attached to the human remains of Native Americans comes from indigenous cultural systems not only as they act alone but as they intersect with dominant systems of power that treated the bones and bodies of "conquered peoples" in ways that they would never treat their own people. In other words, as "cultural items" human remains carry the history of attempted genocide and ethnocide with them and are thus not in any way "merely" or "essentially" biological "specimens." They are symbols of what and who were destroyed and taken and what and who want them back, unconditionally (see Fine and Duke 1993; Zimmerman 1997a: 97–100).

The definition of human remains also becomes problematic when it is considered (and it has been, as the Review Committee minutes reveal) that some parts of the human body occupy a grey area where they may be considered more or less human, or more or less spiritual, or more or less powerful, depending on what body part they are. For example, how should one classify warriors' shirts that are adorned with human hair? What about teeth? How should Lakota birth amulets be treated that contain umbilical cords? Are these items to be considered as human remains or as cultural objects? If they are human remains, they are, as the reader will recall from the discussion in a previous chapter, subject to different penalties if they are illegally possessed than they would be if they were classified as cultural objects (Gulliford 2000: 52).

If human remains are defined by the law as a type of "cultural item," what does the law do with the kind of cultural item that is defined as an "object"? Section 2 of NAGPRA provides a variety of categories:

Sec. 2(3)(A): Associated funerary objects
Sec. 2(3)(B): Unassociated funerary objects
Sec. 2(3)(C): Sacred objects
Sec. 2(3)(D): Cultural patrimony

The definitions are laid out in detail within the law as presented in the appendix. It is easy for readers to see how it would be an interpretive challenge to establish whether objects were associated or unassociated with a burial (especially if they have been separated in the excavation or looting process), or what the meaningful difference is between sacred objects and cultural patrimony. The concept of sacred object seems to imply that it might have been owned by an individual, such as a religious practitioner, while cultural patrimony is always "inalienable" (i.e., it cannot be sold or given away outside of the cultural group) and outside of the control of one individual. Still, there has been a great deal of discussion regarding how these terms should be interpreted. Perhaps the greatest hindrance to cross-cultural application of the law is embodied in the Section 3 category of "Ownership" itself, because of the very different ways that property is defined and ownership established in a European-based context. For instance, are "stewardship" and "caretaking responsibilities" (important concepts undergirding the relationship between Native Americans and their sacred places, cultural objects, and ancestral remains) the equivalent of "ownership" under NAGPRA?

Sometimes in providing legal interpretations the reverse happens, and concepts that seem to be clearly defined in the law are ignored or interpreted well beyond their intent. One example is found in Section 5, which establishes the procedures for creating an "Inventory for Human Remains and Associated Funerary Objects." In Sec. 5(b)(2) it states clearly that

> Upon request by an Indian tribe or Native Hawaiian organization which receives or should have received notice, a museum or Federal agency shall supply additional available documentation to supplement the information required by subsection (a) of this section. The term "documentation" means a summary of existing museum or Federal agency records, including inventories or catalogues, relevant studies, or other pertinent data for the limited purpose of determining the geographical origin, cultural affiliation, and basic facts surrounding acquisition and accession of Native American human remains and associated funerary objects subject to this section. *Such term does not mean, and this Act shall not be construed to be an authorization for, the initiation of new scientific studies of such remains and associated funerary objects or other means of acquiring or preserving additional scientific information from such remains or objects.* (italics added)

Nonetheless, there are those museums and institutions that have ignored this very explicit definition of documentation, which makes it necessary for some tribal organizations to draw attention to this fact at Review Committee meetings (asking, in effect, "which part of 'no new studies' do you not understand?").

4. SCIENTIFIC CHALLENGES

One of the most interesting, telling, and frustrating arenas opened up by the entire repatriation movement has been a polarity between "science" and "Indians." This in many ways is a false dichotomy, as many Indians are in fact scientists, and many scientists are open to other theories of knowledge and truth other than those narrowly delineated by Baconian precepts.[1] However, because NAGPRA is a "Western" law passed by the United States Congress, it is often labeled as a set of concepts and guidelines wholly alien to the "Native world view" and thus incapable of fairly addressing or adjudicating the problem. As Renee M. Kosslak (1999–2000: 142) states, "It is clear that archaeologists, museum officials and American Indians differ widely in the points of view on issues relating to the excavation of archaeological sites, disposition of human remains, and ownership of cultural artifacts."

It is a misconception that Native Americans are a "collective" and have one mind regarding the application, nature, and uses of science. The NAGPRA affiliation and consultation discussions reveal that this is not true, and that there is no categorical opposition to DNA testing. What there is opposition to, in whatever form it takes, is the continued treatment of human remains as if they were objects whose value lies more in their future research potential than in the meaning they hold for living and dead peoples. Native commentators would be correct in pointing out that even the dominant society has recognized the "cultural" aspect of human remains because they have all along been treated as scientific "cultural items," that is, as laboratory specimens, as data, as property, as "Exhibit A," and as everything but what the original spirits that animated those remains would have considered them to be. Review Committee member William Tallbull asked at the seventh Review Committee meeting whether the American people would agree to Vietnamese scientists studying the remains of American servicemen for five years or more before sending them home (NAGPRA Review Committee, meeting 7, Rapid City, 1994: 11). Jicarilla tribal judge Carey Vicenti made a simple yet elegant point in Anchorage at the tenth meeting that "human rights exist forever." In other words, "An individual has a right to dignity and respect after death" (NAGPRA Review Committee, meeting 10, Anchorage, 1995: 4). If anyone believes that dignity cannot be achieved while lying in a cardboard box on a museum shelf, it only takes the Vietnam analogy to soldiers missing in action to make the point more salient.

Kennewick Man

Repatriation is defined as bringing something or someone back to the homeland from which it or him or her was alienated or, in the language of NAGPRA, as returning something or someone to those people to whom it or he or she is most closely culturally affiliated. The law thus requires that cultural affiliation be demonstrated when making a claim and states that this demonstration can be based on geography, oral history, or ethnographic reports. Proof with regard to DNA is neither explicitly mentioned nor prioritized, yet it has emerged prominently in some cases, most notably that regarding the affiliation of the human remains found near Kennewick, Washington, on the Columbia River on 28 July 1996. Because so much has already been written about the remains of the individual referred to variously as the Ancient One, Kennewick Man, or Richland Man, and information about various aspects of the case is readily available through video presentations, books, and Web sites, I do not go into detail here.[2] I wish to discuss Kennewick Man as an example of the ways that an emphasis on "biological affiliation" not only serves to prioritize biological evidence in a manner not in accordance with NAGPRA but also points to our society's seeming inability to consider culture independently of the concept of "race" (see Malcomson 2000).

The controversy surrounding Kennewick Man can be boiled down to this: how can living, extant tribes claim affiliation with nearly 9,500-year-old human remains, especially when scientists claim that these remains do not "look Indian" from a biological perspective? (Widely distributed facial reconstructions of Kennewick Man suggested an affiliation with *Star Trek*'s Captain Picard.) This is precisely what has taken place with the Kennewick controversy, as five tribes in the Pacific Northwest—the Confederated Tribes of the Umatilla Reservation, the Confederated Tribes and Bands of the Yakama Indian Nation, the Nez Perce Tribe of Idaho, the Confederated Tribes of the Colville Reservation, and the Wanapum Band—believe themselves to be affiliated with the remains of a man who, according to forensic anthropologist James Chatters, does not look Indian. This does not mean that the Ancient One was necessarily "white," only that his remains predate the kinds of "craniofacial divisions" that correspond to what are today labeled as modern "races" (Malcomson 2000: 43). According to Robson Bonnichsen, an Oregon State University professor of anthropology and director of the Center for the Study of First Americans, "This is a battle over who controls America's past. . . . We have always used the term paleo-Indian to describe remains of this era. But this may be the wrong term. Maybe some of these guys were really just paleo-American" (Egan 1996).

If Kennewick Man was indeed "not Indian," in the modern sense, then not only do none of the five Pacific Northwest tribes have a claim to the remains, but non-Indians could make repatriation claims to these remains. Indeed, some have, as Kennewick stirred up all kinds of suggestions that maybe "someone" was in the Americas before the Indians, and maybe these "someones" were "white." If they were white, then Indians could well have no real claims to territory or rights of sovereignty on this continent. This might mean that the "first peoples" were actually latecomers who usurped land from inhabitants who were here first (see Hibbert 1998–99: 440–41; Johansen 1999).

Those who claim that Kennewick man might have been non-Indian ("Caucasoid" is the term commonly used, which does not mean "white" but refers to a biological ancestry to which European, African, and Polynesian peoples have affinity) object to the suggestion that their work follows anything but a sincere quest for scientific truth. This is not ideology, they claim, but, on the contrary, fact. Proving that Kennewick or any other human remain is racially distinct from living Indians casts no negative light on those Indians; it only points to all the things we as yet do not know about the peopling of the Western Hemisphere (see Lahr 1997). An outspoken opponent of NAGPRA, paleoanthropologist Geoffrey Clark from Arizona State University argues that it is impossible to arrive at any kind of ethnic identification of skeletal remains one way or another. To Clark, " 'Native Americanness' has only a political definition" (e.g., see our discussion in chapter 2) rather than a purely biological one. To make any claims about cultural or tribal ancestry based on human remains is thus to engage in politics or religion, but not in science. Clark sees this as the silencing of science, a "violation of the First Amendment to the Constitution," which guarantees free speech and prohibits the establishment of religion (Clark 1999; see Hibbert 1998–99 for a legal analysis that disagrees with Clark's view).[3]

An interesting aspect of the case is that the U.S. Army Corps of Engineers, on whose land the remains were found, and which has worked on behalf of the tribal coalition claiming to be affiliated with the remains, stated early on (13 September 1996) that they would return the bones to the Indians for reburial. They buried the Kennewick Man site on 6 April 1998 (McDonald 1998). On 16 October 1996, eight scientists filed a claim to stop the repatriation attempt until scientific studies could be undertaken of the remains, claiming that the actions of the Army Corps of Engineers violated not only NAGPRA regulations but the Archaeological Resources Protection Act of 1979 and the Civil Rights Act of 1966 (*Bonnichsen et al. v. United States et al.*; Kosslak 1999–2000; Liberty 1999). On 17 November 1997, a congressional bill was introduced by Washington representative Richard "Doc" Hastings (R) to amend NAGPRA to allow for scientific study of human remains before reburial. In Hasting's words, "Current law governing the treatment of historic human remains is so vague and confusing that it's no surprise authorities have had difficulty reconciling the need for scientific study with respect for the customs and traditions of Indian tribes. . . . It's time to make sound science the deciding factor" (Knickerbocker 1999).

In January 2000, U.S. Secretary of the Interior Bruce Babbitt issued the decision of the Department of the Interior (DOI) that the remains of Kennewick Man are Native American under the meanings established by NAGPRA and are culturally affiliated with the consortium of tribes claiming him as an ancestor (see materials posted at *www.cr.nps.gov/aad/kennewick*). This decision served to activate the Bonnichsen et al. lawsuit, which had been put on hold by a judge until the DOI issued its decision. The hearing began in the summer of 2001, in U.S. District Court in Portland, but as this book went to press no decision had been rendered. The DOI's federal court brief for Judge Jelderks, the judge who has followed the case and in 1997 criticized the Corps of Engineers' handling of the situation, can be found at *www.kennewick-man.com/documents/doi.html*.

In a paper prepared by the Board of Directors of the Society for American Archaeology, objections to the DOI's decision that there is "a continuity between the cultural group represented by the Kennewick human remains and the modern-day claimant tribes" are expressed as follows:

> "Continuity" or "reasonable relationship" is a far weaker criterion than "a shared group identity that can be reasonably traced" [as is stated in NAGPRA], in terms either of their everyday meaning or of their anthropological usage. . . . A "reasonable cultural connection" with some group might reasonably be said to exist even though an individual's group identity is quite different. While many Americans could legitimately argue a reasonable cultural connection with 18th-century English culture . . . few would claim to have a shared

group identity with the English. By substituting these less restrictive terms for the statutory language, the Secretary's decision undermines Congress' effort to balance scientific and Native American interests by limiting repatriation to cases where there is relatively strong connection with a modern tribe (Society for American Archaeology 2000: 7).

5. DISPUTE RESOLUTION ISSUES

Although the Kennewick lawsuit was heard in a federal court, perhaps signaling a trend in that direction, dispute resolution is normally one of the main responsibilities of the NAGPRA Review Committee. Disputes can occur between cultural organizations and museums, or between one cultural organization or tribe and another. Because this issue is colored by legal concerns and pending issues that will likely have changed or be moot by the time this book is published, I will refrain from going into details. But consider, for instance, the dilemma facing the Field Museum of Natural History, which has a wampum belt it must repatriate to the "Oneida" people. Which Oneida? Wisconsin or New York? This question cannot be answered without studying the long history of Oneida divisions and the conditions under which the museum acquired the cultural property.

Other disputes are even more painful and seemingly irresolvable, such as those that have taken place between the Navajo and Hopi peoples. For them, NAGPRA cannot be discussed without considering the larger context and history of their relationship, which has been deeply complicated and made much worse by the actions and policies of the U.S. federal government. To accuse the Hopis and Navajos, as many have done, of making *ad hominem* arguments against each other that "slow down the process" is to engage in the kinds of "tribalism" accusations that have been levied against postcolonial African nations that "can't seem to get along," although it is thought that they should, since they are of the "same race."

The practice of turning the disputes back to the tribes to "duke it out" among themselves is a cynical one that takes the attention away from historical, governmental, procedural, and structural problems and too narrowly focuses on one set of always exaggerated factional poles. Whether the play is cast in terms of the "hang around the forts" versus the "hostiles," or the "traditionals" versus the "moderns," the same result obtains, and justice is set back even further.

This issue is perhaps the most serious, the most difficult to resolve, and one that relates to all the others. By looking at Hopi objections to the cultural affiliation procedures conducted by three entities of the National Park Service, we can better see in both general and specific terms some of the problems not foreseen by those who drafted the regulations for determining cultural affiliation.

At the time of this writing, the Hopis were contesting the accuracy of the Notices of Inventory Completion for Native American Human Remains and Associated Funerary Objects published in the *Federal Register* for Chaco Culture National Historical Park, Aztec Ruins National Monument, and Mesa Verde National Park. Specifically, the Hopis objected to the process by which the three parks arrived at their determination of just which modern American Indian groups can claim to be "affiliated with" or related to, the cultural items in the holdings of those parks. In short, the Hopis objected to the fact that the three parks conducted consultations with tribes not on an individual but on a *group* basis; that the parks did not provide item-by-item affiliations, instead speaking to whole collections; and that the parks gave undue consideration to contemporary cultural associations with geographical places in establishing identity with earlier identifiable groups. To the Hopis, the fact that the parks did not attempt to determine the affiliation of *each* item in their custody rather than loosely matching up a congeries of items with a congeries of tribes is a "misapplication of the statute by the National Park Service" that "constitutes a threat" to Hopi cultural heritage (Taylor 1999).

Although I do not address the procedures undertaken by Chaco Canyon and Aztec Ruins, I can say a few words about the Mesa Verde cultural affiliation report, as I am one of its authors. While it is true that each object was examined and described individually, it is equally true that the final report did not establish affiliation with each object, but with the *archaeological collection*. Jim Judge, one of the coauthors of the Mesa Verde cultural affiliation report, concludes his discussion of archaeological affiliation as follows:

> The similarity of artifacts, the continuity of styles from past to present, the evolution of architecture—all lend ample archaeological evidence to demonstrate that present-day pueblos are the descendants of the

Anasazi. Yet there is little in the archaeological record which will allow us to reliably assign *specific* cultural affiliation to any given archaeological item, be it human remains, associated funerary object, or object of cultural patrimony. Still, we know that prehistoric occupants of the northern and eastern southwest were the ancestors of the pueblos. Thus archaeological evidence does permit a general assignment of cultural affiliation, that of *ancestral Pueblo*. (Fine-Dare and Judge 1995: 48; emphases in original)

As for me, my task to complete in a very limited amount of time was to go through the ethnographic literature and published oral histories to determine which peoples had identified the area encompassed by Mesa Verde as ancestral within recorded memory. I came up with quite a long list of "culturally affiliated present-day Indian tribes" that included many of the contemporary Pueblo groups (Taos, Picuris, San Juan, Santa Clara, Pojoaque, Tesuque, Nambe, San Ildefonso, Cochiti, Santo Domingo, San Felipe, Santa Ana, Zia, Jemez, Sandia, Isleta, Laguna, Acoma, and Ysleta del Sur), as well as the Zunis, the Hopis, and the Navajos. Because the law requires that geographical affiliation also be considered, we listed the Southern Ute and Ute Mountain Ute tribes because of their long-standing residence in the Mesa Verde/Southwest Colorado region (Fine-Dare and Judge 1995: 10). The list of twenty-four tribes was collectively "mapped onto" the collective archaeological and human remains holdings of Mesa Verde National Park. In this respect, the Hopis are right. Two questions remain: What does the law *say*? How should what it says be *interpreted*?

In preparing my part of the report for Mesa Verde, I carefully read Section 5 of the law, "Inventory for Human Remains and Associated Funerary Objects." The final regulations were not published as yet, so I had only the letter of the law to go on, and, I admit, it was unclear. What it says is this: "Sec. 5(a) IN GENERAL.—Each federal agency and each museum which has possession or control over holdings of Native American human remains and associated funerary objects *shall compile an inventory of such items* and, to the extent possible based on information possessed by such museum or Federal agency, identify the geographical and cultural affiliation *of such item*" (emphases mine).

The wording is odd. Either the last two words should have read "such items," which would continue the parallelism with the first time the collective phrase "such items" appeared, or it should have read "*each item*," which would have made it clear that the inventory and its associated affiliation would be made on an item-by-item basis and not made for "such items" collectively. Either there was a typographical error in the statute, or it was written ungrammatically. I asked others what they thought, and the consensus was that it "must mean" collectively, because the item-by-item affiliation would be virtually impossible to ascertain within the time limits established by the statute.

Because I was given only about a month to complete my end of things, and because I was not assigned to view or analyze the actual holdings (I have still never seen them), I produced what I still believe was a good-faith report that covered the literature as exhaustively as possible. As a cultural anthropologist, I knew that ethnographic work at each of the twenty-five possibly affiliated tribes would have been the ideal research strategy (the Jicarilla Apaches were under consideration as possible affiliates, but I found no evidence in the literature for their ancestral association with the Mesa Verde area). As a cultural anthropologist, I also knew that I would not be the one to conduct the ethnographic work, as I am not a trained "Southwest Native specialist." The issue was moot, however, as the park did not have the funds for twenty-five ethnographic studies to be conducted.

When I first learned that the Hopis had raised the issue of procedure, I was not completely surprised. At the time that I wrote the report I had honestly not believed that a valid inventory should be done item by item. But by the time the first objections were raised to the Chaco report, the Final Rule was out, which clarifies the statute's original murky wording: "Sec. 10.9 Inventories. (a) General. This section carries out section 5 of the Act. Under section 5 of the Act, each museum or Federal agency that has possession or control over holdings or collections of human remains and associated funerary objects must compile an inventory of such objects, and, to the fullest extent possible based on information possessed by the museum or Federal agency, must identify the geographical and cultural affiliation *of each item*" (emphasis mine).

The Hopis have been right about this all along and have the right to state that the affiliation reports were written incorrectly. However, the legal hang-ups continue in two ways. First, the section quoted above states that the inventory must be compiled "to the fullest extent possible." Does that mean to the fullest extent possible "given world enough and time" (not to mention funding), or does it mean to the fullest extent possible "given the existing resources of the institution"? Of course, the museums would probably like the second interpretation to be the operant one, while the Hopis (and perhaps other tribes) are tired of the excuses. How many billion dollars in the black was the U.S. budget in 1999? Can't some of that money be allocated to this process so that accurate, item-by-item, ethnographically grounded inventories can be produced that fulfill the letter of NAGPRA?

There are those who say that the Hopis are using legal roadblocks to stop any Navajo claims to cultural affiliation within the Southwest and particularly within the disputed Navajo-Hopi Joint Use Area. Whether this is true or not, the larger truth remains that the Hopis, a sovereign people who have long been suspicious of any kind of U.S. legal erosions to their sovereignty (recall their opposition to the 1924 Citizenship Act), are reading the law carefully and objecting to its misapplication for reasons they are entitled to both articulate and keep to themselves because it is their survival as a people that is at stake.

Other procedural issues that have surfaced in the reports include the important but difficult issue (and very much a concern to the Hopis and to other groups) of whether affiliation is a yes/no question or one of *degree*. In other words, should affiliation reports be designed like a checklist (which is similar to what I did, in retrospect) that says "Navajo: yes; Apache: no." Or should reports be more nuanced concerning the *weighting of evidence* as regards one claim to an item relative to another?

Other issues regarding cultural affiliation have surfaced in the reports that can be considered cultural rather than procedural in nature, including whether oral histories taken outside of living ethnographic contexts can be valid; whether DNA should be a valid determinant of cultural relationship when many tribes have practiced adoption of nontribal or even non-Indian persons into their kinship groups; whether geographical location alone is sufficient to establish affiliation, since there are tribes with long histories of quite distant migrations; and whether "tribal" affiliation makes sense for peoples whose primary identity was based on cosmic and kin groups such as clans.

7. CULTURAL INTERPRETATION ISSUES

One of the most bitter complaints about NAGPRA has been what Mr. Edward Halealoha Ayau termed the law's "fail[ure] to recognize the legitimacy of spirituality" (NAGPRA Review Committee, meeting 4, Honolulu, 1993: 6). In this way it is seen, as mentioned above, as a very Western document that squeezes Native American experience into inappropriate categories such as "ownership" and "property" and that urges practice into dangerous domains. For instance, many tribal peoples are concerned about the illnesses that can and do occur from handling remains of the dead. They are concerned for not only themselves but also for the thousands of non-Indian museum personnel that work with these items. In addition, the pesticides and poisons such as arsenic that have been used to preserve artifacts pose biological threats. According to an article published in *Indian Country Today* ("Artifacts Returned to Tribes" 2000: C5), "the Hopis will call for a halt to repatriation until the contamination issue is settled."[4]

To return to the problem of ownership, the Zunis believe that any object that has been made using Zuni cultural knowledge is Zuni property. Whether the object in question is an Ahayu:da like the one Frank Hamilton Cushing made to send to British anthropologist Edward Tylor, or whether it is a museum model of an Ahayu:da shrine, the objects matter less than the cultural knowledge, or the intellectual property, without which they could not have been conceived or executed. The idea is rather like a patent on an invention, only it goes deeper because a real, spiritual connection gets established with the object on the basis of the wisdom that animates it and makes it work (Merrill, Ladd, and Ferguson 1993: 546–47).[5]

In a sensitive and insightful article written primarily for the museum and arts community, Claire R. Farrer, an anthropologist who has worked with the Mescalero Apache people of south central New Mexico for over three decades, raises one of the most crucial and telling issues that illuminates a key problem with Public Law 101–601: the question of whether "property" is only a material, tangible thing, or whether it extends into the realm of words, ideas, and spiritual phenomena. At first, the reader might wonder whether or not this issue is a "real" or "non" issue, but if one first considers the question of copyright law in the United States and the phenomenon of "intellectual" or "artistic" property, then the issue immediately becomes much clearer. (Think, for instance, of the furor over Napster, an online service that allowed individuals to download practically any piece of music they wanted without paying any fees). So clear, in fact, that one wonders why discussion of such was not included in the original wording of the law, particularly when one understands (as the architects of the law might have if they had conducted more research on Native American beliefs and language) that some notion comparable to "copyright" is only the tip of a vast cosmological if not juridical iceberg.

Farrer's (1994) point of departure in "Who Owns the Words?" is Section 2(3)(D) of NAGPRA ("Definitions"), which defines "cultural patrimony" as "an object having ongoing historical, traditional, or cultural importance central to the Native American group or culture itself, rather than property owned by an individual Native American, and which, therefore, cannot be alienated, appropriated, or conveyed by any individual regardless of whether or not the individual is a member of the Indian tribe or Native Hawaiian organization and such object shall have been considered inalienable by such Native American group at the time the object was separated from such group."

The problem with this definition, according to Farrer, is that while "cultural patrimony" implies tangible property to mainstream Americans, to most Indians cultural patrimony includes "intangible property such as words, songs, and . . . the words in songs, that are considered to be tantamount to objects that are necessary to certain cultural practices, usually of a ritual or ceremonial nature" (Farrer 1994: 318). Farrer illustrates this statement by examining closely her experience working with Mr. Bernard Second, a Mescalero singer and intellectual who became Farrer's research partner regarding the meaning and importance of Mescalero songs that were recorded in 1931 on wax cylinders during a training project conducted by anthropologist Ruth Benedict. These cylinders had disappeared until 1980, when they were located, along with partial transcriptions of the songs, in a storage facility at the School of American Research in Santa Fe, New Mexico. Once the cylinders and accompanying documents were found, they were sent to the Library of Congress to be incorporated with the Federal Cylinder Project; taped copies were returned to the School of American Research and only later to the tribe (319).

In the early 1980s Farrer and Second prepared an introduction and index to the taped materials and began the difficult task of deciding what would or would not be appropriate to translate. It was immediately clear to Second that what he recognized as "holy songs" could and should not be translated by anyone, including himself, as they contained powerful words (and, by extension, thoughts) given to the Apaches at the time of creation and expressed in ritual ("root") Apache language. Although these songs are still sung today in a variety of ceremonial, ritual, and religious contexts, Second was not able to do what would be the equivalent of "playing God," which would be to unleash the power of the words by translating them word for word. Farrer explains the power inherent in both everyday and ritual language:

> There is, for example, no way to swear in Apache, not even in everyday, colloquial Apache; that would be a blatant misuse of words. Words, or at least some of them, have inherent Power, such that pronouncing them calls their referents into immediate being—usually to the detriment of mere mortal people. Words in the root language carry even more Power; oftentimes it is not even necessary to use a complete word—a portion of it will do. Or a particularly Powerful concept will be alluded to through metaphor or illusion rather than be explicitly stated. Therefore to have root words fixed forever and forever playable, even by those who do not understand them and their Power, is to potentiate unbridled chaos and to threaten destruction through blasphemy. (Farrer 1994: 320)

While everyday personal and social songs and lyrics may be translated or conveyed by individual composers and owners, this is not the case for ritual songs, which belong to no one but instead are "carried in trust for the tribe as a whole" (Farrer 1994: 321). While it is the case that a head singer may add to the corpus of songs with one he has created himself, the fact that this new song was inspired by the Creator and "encapsulate[s] the experiences of the tribe during the period of time that the particular head singer held his position" (322) means that the head singer can lay no claim to it singly but must forever consider it as part of the cultural patrimony of the tribe. The original wax cylinders and the taped copies should therefore not remain in the hands of outsiders. Like "more tangible objects," the words embodied in the recorded songs "cannot be alienated from the tribe; they are not individually owned, as Anglos understand the idea of ownership, but rather are held in trust by an individual, or several of them, for the tribe as a whole. Therefore, by the terms of P.L. 101-601, they are repatriable" (323).

8. REBURIAL AND PRESERVATIONIST CONCERNS

For many people the most pressing issue entailed by NAGPRA and the repatriation movement is the reburial of the remains of the dead. The law, however, does not specify how this process is to take place or what provisions are to be made in cases where it is impossible to rebury the dead (or, in many cases, to bury them for the first time) in a culturally and spiritually appropriate and safe locale. Discussions have emerged regarding the creation of special regional burial sites or a national cemetery, but many people believe that the dead should be buried as close to their spiritual home as possible. Some tribes, like the Southern Ute of Colorado, have offered to act as mediators or facilitators in the case of contested or culturally unidentifiable human remains, but this offer has not been taken up by the majority of tribes in the Southwest.

A related issue has to do with the disposition of repatriated cultural items and the surveillance tactics that are often exerted by the scientific and other realms of the dominant society to make certain that repatriation results in proper "conservation" or "preservation" of the items in question. Although the law does not specifically deal with this issue (just as it does not deal with reburial), this does not prevent discussion and debate from focusing on what many see as key to the success of NAGPRA: ensuring that cultural items do not end up being destroyed, mistreated, or peddled over eBay. The many feel-good stories being published regarding the return of cultural items may come to be viewed as invasions of cultural privacy, particularly if decisions are made that result in nonpreservation. To put the issue bluntly: it may, in fact, be no one's business whether repatriated items are put in a home, a grave, a museum, a fire, or on the market.[6]

9. "BALANCING" HUMAN RIGHTS

A related issue that must be broached is the recurring question regarding whether the NAGPRA process must achieve a kind of "balance" wherein the interests of the scientific community are treated with the same respect and concern as those of Native Americans. This question is a rather unfortunate one, as it lodges discussion, once again, in false polarities. Who are the "good guys" and the "bad guys?" Is it Indians versus scientists? As mentioned above, what about the fact that many Indians *are* scientists, and not only scientists but archaeologists, ethnologists, biological anthropologists, and museum personnel? How are we to think about the fact that the Army Corps of Engineers and the National Park Service seem to be supporting Indian claims over those of some scientists? My point is an obvious one that raises the question of advocacy and justice rather than of Us versus Them, and it is one to which I return below. Nevertheless, I must also argue that the issue in question, the one that must not be forgotten, is that the human bodies and body parts and cultural treasures and burial offerings and clothing stripped from the dead must be repatriated to those peoples who continue to suffer the legacies of colonialism: genocide, ethnocide, cultural disintegration, and territorial degradation and dispossession. This is the point of the law, not "balancing" the interests of the possessors and the dispossessed. Nowhere in American history can it be said that the "scientific community" (as if there is such a thing) has been discriminated against, prevented from recognizing its heritage, or stripped of its personnel and products by marauding invasive forces. And nowhere in NAGPRA is anything said about achieving balance. Summaries and inventories are to be produced with the consultation of Native Americans. No new studies are to be conducted. Inventories are to be published so that claims can be made. Notices of intent to repatriate the cultural items are to be published, and repatriation is to occur. That is the law.

10. INTERNATIONAL LAW AND SOVEREIGNTY ISSUES

If Indian tribes are sovereign nations, why can they not regain their cultural property on the basis of international law? Why must they succumb to NAGPRA? If they do "play by" NAGPRA rules, will they be jeopardizing the recognition of their sovereignty? The answer to these questions is complex, but by no stretch of the imagination should it be assumed that anything having to do with NAGPRA should jeopardize sovereignty. To return to our earlier discussion of Kennewick Man, it was suggested on a 60 *Minutes* television program that if it were proven that the Kennewick remains were "really" Caucasian, then this would undermine claims to Indians' special status as first, sovereign peoples with a special relationship to the governments that dominate the North American continent. This is just not the case, as sovereignty is a political issue, based on agreements made between sovereign nations, and not a racial issue based on some kind of essentialist, biological entitlement. That the nations who signed treaties differed in some complex biological, linguistic, and cultural aspects is part of the political history of sovereignty, but it does not form some simple sort of checklist that can be invalidated because of ancient human remains or any other piece of "evidence" today.

The question of sovereignty is an important one for the repatriation movement because it reminds us that Native peoples are entitled to their cultural patrimony, their sacred objects, their burial offerings, and their ancestors' human remains not only under United States law but under a variety of international laws and covenants. The repatriation movement is at once part of the American Indian movement, part of a hemispherical pan-Indian movement, and part of an international indigenous rights movement.

One issue that has surfaced in Review Committee hearings has been whether NAGPRA can have any bearing on the display of human remains in the United States that come from other countries, the most notable being the "Inca ice princess" mummy displayed in Florida. While the answer is no, that NAGPRA per se has no jurisdiction over this, the broader repatriation movement can work to prevent *National Geographic* and other entities from exploiting human remains for profit.

11. THE NATIONAL PARK SERVICE, CONFLICT OF INTEREST, AND STRUCTURAL CONTRADICTION

A final problem that brings us back to the first one discussed above, administrative and procedural matters, is one that might be subsumed under the category of "bureaucratic" or "institutional" contradictions. As discussed above, the fact that the Smithsonian has its own set of guidelines and procedures to follow as a result of the 1989 NMAI Act is confusing to tribes that have to deal with two different processes.

A more significant bureaucratic problem has to do with what many people see as a major conflict of interest. Should the National Park Service be in charge of implementing a law that also applies to its own museums? The National Congress of American Indians (NCAI), for instance, finds that the consultation process is deeply flawed because the NAGPRA Final Rule was drafted under the aegis of the departmental consulting archaeologist for the secretary of the interior (see also the testimony given by Ernie Stevens Jr., first vice president of the NCAI, during the Senate hearings; U.S. Senate 1999). According to the NCAI, "keeping the NAGPRA Program within the National Park Service unbalances the delicate compromise originally struck during the drafting of NAGPRA; thereby, subjecting tribes to undue pressure in the name of science, based on the needs of the museums, the agencies, and the states. Furthermore, to place this program under the authority of the Departmental Consulting Archaeologist is clearly erroneous due to obvious potential for conflict of interest" (U.S. Senate 1999, NCAI testimony).

This issue is so important to the NCAI that it was passed as Resolution PSC-99-128 by the NCAI General Assembly (see NCAI 1999). It was also reformulated as NCAI Resolution MRB-98-102. A response is included in the minutes of the eighteenth NAGPRA Review Committee meeting held 18–20 November 1999, in Salt Lake City:

> The Assistant Secretary of the NPS sent a memorandum to the Chief of Staff for the DOI recommending that the NPS is the proper bureau to implement NAGPRA and that the Archaeology and Ethnography Program is the appropriate office to carry out the functions of NAGPRA implementation. In order to address criticisms of potential conflicts of interest, the NPS recommended clarification regarding information presentation and program organization. In addressing concerns about the lack of adequate resources, the proposal provides for some additional one-year positions to begin the process of overcoming backlogs and delays in NAGPRA implementation (NAGPRA Review Committee, meeting 18, Salt Lake City, 1999: 4; also see Stevenson 2000).

It is clear from the understandable complaint and perhaps understandable responses that problems and issues do not emerge just from history, from culture, from racism, or from willful misunderstanding, but also from unexamined contradictions in institutions and structures. Although the NPS may have been the most logical federal entity to administer the implementation of the law, it is unfortunate that a simple sociological analysis of institutional contradictions was not undertaken at the outset. What might have been thought through in terms of structural contradiction will unfortunately remain in people's minds as the institutionalization of bias within a process that has often exerted herculean efforts to be fair. Much discussion has therefore emerged regarding the possibility of making amendments to NAGPRA, but at the time of this writing there was no legislation pending to change any sections of the law.

Weighing the Evidence

The eleven issues summarized above do not by any means cover the entire range of what was said and, perhaps more importantly, what was not said in public in the various contexts under consideration. I would like to return, however, to the contexts where I was actually present—Fort Lewis College and Mesa Verde National Park—to provide an attempt to synthesize and link these issues.[7]

First, it must be emphasized that the tribal consultants (many of whom are academically trained or are skilled experts in other intellectual domains) are speaking to academics about who they are, and they want to remind anthropologists and historians of the complex ways that "Native American" as a category of identity has been constituted for more than five hundred years. Although in terms of NAGPRA Native Americans are expected to act in concert as "American Indians," these same Indians provide an implicit critique of that totalizing category every time they qualify it, which is nearly constantly. It bears repeating that the comments made during consultation, cultural affiliation, federal hearings, and Review Committee meetings also tell us that what may be more important than "cultural" differences are the structural inequalities and differing degrees of sovereignty Native Americans experience within the federal system. The disparities between the ways that cultural identities are constituted in the face of historical oppression and biologically defined "blood quantum" definitions of "Indian-ness" mean that Native Americans often have to justify their primordial claims to land, while simultaneously talking like nomads who must be invented for mainstream America over and over again. They talk a certain kind of essentialist talk, not necessarily because they believe it, but because they need it to deal with state and federal governments. Among American Indians, of course, other kinds of essentialist notions prevail, as suggested in the previous section. One hears about "full-bloods" and "mixed-bloods" in Plains towns and communities, while on the Hopi mesas labels distinguishing "traditionalists" from "progressives" are sometimes heard (see Fine 1994 regarding the uses of pragmatic essentialism among the Southern Utes).

Recognize, however, that although it may be problematic that the categories used in NAGPRA can be reductionistic and limiting, the very use of the repatriation concept implies the existence of a plurality of nations within the so-called U.S. nation-state, however asymmetrical. It thus begs the question of what it means *to have a nation to which to repatriate something.* NAGPRA's use of the discourse of nationalism to talk about Indian tribes and Native Hawaiian organizations has opened up arenas for contestation that may not previously have been available to most Native Americans. In other words, if the U.S. government is mandating the return of cultural and biological items to their respective *patriae,* or native lands, it is formally endorsing the possibility that these nations not only legitimately exist within the larger nation but have a status that exceeds that of the provincial states, which attempt to limit access to burial grounds (as well as, in a different vein, to prohibit casino gambling.)

WEAK LAW BUT POWERFUL SYMBOL?

Something else is painfully obvious to most Native Americans. Despite the ways that NAGPRA opens a door for contestation and property claims, it is also a symbol and embodiment of nationalist ideologies and practices that are "continually represented in state institutions such as courts, schools, bureaucracies, and museums, which employ the icons and symbols of the nation" (Gupta 1992: 72–73). Because of the money it is costing, the resources it is draining, and the frustrations it is engendering, NAGPRA has driven itself into the position of arousing the suspicions of Native Americans and becoming what Alcida Rita Ramos (1994: 168) has termed an "exercise in anthropological suspicion" concerning the extent to which it can actually achieve the ends of justice that it claims.

Much of this suspicion is grounded in the fact that, although high hopes were expressed around the country for the power of this law to address human rights issues with expediency, increasing numbers of participants are beginning to see it in more jaded terms, characterizing it as too little, too late. And although the law takes steps to redress historical wrongs and represents a successful case of Native American political lobbying, some feel that right after the legislators passed the law they said, "Well, we did this good thing in response to your pressing concerns, but now it's up to you to come up with time, money, and quick decisions." As Cherokee judge Steve Russell commented, regarding institutions' claims that they lack proper funds to carry out the process: "Some scientists seem oblivious to the absurdity of simultaneously claiming that they are holding items of such great scientific and historic significance as to outweigh simple human dignity and that they have no idea exactly what they are holding without spending a lot of money" (Russell 1995: 210, note 66).

As infuriating and difficult as this task has been, what still makes NAGPRA compelling to many Native Americans is that it is also about American constitutional rights and represents an attempt to provide more protection of Native American religious freedom, especially for sacred sites and objects. My frustration over having no real "four-fielders" (i.e., anthropologists versed in all four subfields of anthropology: biological, archaeological, linguistic, and cultural) to tackle the job of meaningful consultation and assignment of cultural affiliation pales in comparison to the frustrations the tribal representatives have felt while participating in these consultations. One reason this process has been so grueling for them is that virtually no one with whom they consult considers himself or herself "expert" enough to offer any decisive opinions, because he or she is not an archaeologist, or has not been trained in the Southwest, or thinks anthropology should no longer make authoritative statements on cultural affiliation matters.

These frustrated responses are not just about the decisions someone makes about what material objects and human remains belong to whom but are symptomatic of issues that beset not only the field of anthropology but academic disciplines in general. This was brought home to us by the consultants when they said some of the kinds of things they are used to hearing, as discussed above, when "tribalism" is invoked against them in the press: "Why can't you people get it together? Don't you ever talk to each other? Can't you work as a team?"

Recognizing the members of any team in a multidimensional field is difficult, as it is clear that all parties—academics and tribal representatives alike—are aware of the ways in which the law has created collusions that have been unexpected and sometimes less than desirable. For the tribes, these may include pressure to use the language of archaeology, or of the federal bureaucracy, to get their views across. For anthropologists, this may mean that they appear to support the federal government when they cannot meet Native demands. Because many of the parties involved in the federal government possess degrees in anthropology, the differences between academic and federal anthropology can take on accusations of betrayal, brainwashing, and selling out.

When Indians ask anthropologists to provide a scientifically grounded rationale for their religious and political claims, this can also be quite confusing. As discussed above, the standard view held by much of the public is that science and Indian beliefs do not mix. This is not necessarily the case if one recognizes that resistance to "science" may mean only resistance to discourses of domination. The nature of this domination has been one where the language of control (over human remains and objects) has been couched in terms of the importance of universal science and the pursuit of truth. In reality, many people making those claims are doing so in the absence of any working theories regarding the ends to which research over these items held in hostage are being put. They point to a future time when improved technology can yield heretofore undreamed-of secrets, but they do not connect propositions in present time to theories that can be linked, as all social theories must, to ethical ramifications of the uses of the particular knowledge in question. In such a context, the invocation of ecumenical science as a rationale for holding onto bones and artifacts in perpetuity can therefore only sound like the invocation of religious dogma, which, in fact, it is.

Resistance to the hegemonic assertion of one set of principles at the expense of another is what the "resistance to science" phenomenon is largely about, in my view. When some cultural anthropologists have attempted to remain above the fray into which some archaeologists and physical anthropologists have fallen, they have often done so by mistakenly adopting the view that scientific authority is not something Native Americans are particularly interested in hearing. When they have come across evidence to the contrary, they have expressed a great deal of surprise and shock (I know; I've been one of them).

To express what I said above a bit differently, when Native Americans attempt to create emancipatory accounts of their past, present, and future, they must often frame their views in terms of oversimplified dichotomies that lump science in with all other oppositional forces. As Michel Foucault puts it, (1980: 83–84), these dichotomies express resistance to "the effects of the centralising powers which are linked to the institution and functioning of an organised scientific discourse within a society such as ours." Tribal members may give the impression of collusion when they utilize science, or rejection of it when they provide a critique, but ultimately their dilemma illuminates the complexity of race politics and moves into the overlapping and mutually constitutive arenas of local, national, and global politics.

NAGPRA AS NIGHTMARE

Finally, the comments concerning partnership, meaningful consultation, and willingness to help us educate our students indicate Native Americans' growing interest in extending the law beyond repatriation issues and institutional and cultural boundaries to tell academics things they have long thought we should hear. Although not one of the tribal representatives at the sessions I attended said it aloud, I thought I could feel the words in the air: "You've invited us here because you had to, and now you're going to listen." The words are appearing everywhere now and reaching a widening audience: at the consultation meetings across the country, on the Internet, in print, in law briefs, and at conference sessions. To make absolutely certain that the academy hears, some tribes, such as Zuni, Hopi, and Cochiti, have issued statements concerning cultural privacy and property protocol.[8] Tribal members and tribal employees are on the conference circuit as well, giving talks at the Society for Applied Anthropology, Society for American Archaeology, and American Anthropological Association annual meetings. The contexts of these various meetings supply further opportunities for consultation and expression of conflict. For example, talks on NAGPRA-related issues were given at the Navajo Studies Conference, a regional set of meetings that took place at Fort Lewis College in April 1996.

One morning I attended a session on the land and politics of Dinétah (Athabascan cultures' designation for their homeland, said to exist in an area that lies somewhere in northern New Mexico and southern Colorado), mainly because I wanted to hear a paper written by two archaeologists working with the Navajo Nation Archaeology Department in Flagstaff, entitled "Navajo, Anasazi, and NAGPRA." As the authors could not be present to read their paper, a young Navajo colleague from their office read the authors' argument for looking more closely at the ethnography of Washington Matthews and others who indicate that several Navajo clans have a much longer history of existence in the Southwest than archaeologists have previously supposed. Evidence from oral history and the origin stories embedded in the Nightway, Beadway,

Flintway, Beautyway, and other ceremonies was forwarded to support direct links between the Navajo and the prehistoric people labeled with the Navajo-derived term "Anasazi," which now has largely been replaced by "Ancestral Pueblo." The paper suggested that since the prehistory of the Southwest was clearly one of massive migratory waves, perhaps the degree of cultural "intermingling" via intermarriage and exchange was such that no strict claims to cultural depth or boundaries can be maintained today. In the authors' view, the "fluidity of ethnicity needs to be researched" to widen repatriation claims in the Southwest to include the Athabascans more broadly (Begay and Warburton 1996).

After the talk, questions were entertained, but none were offered by the Hopi group who had driven up for the meetings to hear what would be said on this issue. After the session I bumped into an anthropology graduate of Fort Lewis College who was working as an archaeologist for the Navajo Nation. This young man told me how disturbed he was by the paper he had just heard, even though it was about "his culture," and how it made him just want to stop talking about NAGPRA. He said he was worried that the problems would continue to grow without resolution if the path discussed in the paper is taken and if hostilities among some Navajos and Hopis escalate. "This will just create an identity crisis for the Navajo people," he said. "This will just make things worse."

This example is one of many I have come across that illustrate the ways that NAGPRA as law, discourse, ideology, and practice is not only reflective of deep divisions and continuing problems but is perhaps creating new ones (see MacLennan 1995: 52). These problems may not, in fact, be so new, but increasingly it seems that the "good-faith" law that was supposed to help redress centuries of appropriation, theft, and injustice has the qualities of what several Native people have termed a "nightmare" of growing proportions. This sense of nightmare may obtain for all of us, as our national collective unconscious bubbles up, formed in part by all the most horrible experiences endured by oppressed peoples on this continent. One of the "true myths" of anthropology is that Franz Boas is supposed to have said that he was disturbed by "dreams of bones" because of his work excavating human remains for scientific purposes. In Boas's case, we might wish that he had had more such dreams and therefore might not have made the mistakes that he did. But Native Americans certainly dream of vast killing fields of body parts and artifacts through which they must wander, sadly searching piece by piece for the remains of those who went before. What makes this process even more horrific is the sense that they have been set to fight among themselves while the anthropologists and state and federal employees watch, shaking their heads in collusion over their misplaced goal of objective non-involvement.

The public presentations and consultation sessions and private conversations are full of urgency and anguish, as all participants find themselves working to beat some kind of clock and to prevail over some kind of structure that is made of a bewildering intersection of institutions, agencies, laws, and culturally grounded concerns. As one who preaches daily on the constructed nature of knowledge, who believes firmly in the largely invented nature of culture, and who refuses to see hegemony as absolute and irreversible, one might think that I would find this seeming confirmation of postcolonial constructionism somehow intellectually vindicating, as I watch the exciting process of reclamation going on, in both the Spanish and English senses of the term—as claim making, respectively, of justice and property. But watching real people continue to struggle and suffer over the mess that all of us have inherited from the past flattens any sense of delight in the theoretical accuracy. Sometimes this law reminds me of the Spanish Requerimiento, that charming bit of bureaucratize that was yelled out to Indians who did not yet speak Spanish. "Here are the words," the Requirement proclaimed. "Here is the law—deal with it!"

Whether we will ever see an end to the days of one-way speech acts, we must remember that many Native Americans are also deeply implicated in NAGPRA in a variety of ways. Some of them lobbied heavily for NAGPRA, while others have played key roles in improving and clarifying its meaning. They participate significantly in the Review Committee, which oversees the process of compliance and helps settle disputes, and they work as professionals on every aspect of the legislation, as archaeologists, ethnographers, bureaucrats, political activists, spiritual advisers, lawyers, and cultural specialists. They participate because they are American, because they are not Anglo-American, because their territories are located in a hostile United States of America, because they reside in an America that has already taken their territories from them, and because some of them hope that language can persuade as well as it can betray.

This chapter has dealt with only a few of the problems that have arisen in the course of interpreting and enforcing NAGPRA. Laws are written and passed, but it is then incumbent upon others to interpret and enforce the language embodied in these laws. Unfortunately, it is often only after a law has been put into practice that the problems emerge with its wording, conception, or practicality. This is especially the case when a law is written from one cultural context regarding matters that cross into very diverse cultural contexts. Those of us who have been trained in anthropology can appeal to notions that go beyond the "letter of the law," however. These notions are embodied in the American Anthropological Association's Code of Ethics, which states: "Anthropological researchers have primary ethical obligations to the people, species, and materials they study and to the people with whom they work. . . . Anthropological researchers must do everything in their power to ensure that their research does not harm the safety, dignity, or privacy of the people with whom they work, conduct research, or perform other professional activities" (AAA 1998; for the full text of the Code of Ethics, see *www.aaanet.org/committees/ethics/ethcode.htm*).

It is clear that bones, bodies, objects, and words were collected without consideration of these ethical guidelines, which were not articulated within the profession until the 1970s. It is, however, not too late to take them seriously and, as Farrer (1994: 326) suggests, "to sensitize those in other disciplines that the Western model . . . is but one model for belief and behavior."

Conclusion: There Is No Conclusion to the Repatriation Movement

Indigenous peoples have the right to practice and revitalize their cultural traditions and customs. This includes the right to maintain, protect and develop the past, present, and future manifestations of their cultures, such as archaeological and historical sites, artifacts, designs, ceremonies, technologies and visual and performing arts and literature, as well as the right to the restitution of cultural, intellectual, religious and spiritual property taken without their free and informed consent or in violation of their laws, traditions and customs.

Indigenous peoples have . . . the right to the repatriation of human remains. States shall take effective measures, in conjunction with the indigenous peoples concerned, to ensure that indigenous sacred places, including burial sites, be preserved, respected, and protected. — Articles 12 and 13 of the *Draft Declaration on the Rights of Indigenous Peoples*, 1993

Federal Register/Vol. 64, No. 165/Thursday, August 26, 1999/Notices 46719/46720

Notice is hereby given under the Native American Graves Protection and Repatriation Act, 43 CFR 10.10(a)(3), of the intent to repatriate cultural items in the possession of the Wyoming State Museum, Cheyenne, WY which meet the definition of "sacred objects" under Section 2 of the Act.

The cultural items are two arrows with steel points and fletched with feathers; a wooden bow with pink ribbons attached at knocks, front stained blue and belly stained red; and a pipestem.

In 1919, John Hunton of Fort Laramie, WY donated these cultural items to the Wyoming State Museum. Donor information accompanying these cultural items indicates that on December 29, 1890, they were picked up on the Wounded Knee Massacre site by a U.S. Army scout Baptiste "Little Bat" Garnier, who later gave them to John Hunton.

The donor information accompanying these cultural items clearly indicates that they were removed without permission of the owners or relatives following the massacre. Consultation evidence provided by representatives of the Cheyenne River Sioux Tribe states that "mourning [associated with Wounded Knee] . . . cannot end until all of the property stolen away from the dead . . . is returned . . . and all necessary spiritual ceremonies relating to the traditional burial rites of the Lakota have been performed and executed by Lakota spiritual leaders."

Officials of the Wyoming State Museum have determined that, pursuant to 43 CFR 10.2(d)(3), these four cultural items are specific ceremonial objects needed by traditional Native American religious leaders for the practice of traditional Native American religions by their present-day adherents. Officials of the Wyoming State Museum have also determined that, pursuant to 43 CFR 10.2(e), there is a relationship of shared group identity which can be reasonably traced between these items and the Cheyenne River Sioux Tribe, Oglala Sioux Tribe of the Pine Ridge Reservation, Rosebud Sioux Tribe of the Rosebud Indian Reservation, and Standing Rock Sioux Tribe of North and South Dakota.

Representatives of any other Indian tribe that believes itself to be culturally affiliated with these objects should contact . . . [name and address] before September 27, 1999. Repatriation of these objects to the Cheyenne River Sioux Tribe, Oglala Sioux Tribe of the Pine Ridge Reservation, and Rosebud Sioux Tribe of the Rosebud Indian Reservation may begin after that date if no additional claimants come forward.

The National Park Service is not responsible for the determinations within or the content of this notice.

If the early 1990s were marked by discussions regarding the interpretation and implementation of NAGPRA, by the end of the twentieth century procedural discussions would, in some ways, take a back seat to the news of repatriation and reburial across Indian Country. By October of 2000 it was estimated that "some 14,000 human remains out of 200,000" had been repatriated to tribes under NAGPRA (Paulson 2000). News of the Kennewick Man controversy hit every newspaper I opened, including the *Durango Herald*, and a special section on repatriation was created in *Indian Country Today*, the more mainstream of the country's many Indian newspapers. In addition, a flood of Notices of Inventory Completion (NICs) and Notices of Intent to Repatriate (NIRs) were published in the *Federal Register* and made easily accessible online to a global public. The NICs provide information regarding an institution's holdings that fall under NAGPRA regulations and give a date that repatriation can begin. The NICs are also sent to the tribes that are adjudged to be affiliated with the items in question so that they may be informed directly that they can make a repatriation claim to them if they so choose. The NIRs are published after the NIC date has passed and are also sent to the relevant tribes.

The notices of both types are at once fascinating, chilling, and a relief. They give detailed information regarding one item, or a collection of items, unless a tribe requests that the information not be published for religious reasons. The stories that are told about these objects within their strict, three-column format are like a ghost of voices calling home. The act of reading through these notices is never tedious, however. This is my government, to which I pay taxes. This is the report of what they did, will do, and have done. This is history, heartache, and recompense.

The notices begin to open up the silences: An iron spoon taken from a Brule–Sicangu Sioux grave for a medical museum in 1869. A Tlingit canoe prow that survived a U.S. Navy shelling in 1882. A Ute woman's bones taken from the site where she was slain. Ten Apache *Dilzini Gaan* masks, two dance wands, and one medicine man's feathered cap. A carved wooden Ahayu:da removed from a Zuni cave shrine near Thunder Mountain, New Mexico. The remains of thirty-two individuals and 8,138 associated funerary objects excavated in 1959–60 by the University of Illinois from a farm in Rock Island County, Illinois. A scalp lock said to have been taken from a Pawnee Indian. The human remains of a young Ute woman slain during the Beaver Creek Massacre in June 1885. The human remains of seven individuals and 45 funerary objects excavated from Anvik Village, Alaska, in 1903 by a Reverend John W. Chapman.

A Natoas bundle used in the Blackfeet Sun Dance. A HoChunk brass kettle water drum and one carved gourd rattle purchased from Sam Blowsnake by the State Historical Society of Wisconsin in 1958. And the remains of one known individual found in Willamette University's archaeological collections in 1998: "The human remains are a lock of hair tied to a 'ladies' calling card' emprinted with 'Miss Maria(?) Parrish.' Handwritten on the card is 'Scarface Charlie, Modoc (?illegible) June 24, 1875'. . . Scarface Charlie (c. 1837–1896) was the chief advisor, interpreter, and battlefield tactician of Modoc leader Captain Jack and fought during the Modoc War of 1872–1873." (*Federal Register* 64, no. 200 [Monday, 18 October 1999], Notices, 56223)

The Jemez Pueblo–Pecos Pueblo Repatriation

This book opened with a brief discussion of the repatriation of thousands of items to the descendants of Pecos Pueblo, but I did not recount how this process appeared in the *Federal Register*. In its "Notice of Inventory Completion," published in the *Federal Register* on 13 October 1998, the Peabody Museums at Harvard and Phillips Academy reported that they had consulted with representatives of the Apache Tribe of Oklahoma, the Hopi Tribe, the Jicarilla Apache Tribe, the Kiowa Tribe, the Mescalero Apache Tribe, the Navajo Nation, the Jemez Pueblo, the Santo Domingo Pueblo, the Zuni Pueblo, and the Wichita and Affiliated Tribes in determining the cultural affiliation of the objects and human remains in their possession. According to the notice, the human remains of "1,922 individuals of Native American ancestry" and 534 objects "reasonably believed to have been placed with or near individual human remains at the time of death or later as part of the death rite or ceremony" were in the possessions of these museums.

Immediately following the Notice of Intent to Repatriate, the *Federal Register* (vol. 63, no. 197) recorded the Notice of Intent to Repatriate 488 of these items, including:

ceramic vessels, ceramic fragments, medicine bundle contents, stone drills, bone flutes, shell tinklers, shell ornaments, shell necklaces, a concretion bone whistles [*sic*], a crystal, a bone button, effigies, pipes, bone beads, projectile points, stone scrapers, bead bracelets, turquoise pendants, shell pendants, worked shell, cordage, fossils, a clay ball, wrappings, bone tubes, bone knives, stone drills, pieces of obsidian, stone axes, polishing stones, hammerstones, shell fragments, flint chips, pebbles, wooden and copper crosses, a brush, lumps of paint, textiles, buffalo hair, moccasins, sandals, pieces of copper ore and lead ore, bone awls, and a stone pendant. (*Federal Register Online, www.access.gpo.gov/su_docs/aces/aces140.html; Federal Register* documents can be browsed from this URL)

On 14 April 1999 (*Federal Register*, vol. 64, no. 71: 18447) eleven more cultural items were listed as ready for repatriation. The relative swiftness with which Pecos repatriation occurred points to the ways the law has achieved its aims and continues, in slower fashion, to return ancestors and their remains to other Native communities.

Summary of Key Points

This one "success story," however, reminds us that we need to review and summarize the main points made in this work before bringing it to a close.

1. *NAGPRA is part of a broader repatriation movement with a long history.* The war gods stolen from the Zuni people and repatriated to them from the Smithsonian in 1987 have been characterized as "heralds of a new era in the relations between American Indians and museums" (Merrill, Ladd, and Ferguson 1993: 524). As was briefly discussed in chapter 3, the Zunis worked for many years (and are still working) to have their gods "restored to the purpose for which they were created in Zuni culture and society" (523). The return of the gods can in one sense be viewed as a "success story" with a tidy beginning, middle, and end: the gods were stolen from the Zunis; the Zunis fought to get them back; the gods were returned. But the length of time it took for the Ahayu:da to be returned, the fact that so many were missing, and the continued alienation of many of them points to the reality that the repatriation movement is just that—a *movement*, a process that is ongoing with no end in sight, and with no shortage of controversy surrounding it.

2. *Repatriation and reburial justice is not just a legal matter but involves deeply religious, humanitarian, and human rights concerns.* "Pine Ridge 1890–1891" is inscribed on one of the many battle streamers that flutter from

the U.S. Army flag. This particular battle streamer commemorates the only significant military action during this one-year period, the Massacre at Wounded Knee Creek on 29 December 1890, yet it has twenty Congressional Medals of Honor associated with it. This is more than any other streamers carry, including the Battle of the Bulge, Normandy, and Iwo Jima. The National Congress of American Indians passed two resolutions in 1997 asking that this streamer be removed and the "action" be stricken from the Medal of Honor Roll (NCAI n.d.). In 1896 anthropologist James Mooney provided a description of the aftermath of the Wounded Knee Massacre:

> A long trench was dug and into it were thrown all the bodies, piled one upon another like so much cordwood, until the pit was full, when the earth was heaped on them and the funeral was complete. . . . Many of the bodies were stripped by the whites, who went out in order to get the "ghost shirts," and the frozen bodies were thrown into the trench stiff and naked. They were only dead Indians. As one of the burial party said, "It was a thing to melt the heart of a man, if it was of stone, to see those little children with their bodies shot to pieces, thrown naked into the pit." (Mooney 1973: 878–79)

On 19 December 1981, one of the shirts that was taken from the Wounded Knee battleground was donated to the Glasgow Museums in Scotland by George C. Crager, an interpreter who traveled with Buffalo Bill's Wild West Show and who had collected trophies from Wounded Knee shortly after the 1890 massacre. An inventory list describes the shirt as being "of cotton cloth with a feather ornament, blessed by Short Bull, the high Priest to the Messiah, and supposed to render the wearer invulnerable. It was taken from a Sioux Warrior killed at the battle of Wounded Knee" (Little Eagle 1996: C1). A condition report contained this description: "Dark brown/black staining on bottom left of shirt and much holed in this area. Further staining on front centre with small hole 10 mm in length. Black accretion on right shoulder and a number of small pine-type holes. Hole in back of costume 11 x 3 mm within the brown dyed area. Brown staining 8 x 13 mm in area, back left. Area of brown staining, 22mm diameter, back right with a torn area within in" (C1).

Although the authenticity of the shirt was doubted by some (see Spalding 1999), once the Lakotas learned of its existence they began a campaign for its repatriation. The Wounded Knee Survivors Association took the lead in convincing the museum that the return of the shirt would help "to bring about healing for the descendants of the Sioux Nation [and] would help to alleviate the years of suffering and heartache they experience. . . . The humanitarian result of the museums [sic] benevolence cannot be measured" (Little Eagle 1996: C2).

Repatriation of the shirt finally took place in 1998 within a context of controversy and skepticism. The former director of the Glasgow Museums, Julian Spalding, wrote a bitter article in *The Art Newspaper* that expressed his sorrow and anger over the removal of the "Ghost Dance Shirt" after his forced resignation in the summer of 1998. In Spalding's view, taking the shirt from the Kelvin Grove Museum in Glasgow also removed the possibility of educating the public about an act of genocide that should be forever remembered: "Tacked onto the end of a line of genuine 'Ghost Dance' shirts in the future Museum of Wounded Knee, the Glasgow shirt will hardly add a footnote to each visitor's understanding. Prized in Glasgow, it could have made generations of future visitors aware of a tragedy that European values helped to forge and also quickly to transform into entertainment" (Spalding 1999: 21).

Many Lakotas disagree with Spalding. The return of the shirt not only represents one of the few successful repatriations of a cultural item from a foreign museum but also demonstrates the power of an international repatriation movement to appeal to the sense of justice of those in control of European museums to return objects not rightfully theirs. It further underscores a point made forcefully by Echo-Hawk and Echo-Hawk (1994) that religious concerns of Native Americans have most often been pushed aside by the interests of science and, in this case, an "educational institution" such as a museum. The frustration expressed by Spalding is very similar to that heard from scientists who say that reburying bones is like "burning books." The reverse point is rarely made, however, that digging up bones and other forms of ethnocidal practices linked to genocide is its own form of "book burning" when beliefs, languages, and the fabric of human communities go on the museum and laboratory "trail of tears."

3. In addressing human rights issues, the repatriation movement is situated firmly within an international context, which includes recognition of self-determination, tribal sovereignty, and treaty agreements. As I discuss in chapter 3, the United

Nations Working Group on Indigenous Populations (WGIP) was formed in 1982 to work toward developing international standards regarding indigenous peoples (Anaya 1997: 59). By 1988 the WGIP had produced a first draft of a Declaration on the Rights of Indigenous Peoples. What distinguishes this document from the 1948 Universal Declaration of Human Rights is not only that it focuses specifically on indigenous peoples within states, but that it is specifically concerned with group rather than individual rights. Although only two of the forty-five draft articles had been accepted by the Working Group of the Commission on Human Rights by October 1998, it has "already had a considerable impact on the lives of indigenous peoples worldwide," in the view of John Henriksen, an indigenous Norwegian Saami lawyer and activist, as well as a human rights officer for the United Nations (Henriksen 1999a: 50; see, however, Pritchard 2000). Articles 12 and 13 of the Draft Declaration deal with cultural rights and repatriation and are quoted at the opening of this chapter. But probably the most important group right that indigenous peoples want recognized is that of self-determination. Australian Aboriginal lawyer and human rights activist Mick Dodson defines self-determination simply as "the very basic right to determine our own future, to choose how we would live, to follow our own laws" (Jensen 1999: 2).

Dodson, who serves as director of the Indigenous Law Centre at the University of New South Wales, points out that the right to self-determination is supported in Article 1 of the International Convention on Civil and Political Rights and Article 1 of the International Covenant on Economic, Social, and Cultural Rights (Dodson 1999: 35). The idea of self-determination is firmly tied to the right to representation in the United Nations, which became formalized in Vienna in 1993 during the World Conference on Human Rights, where the "idea of a Permanent Forum for indigenous peoples in the UN was proposed" (Tauli-Corpuz 1999: 6). Various workshops and meetings have been held each year around the world regarding the establishment of this forum, the tasks it would undertake, and its placement within the United Nations system. At the 1995 Copenhagen workshop, a draft mission statement was crafted for the Permanent Forum that includes as one of its tasks "[the provision of] a high-level and public forum [for indigenous peoples] to participate in decisions and consider a wide range of matters affecting indigenous peoples in the areas of development, environment, culture, education, economics, social [sic], intellectual property, trade" (Henriksen 1999b: 18).

Indigenous cultural and intellectual property, in fact, has emerged in international circles as one of the most important focuses for lobbying and other activities, and it is appearing in forums that go well beyond the work linked to the United Nations and that provide strong support for internationally backed legal claims to cultural property that has been improperly alienated. Requests for the return of grave goods, cultural items, and human remains are being made on a worldwide scale, by Australian Aboriginals, Polynesians, Melanesians, and Africans, and by Greeks who want the return of the Elgin Marbles. The repatriation movement is part of what Phillip Wearne calls "international indigenism" symbolized by the work of the Quiché Mayan Nobel Peace Prize recipient Rigoberta Menchú and many others who advocate an end to racism, poverty, genocide, violence, and environmental destruction (Wearne 1996).[1] A key element of implementing international law, however, is the recognition of sovereignty and treaty rights. As Pawnee attorney Walter R. Echo-Hawk observes:

> Another legal theory arises under federal Indian law. Regardless of whether dead bodies were removed from ceded treaty areas, tribes also possess the inherent sovereign right to repatriate desecrated remains of deceased members or ancestors—a right that has never been divested by treaty or statute, or by necessary implication. One of the most fundamental attributes of tribal sovereignty is the right to govern the internal affairs and the personal, social and domestic relations of tribal members. Proper disposition of tribal dead and protection of the sensibilities of living members clearly falls within this inherent aspect of tribal sovereignty. Such an exercise of tribal control over deceased tribal members desecrated from graves located outside reservation boundaries may properly be argued to exist in certain narrowly-defined circumstances. (Echo-Hawk 1988: 3)

4. *As a key element of the repatriation movement, with a long history and ongoing development,* NAGPRA *is also a powerful symbol that must be viewed in terms of deeper cultural and political meanings.* The subject matter of this book speaks to the messiness of historical truth, to the difficulty of identifying clearly demarcated "sides" in the debate, or of positing easily achieved solutions.[2] It also speaks to the power of interpretation and to

the humbling lesson that one author writing one book, however well researched, can only contribute one author's viewpoint to the sea of other voices and interpretations. And my viewpoint, my interpretation, that frames this book is this: the treatment of American Indian objects and human remains in this country is a metaphor (an elaborate symbol) and a metonym (an extension) of the treatment of Native American persons and souls in the United States of America since its inception. NAGPRA thus provides a window into the psyche of the nation. It is at once good, bad, and indifferent, both engendering and at times diminishing hope. By paying attention to this law we can understand more of what it means to live in America in ways that go far beyond the American Indian repatriation movement.

5. NAGPRA *must be mobilized to work toward distributive as well as cultural justice for it to an effective piece of "human rights legislation." This means that it must be well funded in a meaningful and ongoing way.* NAGPRA is often described as a type of "human rights legislation" because of the ways it addresses practices historically grounded in racism, religious desecration, and dehumanization. However, following suggestions made by Nancy Fraser in her study of recognition politics in the late twentieth century, legal mechanisms that focus on cultural injustices without addressing the linked economic injustices may not facilitate human rights at all (Fraser 1997). Applying her distinction between "the struggle for recognition of difference" and the "struggle for redistribution" to NAGPRA and other legislation that addresses American Indian rights, I find that she has a point. Unless resources are redistributed in a manner that provides for more funding to tribal repatriation offices, as well as to Native peoples unaffiliated with tribes who also have repatriation claims, the "justice" entailed can only be very limited and even cynical (Fraser 1997: 12). Discussions of NAGPRA in newspapers, classrooms, and video presentations have focused far more on cultural politics than they have on political economy. For Fraser, "democracy today requires both economic redistribution and multicultural recognition" (174). If the existence of NAGPRA lulls us into thinking that justice has been achieved for Indian peoples and that the playing ground is once again even, then we will be creating new kinds of silences regarding the truth of things.

Conservative politicians often speak strongly (with religious fervor) against "throwing money at problems" such as education and health care. For them, local management is key, not tax money, and not federal interference. This attitude has contributed to the Faustian pact with casinos that has developed in many parts of Indian Country, and has been the genius behind the American Indian Ritual Object Repatriation Foundation, which secures sizeable tax breaks for private citizens who "rescue" American Indian patrimony from auction houses, art galleries, and their own collections for repatriation purposes. But these local-level remedies only address a tiny portion of an enormous, historically and internationally rooted set of practices that has removed hundreds of thousands of human remains and cultural property from their rightful owners, caretakers, and descendants. NAGPRA will be a viable "human rights" law only when its implementation is accompanied by a fixed federal budgetary line of many more millions of dollars per year than is currently allocated.

Reflections on Changes in American Anthropology in Response to the Repatriation Movement

Although this book has been designed to be "interdisciplinary" and of interest to a wide range of readers, as an anthropologist I feel a special commitment to provide a retrospective on NAGPRA that relates to the arena of relationships between anthropologists and Native Americans. A great deal has been written on this topic in recent years, much of it in response to Vine Deloria Jr.'s well-known critique of the anthropological enterprise in relationship to Indian peoples. Much of this discussion has centered around the practices of biological and archaeological anthropology, with NAGPRA at its center. I have some other insights to offer.

In the view of John Borneman (1995: 665), American anthropology "has defined itself less in terms of mapping national social structure than in terms of mapping global categories of Otherness." In the United States we enacted a strange foreign policy as we treated Native Americans (under the aegis, for many years, of the War Department and then the Department of Defense) as foreigners whose bodies and objects were to be obliterated or stuffed into museums so that we might exhibit our victory over them. We thus turned the true foreigners into new natives, and truer natives into enemies. By looking more closely at this historical process, NAGPRA offers us the opportunity to rethink our relationship to Indian peoples in constructing revised visions of domestic policy. This is important to a discipline such as anthropology, which has built most of its methodology on scrutinizing the exotic "Other" but which is being "repatriated" to this continent (Rappaport 1995: 235). It is surprising to find, even today, that few edited works on "American culture" include discussions of Indian peoples, who are still mainly anthologized within collections dealing with that always marginalized cultural category as a whole, reflecting their continued foreign status to academic disciplines.

The physical manifestation of what Borneman calls the "centrality of the Indian for the category 'foreign' in the formation of the American national imaginary" (1995: 665) is nowhere more apparent than in the stacks of computer printouts that teeter on cultural preservation officers' desks in crowded Indian tribal offices. "Here's what we took from you," the lists seem to say, "Come and get it." The offer—backed by force of law—is usually sincere, but the fact remains that the task is more enormous than anyone anticipated, and the degree of Indian and Native Hawaiian property theft and purchase is more constitutive of the American cultural psyche than is comfortable to admit. So what directions should we take? How can we create something positive from this? And how can we "use the knowledge we already have" to make this discipline "continue to work for, not against, humanity" (Strathern 1995: 169)?

First, I think it is important to work toward the "collaboration of local knowledges," as Anne Salmond (1995: 24) suggests, based on her experiences with the Maori of New Zealand and her reading of Foucault on knowledge insurrections. Colleges and universities all have local, regional, historical, national, social, and global contexts, and it behooves us to consider them as we do our work and make our pronouncements about "diversity" and "culture" in our classrooms and to our colleagues. Marilyn Strathern emphasizes this cogently in relationship to anthropology:

> Attention to the detail of social relations has always been one of the discipline's strengths. A reason for taking anthropology's focus on local circumstance with a new seriousness is, then, because we know

that is what focus does, and that includes taking as particular and local those bureaucratic structures, nationalist and internationalist ideologies and claims about universal human characteristics that appear everywhere. If we think we have something to share we shall share nothing by claiming to have produced universal insight; each and every one has his or her own vision of what is of universal importance.

Acknowledging the presence of persons is a premise of another order. Those moments when we render knowledge local and people co-eval conserve the global possibilities of that premise (Strathern 1995: 170).

In response to the realization of the historical constitution of the concept of culture within the projects of empire, a great deal of debate has ensued in recent years concerning the wisdom of placing the concept of culture at the heart of anthropology (see, e.g., Abu-Lughod 1991; Dirks, Eley, and Ortner 1994; Fardon 1995). It hardly seems possible that we can jettison this troublesome concept, however, considering the central role the concept plays in ethnic struggles, popular culture, and the funding and hiring requirements of major institutions. We can and must, however, modify our working definitions in such a manner so that we avoid what Strathern (1995: 170) calls, following Stolcke's 1995 discussion, "cultural fundamentalism," wherein the culture concept is used to endorse racism, terrorism, and ethnic cleansing. It can also be used to punish and further exclude dominated peoples when they do not conform to nationalist expectations. Brazilian anthropologist Alcida Rita Ramos has this to say regarding the fundamentalist and essentialist ideal of what she calls the "hyperreal Indian" in Brazil: "Virtuous principles, ideological purity, willingness to die heroically for cherished ideals are no more than white fantasies. Indigenist activists who cultivate such an image do not seem to realize that, by demanding it of the Indians they are, in fact, creating a model of perfection of the honourable, incorruptible Westerner. The contrast between the martyr Indian and the sold-out Indian is a facsimile of the contrast between the honest white and the corrupt white" (Ramos 1994: 162).

This can perhaps be avoided by conceptualizing culture not in terms of fundamental essence but "as emergent from relations of power and domination" (Dirks, Eley, and Ortner 1994: 6). Gerald Sider finds that a concept of culture that is not "trivialized" and that "allows us, indeed encourages us, to address struggles that are simultaneously both against domination and against the dominated" is one that "names a locus of struggle: "The concept of culture as shared meanings and/or values, rather than being a simple descriptive statement about the social landscape, in fact, names an arena of the most profound conflicts, where people struggle to create different and ongoing conceptual and material histories within and against the same general history, a general history that people must continually struggle to create or to transform" (Sider 1994: 116).

Through our collaborations with Native Americans (however one-sided these collaborations sometimes seem to be and, in fact, are) we are becoming more aware of the complexities of history and culture and of the conflicts that will keep driving the reformulations of identity and power. In collaborating more regularly and honestly with Native Americans in doing cultural resource management work, observing American Indian Religious Freedom Act concerns, designing education for Native Americans in public schools and colleges, expanding feminist education to include more Native American women, and the like, we open the door for more types of knowledge to enter the arena of cultural and political struggles, and we enhance the possibilities for local peoples to enter "our territory" and contest the practices and representations that go on there. If this means that we have to change our way of thinking about our "chosen professions," then perhaps we should entertain the possibility that this might not be an altogether bad thing. As ethnologists have had to become archaeologists, and archaeologists have become ethnologists, and everyone, in some sense, has become an Americanist in the face of NAGPRA, we must recognize that the truths of history and the necessity of changing academic practice has changed the "location" (Bhabha 1994) of our respective academic disciplinary cultures. As these move outside of us, we may have had to follow them in nomadic fashion and to internalize these changes in ways that may transform many of our identities (see Willson 1995: 256).

Change, of course, is not always a good thing. In these postmodern times managerial metaphors (and their legislative and accreditation organization carriers) are inserting themselves into the academy (Hill and Turpin 1995), demanding that we assess "outcomes," "subcontract" services, and "downsize our operations." This trend is probably the single largest cause of demoralization in the academy than anything else I know. In addition, the world beyond the ivory tower is questioning scientific research as an organizing center of academic activity (see Downey and Rogers 1995), which also brings a sense that Armageddon may be just around the corner. In the face of all these disturbing threats to our accustomed way of life, it may be a relief to know that some incursions into our familiar world will be of benefit to our students and to those peoples whose societies are made a focus of study and debate.

Anthropologists and historians have disciplinary precedents for this type of work, so it should be relatively easy for us to help Indian peoples interpret the stacks of NAGPRA computer printouts that still must be digested. We should do this not only in terms of what these documents might "mean" in regard to cultural affiliation matters of possession and repossession, but in terms of what they signify on a deeper level, as ideological expressions of what it has meant to American history to naturalize Indians by putting their objects and bodies in natural history museums. We need to tell our students that it is a much shorter step than they might think from idealizing Native Americans as "natural people" to collecting their bodies, dead or alive, for museum exhibits. And when they protest the presence of human remains in their sites of learning, as some are currently doing at Fort Lewis College, we should be prepared to listen, to converse intelligently, and to act reasonably.

Perhaps most importantly, academics need to examine the various *demands* placed on knowledge as we think about the *effects* of knowledge. We need to interrogate the concept of "expert" and realize that it is not ourselves as often as we think. The expertise we should develop is to find more ways to assist in getting Native Americans full access to the documents that will help their struggles to regain land, human remains, and cultural property. We must also consider the possibility that if we proceed blindly in helping implement federal laws, we are in danger of becoming "nationalist academics," to use Anastasia N. Karakasidou's (1994: 38) term, more often producing "good knowledge" for the sake of propping up national, state, and academic applecarts than in finding out ways to the darker truths of things, where each of us may be implicated.

The history of anthropological work in the American Southwest is often narrated in terms of half-truths disguised as bitter jokes. In this breathtaking landscape threaded with rock shops and jewelry stores along an anachronistic and romanticized Route 66, anthropologists have, so the stories go, created a bad reputation for themselves. In their fervor to obtain "information before it got lost," the tales say that they ensconced themselves in every Indian home, paid drunken Indians for secret information, and went native. Still sensitive to these partially true accusations (which are trotted out far more often by the press, other academic disciplines, and New Agers—of all people—than by Indians), we often disappoint our students by not engaging them directly with Indian peoples, issues, and communities. We also disappoint Indians by not performing the task that we have told them we are trained to do, which is to fairly and thoroughly seek the truths of things using methods with which we are most familiar but which we have now become timid about using.

For instance, we were astonished during one of the consultation sessions when academics in general were taken to task by a Hopi official for not being critical enough of oral tradition. He said that he thought anthropologists had gone wrong by being lured into the view that oral narratives can stand alone as an adequate form of truth. What he was asking for, driven by NAGPRA or not, colored by the Navajo-Hopi dispute or not, was for anthropologists to return to the ethnographic method in seeking solutions to important human and Native rights issues (see Weiner 1995 regarding the debate over oral histories and ethnography in Australia for a similar position). The fact that many Native Americans seem to be calling for more ethnographic work, but on their own terms, provides us with an opportunity, and perhaps presents us with an obligation, that we should not ignore. NAGPRA is, therefore, one of several global, national, regional, and local phenomena that confront us each day as we attempt to revitalize our field by integrating our intellectual practices with the social life around us, in all its dimensions. Such challenges could hardly have been imagined by those who used the concept of culture as a critique or defense of empire, and are not addressed well if we forget that external forces are always, in some way, localized and contestable.

Series Editors' Afterword: Rethinking Struggle

One of the most important lessons from Kathy Fine-Dare's presentation and analysis of NAGPRA, as she writes in her conclusions, is "the messiness of historical truth, . . . the difficulty of identifying clearly demarcated 'sides' in the debate, or of positing easily achieved solutions." In plain terms, *Grave Injustice* makes undeniably clear the fact that the struggle for justice is neither defined nor described by the injustices that are committed. Knowing this, what is most broadly and generally at stake, we argue, is what this lesson means to those who wish to ask about the *strategic* possibility of other sorts of struggles that might well and productively be engaged by Native peoples and their allies and supporters in the dominant society, either under NAGPRA, or whatever law comes next. What, we ask, are the social possibilities of future Native struggle, and what, given the "messiness" that such struggles invoke and produce, are its current social (not simply conceptual) limits? Let us put the issues more concretely in terms of NAGPRA itself: suppose someone offered you a chance to get back the bones of your grandmother, and her headstone—and the tree you planted by the grave—that they took to study and display. You could get these bones back if you petitioned for them in appropriate language, and if you treated them in ways you were told were appropriate after they were "given" back to you. Suppose, moreover, that the people who offered to give your grandmother's remains back to you, under their conditions, were the same that killed her? Think about this, and think: could you even name all the different kinds of turmoil, all the feelings that would be running through your thoughts? Could you even name all the difficulties of talking about this with your kin, your neighbors, your friends? Such struggles cannot be engaged without answers to these sorts of questions, which are in the end far more socially pragmatic than they are conceptual or theoretical.

The point to be made is both simple and crucial and follows directly from the conclusions of *Grave Injustice*: for all that "struggle" names (what must be done, both in the hopes of making the world as a whole a little better, and in the hopes of making your own world a little more livable); for all that "struggle" invokes (what cannot be avoided, whether it will make things better or not); for all that, "struggle" remains a problematically simple and overly neat concept. Despite its critical role in so many critical anthropological texts (from Wolf 1959 to Tsing 1993; from Hymes 1969 to Marcus and Fischer 1986), it is this same clarity that makes struggle seem both too simple and too static. The world of dominated people is ordinarily made so messy and complex that the very notion of struggle represents, at best, transient—gossamer—moments of clarity. Let us look more closely at the problems that emerge with such crucial, yet not necessarily clarifying, concepts as "struggle" and at the social possibilities that emerge (and evanesce) with these problems.

We can start with a story that circulated, in multiple and diverse versions, at the height of the most recent period of reservation termination, during the Nixon presidency. The story introduces what seems initially to be a moment of clarity and social hope, for its implications seem deceptively clear. It went like this:

> A group of Menominees [a name echoing with the suffering caused by termination: the Menominees had been reduced by termination from a modestly prosperous and autonomous Native "reservation" to the desperately impoverished citizens of a newly formed, ordinary Wisconsin county] had applied to the National Science Foundation for a grant to dig up the bones from a Puritan cemetery in Massachusetts and study the bones. Since this Puritan cemetery was no older—no more ancient—than Native burial grounds that the NSF routinely gave funds to excavate, and since the importance to Native American citizens of finding out what diseases, etc., the Puritans brought with them was clearly no less, and probably very much greater, than having Euro-Americans put Indian bones and grave goods under the shovel and the microscope, the Menominees let it be known that if their grant request were denied they would go all the way to the Supreme Court, if need be, to enforce their right to equality.

The story that was circulating ended with this Menominee grant application and the associated claims being "quieted"—that is, withdrawn—with the conditional offer to the Menominees of very substantial other kinds of grants by the federal government (medical facilities, roads, education, etc.—that is, most of the things they lost with termination).

In some peculiar and complex way, they got their reservation and their "Indian-ness" back by claiming to be something that was not quite the opposite, by claiming equal standing under law (as citizens) and in science (as "objective" researchers). The story would lose both its appealing irony and its apparent political effectiveness if either of these were missing. In turn, the victory of the dominant society was made through the evasion of these claims to equality and objectivity (the same ideas used to justify the original termination movement itself). What happens to truth, to justice, and to the notion of "sides" in all this, where Natives regain their Indian-ness by claiming critical elements of "whiteness," according to laws and rules created originally to ensure the distinction between these two? Whatever we might usefully know about struggle begins from accepting the impossibility of clearly and unambiguously answering these questions in anything but the most superficial terms.

The veracity of the Menominee story is not the issue here, nor is the strong disappointment of progressive anthropological listeners at the point in the story when the Menominee grant and claim was withdrawn. The issue is what the story reveals: a range of people, from archaeologists to scavenger-profiteers, do not simply dig up Native peoples'—"Indian"—burial grounds. More: it is in good part the thoughtless and unreflective but necessarily "legal" impunity with which such acts were committed that makes the graves of Native people (graves that are absolutely nothing more and nothing less than those of ordinary human beings) into "Indian" graves. Put more directly, a power that constitutes itself though its claims to "legal" impunity creates a legacy that is never completely closed to its victims. While the identity of the victim is partly created by the actions against this identity, the possibility exists (indeed is created simultaneously with this victimization) that those subject to such laws find recourse in them. In the Menominee story (whether fictional or not) the irony that makes us grin, makes us hopeful that someone might at some point tweak the nose of power with such aplomb, is the tying together of both the identity of the victim with the means of its origination and ongoing creation. As Edward P. Thompson notes: "The rhetoric and the rules of society are something a great deal more than sham. In the same moment they may modify, in profound ways, the behaviour of the powerful, and mystify the powerless. They may disguise the true realities of power, but, at the same time, they may curb that power and check its intrusions. And it is often from within that the very rhetoric that a radical critique of the practices of the society is developed" (1975: 265).

As clear (and optimistic) as such a conclusion would seem, it is only part of the picture, and a full picture of the costs of such a strategy for the powerless who take it up seems still to come. *Grave Injustice* is a crucial part of that picture, for it reveals not just the frustrations of those who would take up NAGPRA (or other legal means) in search of redress. It shows the cost of doing so in the ways that people can and might imagine a future for themselves, and how they might talk about such things with one another, or with sympathetic and potentially strategic audiences outside their ranks. In this way Native struggles with and over NAGPRA represent part of a much larger picture of what it means to take up the "rhetoric and rules" (in Thompson's terms) of a particular society in order to try to check the power that these rules seem to create. Women (in past and in some places still today) know this, not just in their thoughts but in their lives: the same beliefs, perceptions, and actions that put them up on a pedestal, that make them special objects and symbols of honor and of value, more and different than just human, simultaneously bind, imprison, and restrict, and ultimately degrade. The desire to possess is just that: it is not science, nor art, nor history, and it is, of course, not just. Nor is it love, nor concern.

Yet neither is the situation so simple for those who would reject it. The alternative is not simply to choose autonomy or independence (of thought, action, or spirit); for it is never true that such things can be simply chosen, no matter how clear the situation of oppression in which one finds oneself. This is not because power has some mystical power to define what people can think about their lives and possibilities. Mystical power of this sort has been greatly exaggerated of late, in anthropology and elsewhere. Rather, when carrots are your primary food (and no one is ever—ever—effectively constrained by the stick), the whole notion of domination being organized by "the carrot and the stick" turns out to shape not just cooperation with domination but equally to shape resistance. And as Thompson points out, law is far more *both* carrot and stick. Struggle in general and struggles that invoke law are, as it were, necessarily simultaneously both against and within the world of carrot and stick. Women must know this, and African Americans, and Native Americans.

Against and within; within and against. We can take this characterization of the struggles and the relationships between dominators and dominated (to give far too neat names to what appears to be the "sides") in many directions. We can productively use the notion of "within and against" to talk about a particular kind of domination, very widespread, but very specific, whose main characteristic is the intense intimacy—often imposed—of dominator and dominated.

But that is not the main point, or the main task here. Following directly from Kathy Fine-Dare's analysis, we address a different set of issues: the point that struggles within as well as against domination ensure that the dominated can never be unified or have a single coherent strategy, or one that will last for very long. Taking up the role of victim, for example, or legal advocate, means taking up the role of a particular figure in the eyes of the dominant group (or, in this case, the eyes of the court) and thus putting aside the claims of some within one's own group in favor of successful "representation." Such strategies necessarily exaggerate existing splits among the powerless and create a host of others—for no strategy guarantees success, and thus every provisional answer serves to further heighten the tensions caused by choosing one role or figuration over another. Such a situation means that those areas of social life we point to when we speak of "struggle"—the actual physical struggles between dominated and dominators and, as importantly, those areas of their lives in and through which people come to decide how and why they do what they might to engage such struggles, and the repercussions this will bring—will always turn in crucial ways on the internal splits and tensions among the dominated and the dominators. And thus, the struggle for "justice," "repatriation," or "legal reparation" unfolds not simply along the lines of opposition over a history of exploitation, abuse, domination, or current versus historic "possession" of bones and grave goods. Nor even, contrary to what Thompson implies above, will they necessarily unfold along the lines laid out by the laws or rules invoked; but rather, struggles like those around NAGPRA proceed along the lines of fracture and incipient alliance within each "side"—along the lines of internal differentiation, which both is and is not produced and shaped by the struggle itself.

In the context of NAGPRA the most revealing incidents are those involving Native "grave goods"—goods put in the ground to honor and accompany the deceased; to be and to express the continuing relations between the living and the dead. Where Native communities have managed to make a case (under the particularly narrow confines that NAGPRA provides for the return of such items), some "grave goods" have actually been returned to the descendants of the people from whom they were taken. But in many of these cases the return was not unconditional. It came with various pressures and inducements to build a museum and in general to display the goods as they had been or might have been displayed among the dominant society. This understandably led to some substantial controversies among the members of the community that received the returned goods. In simple terms we can pose some of that struggle in terms of a characteristic or widespread split within Native communities between those who want to put the objects, or some or many of them, back in the ground where they belong, and those who would agree to put them on display—for reasons that have to do with jobs, with casinos, with pride, with the dignity of having one's own museum, with one's own "culture" on display.

Such conflicts can scarcely ever be reduced to simple factionalism, almost never a simple split between a (by now incredibly clichéd) mostly older generation of "traditionalists" and a younger generation of "progressives." Rather, we begin this task by realizing that the whole social matrix of Native communities is changing, has been changing dramatically for the last thirty years, making it less and less possible for increasing numbers of Native people to live a life drawn from locally derived resources—from locally grown foods to locally earned incomes. Simultaneously we can find, especially over the past thirty years or so, increasing numbers of affluent Native people residing in primarily Native communities. At both ends of the spectrum, but in profoundly different ways, Native people are being drawn into large-scale economies of trade and tourism, wage employment and resource extraction and management. Local controversies over how to deal with repatriated goods often become embedded in this changing matrix of opportunity and constraint.

The case is far more complex when other laws besides NAGPRA come into play, as is the case for most of those groups who possess the resources to finance the claims process involved in the repatriation of these goods. Put bluntly, those who support casinos need the museum to validate a vision of Indian-ness both assumed by the surrounding society and, perhaps more importantly initially, required by the laws set up to govern recognition and reparation (see Sider 1993, Clifford 1988). Casinos, we should point out, can be built on Native lands because Native peoples are considered by the federal government to be governed by the U.S. criminal code but to be exempt from the U.S. civil code, which includes codes about gambling. That exemption is part of Native "residual" sovereignty: a sovereignty that resides not simply in Native self-government but in the legal "specialness" of Native culture and history. Thus it is, ironically, those who are against museums for repatriated grave goods (by wanting, sometimes demanding, that returned goods be reburied) who demand the strongest stand on Native sovereignty: ironic, that is, because this same sovereignty requires (economically and politically) that these goods be used to attract potentially desecrating hordes of tourists who will simultaneously finance from their predictable losses a reinvigoration of Native economy and to justify the efforts of those politicians who have swapped the public's birthright to live in a decent society for the casino mess of pottage (i.e., the jobs, tax revenues, and ancillary industry that follows the scorched earth of organized gaming). It is difficult to say in such circumstances what "should" be done about these things—what ought to be done with the grave goods once received, or whether to even try to engage NAGPRA in the first place. Yet, we argue, it is this very undecidability—the fact that no strategy seems adequate to the tensions, feelings, or real politics of the situation—that sustains and re-creates novel sorts of Native autonomy. Not quite the same as sovereignty (which remains an element in the law of the dominant society), autonomy represents moments of possibility and decision that cannot be reduced to manipulation from the outside; nor can it be predicted from the outside which way they will go, or what sorts of divisions and unities they will entail and make possible. Always momentary, and always provisional, autonomies of this kind are nonetheless critical products of the sorts of struggles we are calling struggles "within and against" the dominant society.

This leads us to what might seem to some to be rather startling conclusions: that the internal differentiation of Native American communities—even though often provoked by external manipulation, and even though it can cause much tension and antagonism within the communities in which it occurs—turns out to be part and parcel of Native peoples having, and developing, their own histories, their own ability to shape the future that is made uncertain for both themselves and those around them by the peculiar autonomy entailed in struggles simultaneously within and against the larger society in which they are situated. Law in general, and laws like NAGPRA in particular, seem good examples of these sorts of struggles, the sort that provide the opportunity for the creation of a form of autonomy by and for those who are, in other ways, made largely powerless by these same struggles. Under such conditions, political strategies might well and productively root themselves within this differentiation, rather than seeking unity; and political support for Native peoples' rights and claims by members of the dominant society might well and productively begin from a more thoroughgoing engagement with the fissures among the dominant. That seems to be among the useful lessons of the struggles for and from NAGPRA.

Gerald Sider

Kirk Dombrowski

REFERENCES

Clifford, James. 1988. *The Predicament of Culture*. Cambridge: Harvard University Press.

Hymes, Dell H. 1999 [1969]. *Reinventing Anthropology*. Ann Arbor: University of Michigan Press.

Marcus, George E., and Michael M. J. Fischer. 1986. *Anthropology as Cultural Critique: An Experimental Moment in the Human Sciences*. Chicago: University of Chicago Press.

Sider, Gerald. 1993. *Lumbee Indian Histories*. New York: Cambridge University Press.

Thompson, Edward P. 1975. *Whigs and Hunters: The Origin of the Black Act*. New York: Pantheon Books.

Tsing, Anna L. 1993. *In the Realm of the Diamond Queen*. Princeton: Princeton University Press.

Wolf, Eric R. 1959. *Sons of the Shaking Earth*. Chicago: University of Chicago Press.

Appendix: Full text
of the NAGPRA Law

PUBLIC LAW 101-601—NOV. 16, 1990 NATIVE AMERICAN GRAVES
PROTECTION AND REPATRIATION ACT

Public Law 101-601
101st Congress
An Act

[104 stat. 3048 public law 101-601—nov. 16, 1990]

Nov. 16, 1990
[H.R. 5237]
To provide for the protection of Native American graves, and for other purposes.

Be it enacted by the Senate and House of Representatives of the United States of America in Congress assembled,

Native American Graves Protection and Repatriation Act.
Hawaiian Natives.
Historic preservation.
25 USC 3001 note.
25 USC 3001.

SECTION 1. SHORT TITLE.

This Act may be cited as the "Native American Graves Protection and Repatriation Act".

SEC. 2. DEFINITIONS.

For purposes of this Act, the term—

(1) "burial site" means any natural or prepared physical location, whether originally below, on, or above the surface of the earth, into

which as a part of the death rite or ceremony of a culture, individual human remains are deposited.

(2) "cultural affiliation" means that there is a relationship of shared group identity which can be reasonably traced historically or prehistorically between a present day Indian tribe or Native Hawaiian organization and an identifiable earlier group.

(3) "cultural items" means human remains and—

(A) "associated funerary objects" which shall mean objects that, as a part of the death rite or ceremony of a culture, are reasonably believed to have been placed with individual human remains either at the time of death or later, and both the human remains and associated funerary objects are presently in the possession or control of a Federal agency or museum, except that other items exclusively made for burial purposes or to contain human remains shall be considered as associated funerary objects.

(B) "unassociated funerary objects" which shall mean objects that, as a part of the death rite or ceremony of a culture, are reasonably believed to have been placed with individual human remains either at the time of death or later, where the remains are not in the possession or control of the Federal agency or museum and the objects can be identified by a preponderance of the evidence as related to specific individuals or families or to known human remains or, by a preponderance of the evidence, as having been removed from a specific burial site of an individual culturally affiliated with a particular Indian tribe,

(C) "sacred objects" which shall mean specific ceremonial objects which are needed by traditional Native American religious leaders for the practice of traditional Native American religions by their present day adherents, and

(D) "cultural patrimony" which shall mean an object having ongoing historical, traditional, or cultural importance central to the Native American group or culture itself, rather than property owned by an individual Native American, and which, therefore, cannot be alienated, appropriated, or conveyed by any individual regardless of whether or not the individual is a member of the Indian tribe or Native Hawaiian organization and such object shall have been considered inalienable by such Native American group at the time the object was separated from such group.

(4) "Federal agency" means any department, agency, or instrumentality of the United States. Such term does not include the Smithsonian Institution.

(5) "Federal lands" means any land other than tribal lands which are controlled or owned by the United States, including lands selected by but not yet conveyed to Alaska Native Corporations and groups organized pursuant to the Alaska Native Claims Settlement Act of 1971.

(6) "Hui Malama I Na Kupuna O Hawai'i Nei" means the nonprofit, Native Hawaiian organization incorporated under the laws of the State of Hawaii by that name on April 17, 1989, for the purpose of providing guidance and expertise in decisions dealing with Native Hawaiian cultural issues, particularly burial issues.

(7) "Indian tribe" means any tribe, band, nation, or other organized group or community of Indians, including any Alaska Native village (as defined in, or established pursuant to, the Alaska Native Claims Settlement Act), which is recognized as eligible for the special programs and services provided by the United States to Indians because of their status as Indians.

(8) "museum" means any institution or State or local government agency (including any institution of higher learning) that receives Federal funds and has possession of, or control over, Native American cultural items. Such term does not include the Smithsonian Institution or any other Federal agency.

(9) "Native American" means of, or relating to, a tribe, people, or culture that is indigenous to the United States.

(10) "Native Hawaiian" means any individual who is a descendant of the aboriginal people who, prior to 1778, occupied and exercised sovereignty in the area that now constitutes the State of Hawaii.

(11) "Native Hawaiian organization" means any organization which—

(A) serves and represents the interests of Native Hawaiians,

(B) has as a primary and stated purpose the provision of services to Native Hawaiians, and

(C) has expertise in Native Hawaiian Affairs, and shall include the Office of Hawaiian Affairs and Hui Malama I Na Kupuna O Hawai'i Nei.

(12) "Office of Hawaiian Affairs" means the Office of Hawaiian Affairs established by the constitution of the State of Hawaii.

(13) "right of possession" means possession obtained with the volun-

tary consent of an individual or group that had authority of alienation. The original acquisition of a Native American unassociated funerary object, sacred object or object of cultural patrimony from an Indian tribe or Native Hawaiian organization with the voluntary consent of an individual or group with authority to alienate such object is deemed to give right of possession of that object, unless the phrase so defined would, as applied in section 7(c), result in a Fifth Amendment taking by the United States as determined by the United States Claims Court pursuant to 28 U.S.C. 1491 in which event the "right of possession" shall be as provided under otherwise applicable property law. The original acquisition of Native American human remains and associated funerary objects which were excavated, exhumed, or otherwise obtained with full knowledge and consent of the next of kin or the official governing body of the appropriate culturally affiliated Indian tribe or Native Hawaiian organization is deemed to give right of possession to those remains.

(14) "Secretary" means the Secretary of the Interior.

(15) "tribal land" means

(A) all lands within the exterior boundaries of any Indian reservation;

(B) all dependent Indian communities;

(C) any lands administered for the benefit of Native Hawaiians pursuant to the Hawaiian Homes Commission Act, 1920, and section 4 of Public Law 86–3.

25 USC 3002.

SEC 3. OWNERSHIP.

(a) NATIVE AMERICAN HUMAN REMAINS AND OBJECTS. — The ownership or control of Native American cultural items which are excavated or discovered on Federal or tribal lands after the date of enactment of this Act shall be (with priority given in the order listed) —

(1) in the case of Native American human remains and associated funerary objects, in the lineal descendants of the Native American; or

(2) in any case in which such lineal descendants cannot be ascertained, and in the case of unassociated funerary objects, sacred objects, and objects of cultural patrimony —

Claims.

 (A) in the Indian tribe or Native Hawaiian organization on whose tribal land such objects or remains were discovered;

 (B) in the Indian tribe or Native Hawaiian organization which has the closest cultural affiliation with such remains or objects and which, upon notice, states a claim for such remains or objects; or

 (C) if the cultural affiliation of the objects cannot be reasonably ascertained and if the objects were discovered on Federal land that is recognized by a final judgment of the Indian Claims Commission or the United States Court of Claims as the aboriginal land of some Indian tribe—

 (1) in the Indian tribe that is recognized as aboriginally occupying the area in which the objects were discovered, if upon notice, such tribe states a claim for such remains or objects, or

 (2) if it can be shown by a preponderance of the evidence that a different tribe has a stronger cultural relationship with the remains or objects than the tribe or organization specified in paragraph (1), in the Indian tribe that has the strongest demonstrated relationship, if upon notice, such tribe states a claim for such remains or objects.

Regulations.

 (b) UNCLAIMED NATIVE AMERICAN HUMAN REMAINS AND OBJECTS.—Native American cultural items not claimed under subsection (a) shall be disposed of in accordance with regulations promulgated by the Secretary in consultation with the review committee established under section 8, Native American groups, representatives of museums and the scientific community.

 (c) INTENTIONAL EXCAVATION AND REMOVAL OF NATIVE AMERICAN HUMAN REMAINS AND OBJECTS.—The intentional removal from or excavation of Native American cultural items from Federal or tribal lands for purposes of discovery, study, or removal of such items is permitted only if—

 (1) such items are excavated or removed pursuant to a permit issued under section 4 of the Archaeological Resources Protection Act of 1979 (93 Stat. 721; 16 U.S.C. 470aa et seq.) which shall be consistent with this Act;

(2) such items are excavated or removed after consultation with or, in the case of tribal lands, consent of the appropriate (if any) Indian tribe or Native Hawaiian organization;

(3) the ownership and right of control of the disposition of such items shall be as provided in subsections (a) and (b); and

(4) proof of consultation or consent under paragraph 2 is shown.

(d) INADVERTENT DISCOVERY OF NATIVE AMERICAN RE-MAINS AND OBJECTS. — (1) Any person who knows, or has reason to know, that such person has discovered Native American cultural items on Federal or tribal lands after the date of enactment of this Act shall notify, in writing, the Secretary of the Department, or head of any other agency or instrumentality of the United States, having primary management authority with respect to Federal lands and the appropriate Indian tribe or Native Hawaiian organization with respect to tribal lands, if known or readily ascertainable, and, in the case of lands that have been selected by an Alaska Native Corporation or group organized pursuant to the Alaska Native Claims Settlement Act of 1971, the appropriate corporation or group. If the discovery occurred in connection with an activity, including (but not limited to) construction, mining, logging, and agriculture, the person shall cease the activity in the area of the discovery, make a reasonable effort to protect the items discovered before resuming such activity, and provide notice under this subsection. Following the notification under this subsection, and upon certification by the Secretary of the department or the head of any agency or instrumentality of the United States or the appropriate Indian tribe or Native Hawaiian organization that notification has been received, the activity may resume after 30 days of such certification.

(2) The disposition of and control over any cultural items excavated or removed under this subsection shall be determined as provided for in this section.

(3) If the Secretary of the Interior consents, the responsibilities (in whole or in part) under paragraphs (1) and (2) of the Secretary of any department (other than the Department of the Interior) or the head of any other agency or instrumentality may

be delegated to the Secretary with respect to any land managed by such other Secretary or agency head.

(e) RELINQUISHMENT.—Nothing in this section shall prevent the governing body of an Indian tribe or Native Hawaiian organization from expressly relinquishing control over any Native American human remains, or title to or control over any funerary object, or sacred object.

SEC. 4. ILLEGAL TRAFFICKING.

(a) ILLEGAL TRAFFICKING.—Chapter 53 of title 18, United States Code, is amended by adding at the end thereof the following new section:

"§1170. *Illegal Trafficking in Native American Human Remains and Cultural Items*

"(a) Whoever knowingly sells, purchases, uses for profit, or transports for sale or profit, the human remains of a Native American without the right of possession to those remains as provided in the Native American Graves Protection and Repatriation Act shall be fined in accordance with this title, or imprisoned not more than 12 months, or both, and in the case of a second or subsequent violation, be fined in accordance with this title, or imprisoned not more than 5 years, or both.

"(b) Whoever knowingly sells, purchases, uses for profit, or transports for sale or profit any Native American cultural items obtained in violation of the Native American Grave Protection and Repatriation Act shall be fined in accordance with this title, imprisoned not more than one year, or both, and in the case of a second or subsequent violation, be fined in accordance with this title, imprisoned not more than 5 years, or both.".

(b) TABLE OF CONTENTS.—The table of contents for chapter 53 of title 18, United States Code, is amended by adding at the end thereof the following new item:

"1170. Illegal Trafficking in Native American Human Remains and Cultural Items.".

Museums.

25 USC 3003.

SEC. 5. INVENTORY FOR HUMAN REMAINS AND
ASSOCIATED FUNERARY OBJECTS.

(a) IN GENERAL. — Each Federal agency and each museum which
has possession or control over holdings or collections of Native
American human remains and associated funerary objects shall
compile an inventory of such items and, to the extent possible
based on information possessed by such museum or Federal
agency, identify the geographical and cultural affiliation of such
item.

(b) REQUIREMENTS. — (1) The inventories and identifications
required under subsection (a) shall be —

(A) completed in consultation with tribal government and
Native Hawaiian organization officials and traditional religious leaders;

(B) completed by not later than the date that is 5 years after
the date of enactment of this Act, and

(C) made available both during the time they are being
conducted and afterward to a review committee established
under section 8.

(2) Upon request by an Indian tribe or Native Hawaiian organization which receives or should have received notice, a museum
or Federal agency shall supply additional available documentation to supplement the information required by subsection (a)
of this section. The term "documentation" means a summary
of existing museum or Federal agency records, including inventories or catalogues, relevant studies, or other pertinent data
for the limited purpose of determining the geographical origin,
cultural affiliation, and basic facts surrounding acquisition and
accession of Native American human remains and associated funerary objects subject to this section. Such term does not mean,
and this Act shall not be construed to be an authorization for, the
initiation of new scientific studies of such remains and associated funerary objects or other means of acquiring or preserving
additional scientific information from such remains and objects.

(c) EXTENSION OF TIME FOR INVENTORY. — Any museum
which has made a good faith effort to carry out an inventory and
identification under this section, but which has been unable to
complete the process, may appeal to the Secretary for an exten-

sion of the time requirements set forth in subsection (b)(1)(B). The Secretary may extend such time requirements for any such museum upon a finding of good faith effort. An indication of good faith shall include the development of a plan to carry out the inventory and identification process.

(d) NOTIFICATION—(1) If the cultural affiliation of any particular Native American human remains or associated funerary objects is determined pursuant to this section, the Federal agency or museum concerned shall, not later than 6 months after the completion of the inventory, notify the affected Indian tribes or Native Hawaiian organizations.

(2) The notice required by paragraph (1) shall include information—

(A) which identifies each Native American human remains or associated funerary objects and the circumstances surrounding its acquisition;

(B) which lists the human remains or associated funerary objects that are clearly identifiable as to tribal origin; and

(C) which lists the Native American human remains and associated funerary objects that are not clearly identifiable as being culturally affiliated with that Indian tribe or Native Hawaiian organization, but which, given the totality of circumstances surrounding acquisition of the remains or objects, are determined by a reasonable belief to be remains or objects culturally affiliated with the Indian tribe or Native Hawaiian organization.

Federal Register publication

(3) A copy of each notice provided under paragraph (1) shall be sent to the Secretary who shall publish each notice in the Federal Register.

(e) INVENTORY.—For the purposes of this section, the term "inventory" means a simple itemized list that summarizes the information called for by this section.

25 USC 3004

SEC. 6. SUMMARY FOR UNASSOCIATED FUNERARY OBJECTS, SACRED OBJECTS, AND CULTURAL PATRIMONY.

Museums.

(a) IN GENERAL.—Each Federal agency or museum which

has possession or control over holdings or collections of Native American unassociated funerary objects, sacred objects, or objects of cultural patrimony shall provide a written summary of such objects based upon available information held by such agency or museum. The summary shall describe the scope of the collection, kinds of objects included, reference to geographical location, means and period of acquisition and cultural affiliation, where readily ascertainable.

b) REQUIREMENTS. — (1) The summary required under subsection (a) shall be—

(A) in lieu of an object-by-object inventory;

(B) followed by consultation with tribal government and Native Hawaiian organization officials and traditional religious leaders; and

(C) completed by not later than the date that is 3 years after the date of enactment of this Act.

(2) Upon request, Indian Tribes and Native Hawaiian organizations shall have access to records, catalogues, relevant studies or other pertinent data for the limited purposes of determining the geographic origin, cultural affiliation, and basic facts surrounding acquisition and accession of Native American objects subject to this section. Such information shall be provided in a reasonable manner to be agreed upon by all parties.

25 USC 3005.

SEC. 7. REPATRIATION.

(a) REPATRIATION OF NATIVE AMERICAN HUMAN REMAINS AND OBJECTS POSSESSED OR CONTROLLED BY FEDERAL AGENCIES AND MUSEUMS. — (1) If, pursuant to section 5, the cultural affiliation of Native American human remains and associated funerary objects with a particular Indian tribe or Native Hawaiian organization is established, then the Federal agency or museum, upon the request of a known lineal descendant of the Native American or of the tribe or organization and pursuant to subsections (b) and (e) of this section, shall expeditiously return such remains and associated funerary objects.

(2) If, pursuant to section 6, the cultural affiliation with a particular Indian tribe or Native Hawaiian organization is shown with respect to unassociated funerary objects, sacred objects

or objects of cultural patrimony, then the Federal agency or museum, upon the request of the Indian tribe or Native Hawaiian organization and pursuant to subsections (b), (c) and (e) of this section, shall expeditiously return such objects.

(3) The return of cultural items covered by this Act shall be in consultation with the requesting lineal descendant or tribe or organization to determine the place and manner of delivery of such items.

(4) Where cultural affiliation of Native American human remains and funerary objects has not been established in an inventory prepared pursuant to section 5, or the summary pursuant to section 6, or where Native American human remains and funerary objects are not included upon any such inventory, then, upon request and pursuant to subsections (b) and (e) and, in the case of unassociated funerary objects, subsection (c), such Native American human remains and funerary objects shall be expeditiously returned where the requesting Indian tribe or Native Hawaiian organization can show cultural affiliation by a preponderance of the evidence based upon geographical, kinship, biological, archaeological, anthropological, linguistic, folkloric, oral traditional, historical, or other relevant information or expert opinion.

(5) Upon request and pursuant to subsections (b), (c) and (e), sacred objects and objects of cultural patrimony shall be expeditiously returned where—

(A) the requesting party is the direct lineal descendant of an individual who owned the sacred object;

(B) the requesting Indian tribe or Native Hawaiian organization can show that the object was owned controlled by the tribe or organization; or

(C) the requesting Indian tribe or Native Hawaiian organization can show that the sacred object was owned or controlled by a member thereof, provided that in case where a sacred object was owned by a member thereof, there are no identifiable lineal descendants of said member or the lineal descendants, upon notice, have failed to make a claim for the object under this Act.

(b) SCIENTIFIC STUDY. —If the lineal descendant, Indian tribe, or Native Hawaiian organization requests the return of culturally affiliated Native American cultural items, the Federal agency or museum shall expeditiously return such items unless such items are indispensable for completion of a specific scientific study, the outcome of which would be of major benefit to the United States. Such items shall be returned by no later than 90 days after the date on which the scientific study is completed.

(c) STANDARD OF REPATRIATION. — If a known lineal descendant or an Indian tribe or Native Hawaiian organization requests the return of Native American unassociated funerary objects, sacred objects or objects of cultural patrimony pursuant to this Act and presents evidence which, if standing alone before the introduction of evidence to the contrary, would support a finding that the Federal agency or museum did not have the right of possession, then such agency or museum shall return such objects unless it can overcome such inference and prove that it has a right of possession to the objects.

(d) SHARING OF INFORMATION BY FEDERAL AGENCIES AND MUSEUMS. — Any Federal agency or museum shall share what information it does possess regarding the object in question with the known lineal descendant, Indian tribe, or Native Hawaiian organization to assist in making a claim under this section.

(e) COMPETING CLAIMS. — Where there are multiple requests for repatriation of any cultural item and, after complying with the requirements of this Act, the Federal agency or museum cannot clearly determine which requesting party is the most appropriate claimant, the agency or museum may retain such item until the requesting parties agree upon its disposition or the dispute is otherwise resolved pursuant to the provisions of this Act or by a court of competent jurisdiction.

(f) MUSEUM OBLIGATION. — Any museum which repatriates any item in good faith pursuant to this Act shall not be liable for claims by an aggrieved party or for claims of breach of fiduciary duty, public trust, or violations of state law that are inconsistent with the provisions of this Act.

5 USC 3006.

SEC. 8. REVIEW COMMITTEE.

(a) ESTABLISHMENT.—Within 120 days after the date of enactment of this Act, the Secretary shall establish a committee to monitor and review the implementation of the inventory and identification process and repatriation activities required under sections 5, 6 and 7.

(b) MEMBERSHIP—(1) The Committee established under subsection (a) shall be composed of 7 members,

(A) 3 of whom shall be appointed by the Secretary from nominations submitted by Indian tribes, Native Hawaiian organizations, and traditional Native American religious leaders with at least 2 of such persons being traditional Indian religious leaders;

(B) 3 of whom shall be appointed by the Secretary from nominations submitted by national museum organizations and scientific organizations; and

(C) 1 who shall be appointed by the Secretary from a list of persons developed and consented to by all of the members appointed pursuant to subparagraphs (A) and (B).

(2) The Secretary may not appoint Federal officers or employees to the committee.

(3) In the event vacancies shall occur, such vacancies shall be filled by the Secretary in the same manner as the original appointment within 90 days of the occurrence of such vacancy.

(4) Members of the committee established under subsection (a) shall serve without pay, but shall be reimbursed at a rate equal to the daily rate for GS-18 of the General Schedule for each day (including travel time) for which the member is actually engaged in committee business. Each member shall receive travel expenses, including per diem in lieu of subsistence, in accordance with sections 5702 and 5703 of title 5, United States Code.

(c) RESPONSIBILITIES.—The committee established under subsection (a) shall be responsible for-

(1) designating one of the members of the committee as chairman;

(2) monitoring the inventory and identification process con-

ducted under sections 5 and 6 to ensure a fair, objective consideration and assessment of all available relevant information and evidence;

(3) upon the request of any affected party, reviewing and making findings related to—

(A) the identity or cultural affiliation of cultural items, or

(B) the return of such items;

(4) facilitating the resolution of any disputes among Indian tribes, Native Hawaiian organizations, or lineal descendants and Federal agencies or museums relating to the return of such items including convening the parties to the dispute if deemed desirable;

(5) compiling an inventory of culturally unidentifiable human remains that are in the possession or control of each Federal agency and museum and recommending specific actions for developing a process for disposition of such remains;

(6) consulting with Indian tribes and Native Hawaiian organizations and museums on matters within the scope of the work of the committee affecting such tribes or organizations;

(7) consulting with the Secretary in the development of regulations to carry out this Act;

(8) performing such other related functions as the Secretary may assign to the committee; and

(9) making recommendations, if appropriate, regarding future care of cultural items which are to be repatriated.

(d) Any records and findings made by the review committee pursuant to this Act relating to the identity or affiliation of any cultural items and the return of items may be admissible in any action brought section 15 of this Act.

(e) RECOMMENDATIONS AND REPORT.—The committee shall make the recommendations under paragraph (c)(5) in consultation with Indian tribes and Native Hawaiian organizations and appropriate scientific and museum groups.

(f) ACCESS.—The Secretary shall ensure that the committee established under subsection (a) and the members of the committee have reasonable access to Native American cultural items under review and to associated scientific and historical documents.

Regulations.

(g) DUTIES OF SECRETARY.—The Secretary shall—

(1) establish such rules and regulations for the committee as may be necessary, and

(2) provide reasonable administrative and staff support necessary for the deliberations of the committee.

(h) ANNUAL REPORT.—The committee established under subsection (a) shall submit an annual report to the Congress on the progress made, and any barriers encountered, in implementing this section during the previous year.

(i) TERMINATION.—The committee established under subsection (a) shall terminate at the end of the 120-day period beginning on the day the Secretary certifies, in a report submitted to Congress, that the work of the committee has been completed.

Museums.

25 USC 3007.

SEC. 9. PENALTY.

(a) PENALTY.—Any museum that fails to comply with the requirements of this Act may be assessed a civil penalty by the Secretary of the Interior pursuant to procedures established by the Secretary through regulation. A penalty assessed under this subsection shall be determined on the record after opportunity for an agency hearing. Each violation under this subsection shall be a separate offense.

(b) AMOUNT OF PENALTY.—The amount of a penalty assessed under subsection (a) shall be determined under regulations promulgated pursuant to this Act, taking into account, in addition to other factors—

(1) the archaeological, historical, or commercial value of the item involved;

(2) the damages suffered, both economic and noneconomic, by an aggrieved party, and

(3) the number of violations that have occurred.

Courts.

(c) ACTIONS TO RECOVER PENALTIES.—If any museum fails to pay an assessment of a civil penalty pursuant to a final order of the Secretary that has been issued under subsection (a) and not appealed or after a final judgment has been rendered on appeal of such order, the Attorney General may institute a civil action in an appropriate district court of the United States to collect the penalty. In such action, the validity and amount of such penalty shall not be subject to review.

(d) SUBPOENAS.—In hearings held pursuant to subsection (a), subpoenas may be issued for the attendance and testimony of witnesses and the production of relevant papers, books, and documents. Witnesses so summoned shall be paid the same fees and mileage that are paid to witnesses in the courts of the United States.

25 USC 3008.

SEC. 10. GRANTS.

(a) INDIAN TRIBES AND NATIVE HAWAIIAN ORGANIZA-TIONS.—The Secretary is authorized to make grants to Indian tribes and Native Hawaiian organizations for the purpose of assisting such tribes and organizations in the repatriation of Native American cultural items.

(b) MUSEUMS.—The Secretary is authorized to make grants to museums for the purpose of assisting the museums in conducting the inventories and identification required under sections 5 and 6.

25 USC 3009.

SEC. 11. SAVINGS PROVISIONS.

Nothing in this Act shall be construed to—

(1) limit the authority of any Federal agency or museum to—

(A) return or repatriate Native American cultural items to Indian tribes, Native Hawaiian organizations, or individuals, and

(B) enter into any other agreement with the consent of the culturally affiliated tribe or organization as to the disposition of, or control over, items covered by this Act;

(2) delay actions on repatriation requests that are pending on the date of enactment of this Act;

(3) deny or otherwise affect access to any court;

(4) limit any procedural or substantive right which may otherwise be secured to individuals or Indian tribes or Native Hawaiian organizations; or

(5) limit the application of any State or Federal law pertaining to theft or stolen property.

25 USC 3010.

Appendix

SEC. 12. SPECIAL RELATIONSHIP BETWEEN
FEDERAL GOVERNMENT AND INDIAN TRIBES.

This Act reflects the unique relationship between the Federal Government and Indian tribes and Native Hawaiian organizations and should not be construed to establish a precedent with respect to any other individual, organization or foreign government.

25 USC 3011.

SEC. 13. REGULATIONS.

The Secretary shall promulgate regulations to carry out this Act within 12 months of enactment.

25 USC 3012.

SEC. 14. AUTHORIZATION OF APPROPRIATIONS.

There is authorized to be appropriated such sums as may be necessary to carry out this Act.

25 USC 3013.

SEC. 15. ENFORCEMENT.

Courts.

The United States district courts shall have jurisdiction over any action brought by any person alleging a violation of this Act and shall have the authority to issue such orders as may be necessary to enforce the provisions of this Act.

Approved November 16, 1990.

LEGISLATIVE HISTORY—H.R. 5237: HOUSE REPORTS: No. 101–877 (Comm. on Interior and Insular Affairs).
CONGRESSIONAL RECORD, Vol. 136 (1990):
Oct. 22, considered and passed House.
Oct. 25, considered and passed Senate; passage vitiated.
Oct. 26, reconsidered and passed Senate, amended.
Oct. 27, House concurred in Senate amendments.

Notes

1. MUSEUMS AND OBJECTS OF EMPIRE

1. The British Museum holds many Native American objects. For example, a campaign is currently underway to repatriate Kwakwaka'wakw transformation masks from the British Museum to the U'Mista Cultural Centre (see Buckthought 2000).

2. Interestingly, art historian George Kubler (1962: 4–8) argues that an anthropological account of New World cultural expressions is incomplete and often misleading on two grounds. First, archaeology in the New World necessarily became lodged in the practices of science rather than the humanities because of the paucity of other sorts of information about American antiquity that could temper evolutionism. Second, the study of "culture" creates the kind of deterministic framework that excludes or marginalizes the study of individual, nuanced creative impulses. Although art history does not exist to flesh out the details of culture and in fact treats far fewer domains of human manufacture than does anthropology, the latter discipline is not a satisfactory source of information and insight regarding those arenas of human existence where culture engenders but does not determine the final expressive form: "Hence archaeology in America joins with ethnology (the study of living peoples) and with linguistic science as a section of anthropology, dedicated to the study of 'primitive' peoples. Archaeology is a scientific technique rather than a fully autonomous discipline. It is important whenever documents fail to yield direct evidence of the past. In the hands of the anthropologists, it is applied to the recovery of information about social structure and economic life. In this context works of art are used as sources of information rather than as expressive realities" (Kubler 1962: 7–8).

3. The concept for the Midway exhibits was essentially copied from the 1889 Paris World's Fair, particularly the Java, Cairo, and Algeria/Tunis "villages" (see Appelbaum 1980: 95–102). Photographs of the World's Columbian Exposition were produced by a wide variety of companies. The 240 portraits found in *Midway Types* were published without ascription, but they were probably made by Canadian portrait photographer James J.

Gibson (Brown 1994: 83, 150 n. 63). Although the anonymous writer(s) of the captions "catered to the less-than-tolerant prevailing attitudes," Gibson's portraits of national groups on the Midway are characterized as "distinctively individual, empathetic, and dignified" by historian Julie K. Brown (1994: 83).

4. A friend reports that during a recent trip through the back roads of Missouri he visited a beat-up, privately owned museum that was designed along the "collection of oddities" model. In a back room were displayed severed heads of Native Americans that looked to have been exhumed from graves.

5. For information on the scandal surrounding the circumstances under which the brain of Ishi, last of the California Yahis, was taken from his body after his death from tuberculosis in 1916, sent by scientists to the Smithsonian, and finally returned to Native people in California for reburial after eighty-three years, see Norrell (1999a, 1999b, 1999c) and Shea (2000).

6. Perhaps ironically, this viewpoint is more similar to that of some Native Americans than it is to that of most Christians. In the great Council Book, or *Popol Vuh*, of the Quiché Maya a story unfolds regarding the many failed attempts of the gods to "get it right" when it came to creating human beings. The failures remain today, however, not in the form of inferior "races," but in the form of monkeys and other creatures that have been transformed into something more appropriate to their talents.

7. It is believed that the founder of Mormonism, Joseph Smith, was influenced a great deal by the experience of growing up around the mounds of western New York, and that he may have been inspired to write *The Book of Mormon* by the "folk-anthropology concerning the origin of the mound builders" (Hallowell 1960: 77).

2. HISTORY OF THE REPATRIATION MOVEMENT, 1880S TO 1970S

1. This complexity extends to the United States as a whole. Because people could choose more than one race on the 2000 census form, 6.8 million people listed themselves as biracial or multiracial. Although this indicates the increasing widening of racial conceptions as a whole in the United States, it does not tell us how each of these individuals thinks of himself or herself primarily. In the most recent National Health Interview Survey, 25.2 percent of the people who described themselves as both black and white considered themselves white, while "80.0 percent who designated themselves as white and Indian believed themselves to be white"

(Holmes 2001). While this might suggest that Indians may be assimilating into the urban landscape, the 2000 census also reports "that there are now more Indians and bison on the Plains than at any time since the late 1870's," even as the white depopulation of some counties in North and South Dakota is decelerating (Egan 2001). As *New York Times* reporter Timothy Egan indicates, " 'The people are coming back, they get their degrees and they start their own businesses, or take jobs as teachers here on the reservation,' said Anita Blue of the Turtle Mountain Reservation in North Dakota, where the population in the Indian-dominated county grew 7.1 percent." Egan also states that a "third of the nation's 31 accredited Indian colleges offer bison management" (Egan 2001).

2. Thanks go to Thomas H. Shipps for bringing this document to my attention.

3. Resistance to Collier's IRA-established form of tribal government continues to this day. A group of traditionalists based on the Pine Ridge Reservation are working to change what they feel is a genocidal system of government because of the ways it contradicts the traditional system of government, which was based on consensus and the Lakota way ("Ableza Oyate" 1999).

4. The Cayuga, Mohawk, Oneida, Onondaga, Seneca, and Tuscarora nations constitute the Six Nations, formerly the Iroquois Nation.

5. In 1974 the Archaeological and Historic Preservation (Moss-Bennett) Act was passed. The bill that led to the act was designed primarily by archaeologists who believed that the full protection of archaeological sites could not take place unless agencies were authorized to spend funds at the time that resource-protection emergencies presented themselves. Rather than speculate a year in advance how much money might be needed from Congress via the National Park Service to finance archaeological projects and mitigate crises that would almost certainly emerge after fixed funds were granted, the 1974 Act "supplied the rationale for ongoing funds tied to programs and projects as they develop" (McGimsey 1999: 11).

3. HISTORY OF THE REPATRIATION MOVEMENT, 1980S

1. La Flesche was closely associated with anthropologist and humanitarian Alice Fletcher, whose belief in and activity toward achieving education and civilization for the Omahas directly led to the Dawes General Allotment Act of 1887, which was applied to tribes across the United States (Lurie 1999: 22–23).

2. The percentages of indigenous peoples that make up the popula-

tions of nation-states of the Western Hemisphere varies widely. Theodore MacDonald Jr. (1997: 22–23) reports the following Indian populations and Indian percentage of the total populations: Bolivia, 3,755,228 (63 percent); Brazil, 248,333 (0.2 percent); Colombia, 441,356 (1.8 percent); and Ecuador, 2,941,549 (38 percent).

3. One section of the UDHR that comes close to providing the basis for the kind of collective rights sought by the repatriation movement is Article 17(1): "Everyone has the right to own property alone as well as in association with others. (2) No one shall be arbitrarily deprived of his property" (Morsink 1999: 333).

4. The WGIP is part of the United Nations Sub-Commission on Prevention of Discrimination and Protection of Minorities. This group, in turn, reports to the Commission on Human Rights. Major decisions from these groups must be approved to the Economic and Social Council (ECOSOC) or the General Assembly. The WGIP meets in Geneva for five days a year with heavy attendance by representatives from indigenous peoples and their organizations. These meetings have become extremely important as a way for indigenous peoples to exchange ideas and plan pan-indigenous undertakings (Alfredsson 1989: 255).

4. NAGPRA AND REPATRIATION EFFORTS IN THE 1990S

1. Space restrictions prohibit addressing the Native Hawaiian struggles in more detail. Most Americans are virtually unconscious of Native Hawaiian opposition to territorial and sacred property theft, human remains desecration, cultural misrepresentation, racism, and human rights abuses. The fact that Hawaii is a state of the union that is key to the American military presence in the Pacific, and the additional fact that it figures so prominently in the American romantic and touristic imagination, contribute to an even more aggressive colonial amnesia and whitewashing regarding Native Hawaiians. For an introduction to these issues, see Coffman 1998; LaDuke 1996; Pennybacker 1999; Trask 1999; and Young 1998.

2. For Review Committee meeting documentation, see *www.cast.uark.edu/other/nps/nagpra/rcm.html* (accessed 4 November 2001).

3. Some of this account appeared in Fine-Dare 1997. See also Fine-Dare and Judge 1995.

4. Archaeological training at Fort Lewis College extends beyond Ancestral Pueblo excavations. Philip Duke has also conducted survey and analysis of high-altitude sites that are likely Ancestral Ute, sometimes with Southern Ute participation and always with their consultation. Duke has

also conducted historical work at Ludlow, Colorado, site of a massacre of non-Indian miners (see Duke and Matlock 1999).

5. See, e.g., Butler 1995: 440; Fardon 1995: 12; or Silber 1995 regarding the increasing use of spatial metaphors in talking about cultural conflict, identity, and other interpretive issues.

6. Franz Boas was briefly introduced in chapter 1. Widely considered to be the founder of modern anthropology, he stressed broad training in all of the subfields—archaeological, linguistic, biological, and cultural anthropology.

7. Grant #08–95-GP-052 from the National Park Service of the United States Department of Interior. Fort Lewis College was one of forty-two institutions that were funded that cycle. The amount awarded to FLC was $54,460.

As part of the grant proposal package, we included letters from tribes that agreed to participate in the project if it was funded. We solicited letters of support with the understanding that full consultation would occur even if we did not receive the funding, in compliance with the law. The statement of commitment signed by the tribes included the following elements:

—inspection of collections;—consultation regarding the proper care, treatment, and disposition of Native American human remains and cultural items;

—internships for Native American students at Fort Lewis College to assist with and learn from the consultation process;

—consultation with Fort Lewis College staff and faculty regarding cultural property and cultural privacy issues, not only in the museum but in the classroom;

—assistance in the production of a written document to be distributed in the tribal offices and at the college providing some clarity on matters of ethics, treatment of human remains and cultural objects, representation of Native peoples in the classroom, cultural property and cultural privacy issues, etc.

8. It should be mentioned that the second group of consultants did not like the fact that there was more than one consultation session. They wanted to know in detail what had happened at the first session, and at the end of the day they expressed their desire that all further sessions be joint sessions. The reason that we designed two sessions was purely one of convenience and inclusion, knowing that no one date would serve everyone equally well, and that we had to include as many tribes as possible in the process.

9. The discussions over the revision of the International Labor Organization (ILO) Convention 107 held in Geneva are instructive when thinking about NAGPRA consultation problems. As the *IWGIA Yearbook for 1986* reported, "Several people have put in a plea for the concept of participation. This is a two-edged sword because the meaning of participation is dangerously vague. One area of meanings would put indigenous people as participants in a plan which had already been decided. This is a sophisticated form of forced labour" (International Work Group for Indigenous Affairs 1987). And before Geoff Clark from the Australian Aboriginal group walked out of the ILO Convention meetings in Geneva, he had this to say: "Do you think that we are unaware of the actual meaning of words like consultation, participation and collaboration? Would you be satisfied with 'consultation' as a guarantee for your rights? Unless governments are obligated to obtain our consent, we remain vulnerable to legislative and executive whims that inevitably will result in further dispossession and social disintegration of our peoples. The victims are always the first to know how the system operates" (IWGIA 1989: 184, quoted in Bodley 1994: 378).

10. See, for instance, this discussion of the dispute from someone who has developed a pro-Navajo stance in the course of carrying out his work: Brugge 1994.

11. In a letter to Fort Lewis College from the Hopi Tribe, dated 12 February 1996, in which NAGPRA concerns were highlighted, point 10 states the following: "Public education institutes should assist in identifying lands for reburial. This addresses the responsibility that has yet to be addressed by institutions sponsoring activities such as field schools. While these institutions reap a reward valuable to themselves, there is no reward to the tribes that currently must claim affiliation, repatriate and reinter human remains at their own expense. This needs to be addressed as NAGPRA merely addresses the symptoms of what has long been a problem to our people."

12. "The proposed rule (43 CFR Part 10) for carrying out the Act was published in the Federal Register on 28 May 1993 (58 FR 31122). Public comment was invited for a 60-day period, ending on 27 July 1993. Copies of the proposed rule were sent to the chairs or chief executive officers of all Indian tribes, Alaska Native villages and corporations, Native Hawaiian organizations, national Indian organizations and advocacy groups, national scientific and museum organizations, and State and Federal agency Historic Preservation Officers and chief archaeologists.

"Eighty-two written comments were received representing 89 specific organizations and individuals. These included thirteen Indian tribes, ten Native American organizations, nine museums, seven universities, three national scientific and museum organizations, eleven state agencies, nineteen Federal agencies, nine other organizations, and eight individuals. Several letters represent more than one organization. Comments addressed nearly all sections and appendices of the proposed rule. All comments were fully considered when revising the proposed rule for publication as a final rulemaking" (U.S. Department of the Interior 1995).

5. NAGPRA AS A CULTURAL AND LEGAL PRODUCT

1. For an interesting discussion of American Indian science education see Garroutte 1999.

2. See, for instance, Thomas 2000; articles in *Indian Country Today* and most other major newspapers, including the *New York Times*, which ran a feature story in its Sunday magazine (Malcomson 2000); *www.kennewickman.com*, *www.pbs.org/wgbh/nova/first/kennewick.html*, and *www.cr.nps.gov/aad/kennewick* (accessed 4 November 2001).

3. Amendments to the Constitution, Article I: "Congress shall make no law respecting an establishment of religion, or prohibiting the free exercise thereof; or abridging the freedom of speech, or of the press; or the right of people peaceably to assemble, and to petition the Government for a redress of grievances."

4. A program on this issue, "Hopi Repatriation," aired on National Public Radio's *Weekend Edition* program for 8 April 2001. In this program, Native Americans expressed the reasons why they cannot fully repatriate many of their cultural items—which, among other things, would mean reintroducing them into ceremonial life. One reason was because of their contamination with dangerous chemicals.

5. An excellent discussion of the discourse of the sacred, particularly as it relates to arguments presented in courtroom settings regarding sacred sites, can also be found in Miller 1998.

6. I am grateful to an anonymous reviewer of this manuscript for pointing out this important issue.

7. Much of this section originally appeared in Fine-Dare 1997.

8. For example, "The Hopi people desire to protect their rights to privacy and in and to Hopi intellectual resources. . . . Towards this end, the Hopi Tribe shall be consulted by all projects or activity involving Hopi intellectual resources. . . . Enforcement of this protocol requires a cooperative spirit.

The Hopi people may share the right to enjoy or use certain elements of its cultural heritage, under its own laws and procedures, but always reserves a right to determine how shared knowledge and information will be used. The collective right to manage our cultural heritage is crucial" (Hopi Tribe Office of Historic and Cultural Preservation 1995).

CONCLUSION

1. See also the Winter 2001 special issue of *Cultural Survival Quarterly*, "Intellectual Property Rights: Culture as Commodity"; "World's Indigenous People" 2000; Macdonald 1997; Anaya 1997.

2. For examples of archaeological viewpoints in solidarity with those of Native Americans, see Anyon et al. 1997; Klesert and Powell 1993; McGuire 1992, 1997; Zimmerman 1997a, 1997b.

References

Ableza Oyate: Prepare for the Year 2008. *Indian Country Today* (21–28 June). Paid Advertisement.

Abu-Lughod, Lila. 1991. Writing against Culture. In *Recapturing Anthropology: Working in the Present*, 137–62. Richard G. Fox, ed. Santa Fe NM: School of American Research Press.

Adams, David Wallace. 1995. *Education for Extinction: American Indians and the Boarding School Experience, 1875–1928*. Lawrence: University Press of Kansas.

Alfredsson, Gudmundur. 1989. The United Nations and the Rights of Indigenous Peoples. *Current Anthropology* 30(2): 255–59.

Allen, James, Hilton Als, John Lewis, and Leon F. Litwack. 2000. *Without Sanctuary: Lynching Photography in America*. Santa Fe NM: Twin Palms.

American Association of Physical Anthropologists (AAPA). 2000. Statement by the American Association of Physical Anthropologists on the Secretary of Interior's Letter of 21 September 2000 Regarding Cultural Affiliation of Kennewick Man. Electronic document, www.physanth.org/positions/kennewick.html, accessed 4 November 2001.

Anaya, S. James. 1997. Indigenous Peoples in International Law. *Cultural Survival Quarterly* 21(2): 58–61.

Anyon, Roger. 1996. Zuni Protection of Cultural Resources and Religious Freedom. *Cultural Survival Quarterly* 19(4): 46–49.

Anyon, Roger, T. J. Ferguson, Loretta Jackson, Lillie Lane, and Philip Vicenti. 1997. Native American Oral Tradition and Archaeology: Issues of Structure, Relevance, and Respect. In *Native Americans and Archaeologists: Stepping Stones to Common Ground*, 77–87. Nina Swidler, Kurt E. Dongoske, Roger Anyon, and Alan S. Downer, eds. Walnut Creek CA: Altamira Press.

Appelbaum, Stanley. 1980. *The Chicago World's Fair of 1893: A Photographic Record*. New York: Dover.

Artifacts Returned to Tribes May Pose Health Risk. 2000. *Indian Country Today*, 10 April 10: C5.

References

Assu, Harry, with Joy Inglis. 1989. *Assu of Cape Mudge: Recollections of a Coastal Indian Chief.* Vancouver: University of British Columbia Press.

Axtell, James. 1981. *The European and the Indian: Essays in the Ethnohistory of Colonial North America.* New York: Oxford University Press.

Baca, Kim. 1999. Historical Jemez Walk Comes to a Close. *Santa Fe New Mexican*, 22 May.

Baca, Lawrence. 1988. The Legal Status of American Indians. In *History of Indian-White Relations*. William C. Sturtevant, gen ed. Vol. 4: *Handbook of North American Indians*, 230–37. Wilcomb E. Washburn, ed. Washington DC: Smithsonian Institution Press.

Bad Wound, Barbara. 1999a. A New Millennium: We Look Back at the Last 100 Years: The First Decade. *Indian Country Today* 19(19; 1–8 November): A1, A3.

———. 1999b. Millennium Countdown Reviews Progress: Lands Diminish in 1920s. *Indian Country Today* 19(20; 9–14 November): A1, A3).

———. 1999c. Millennium Countdown: The 1930s. *Indian Country Today* 19(22; 24 November): A6.

———. 1999d. Millennium Countdown: The 1940s. *Indian Country Today* 19(23; 1 December): A6.

———. 1999e. Millennium Countdown: The 1950s. *Indian Country Today* 19(24; 8 December): A6–7.

———. 1999f. Millennium Countdown: The 1960s. *Indian Country Today* 19(25; 15 December): A6.

———. 1999g. Millennium Countdown: The 1970s. *Indian Country Today* 19(26; 22 December): B4–5.

———. 1999h. Millennium Countdown: The 1980s. *Indian Country Today* 19(27; 29 December): A6.

Baker, Lee D. 1998. *From Savage to Negro: Anthropology and the Construction of Race, 1896–1954.* Berkeley: University of California Press.

Begay, Richard, and Amanda Warburton. 1996. Navajo, Anasazi, and NAGPRA. Paper prepared for the Ninth Annual Navajo Studies Conference, Fort Lewis College, Durango CO.

Benjamin, Walter. 1968[1955]. Theses on the Philosophy of History. In *Illuminations*. Hannah Arendt, ed. and intro. New York: Schocken Books.

Bhabha, Homi K. 1994. *The Location of Culture.* New York: Routledge.

Boas, Franz. 1962[1928]. *Anthropology and Modern Life.* Ruth Bunzel, intro. New York: W. W. Norton.

References

Bodley, John H. 1994. *Cultural Anthropology: Tribes, States, and the Global System*. Mountain View CA: Mayfield.

Boorstin, Daniel J. 1983. *The Discoverers: A History of Man's Search to Know His World and Himself*. New York: Random House.

Borneman, John. 1995. American Anthropology and Foreign Policy. *American Anthropologist* 97(4): 663–72.

Bray, Tamara, and Thomas Killion, eds. 1994. *Reckoning with the Dead: The Larsen Bay Repatriation and the Smithsonian Institution*. William Fitzhugh, foreword. Washington, DC: Smithsonian Institution Press.

Bray, Tamara, Jacki Rand, and Thomas Killion. 1996. Smithsonian Institution Repatriation Procedures. In *Mending the Circle: A Native American Repatriation Guide*, 47–53. Barbara Meister, ed. New York: American Indian Ritual Object Repatriation Foundation.

Brooks, James F. 1998. Confounding the Color Line: Indian-Black Relations in Historical and Anthropological Perspective. *American Indian Quarterly* 22(1/2): 125–33.

Brown, Dee. 1970. *Bury My Heart at Wounded Knee: An Indian History of the American West*. New York: Holt, Rinehart and Winston.

Brown, Julie K. 1994. *Contesting Images: Photography and the World's Columbian Exposition*. Tucson: University of Arizona Press.

Brugge, David M. 1994. *The Navajo-Hopi Land Dispute: An American Tragedy*. Albuquerque: University of New Mexico Press.

Buckthought, Mike. 2000. We're Taking It Back: First Nations and Repatriation. *Peace and Environment News*, supplement, 4 October. Electronic document, http://perc.ca/PEN/2000–06/supplement/buckthou.html, accessed 4 November 2001.

Bushnell, David Ives, Jr. 1920. *Native Cemeteries and Forms of Burial East of the Mississippi*. Smithsonian Institution Bureau of American Ethnology Bulletin 71. Washington DC: Government Printing Office.

Butler, Judith. 1995. Collected and Fractured: Responses to Identities. In *Identities*, 439–47. Kwame Anthony Appiah and Henry Louis Gates Jr., eds. Chicago: University of Chicago Press.

Champagne, Duane. 1997. Self-Determination and Activism among American Indians in the United States, 1972–1997. *Cultural Survival Quarterly* 21(2): 32–35.

Chicago Times. 1893. *The Chicago Times Portfolio of Midway Types*. Chicago: American Engraving. (Chicago Historical Society; Library Collection)

Churchill, Ward, and Glenn T. Morris. 1992. Key Indian Laws and Cases.

In *The State of Native America: Genocide, Colonization, and Resistance*, 13–21.
M. Annette Jaimes, ed. Boston: South End Press.

Civil Penalty Rule Takes Effect to Penalize Non-Compliance with NAGPRA.
1997. *Common Ground* 2(1): 61.

Claiborne, William. 1992. The Skeleton in the Museum's Closet: An Eskimo
Boy's Tragedy in the Name of Science. *Washington Post*, 5 April: F01.

Clark, Geoffrey A. 1999. NAGPRA, Science, and the Demon-Haunted
World. *Skeptical Inquirer* 23(3): 44–48.

Clifford, James. 1991. Four Northwest Coast Museums: Travel Reflections.
In *Exhibiting Cultures: The Poetics and Politics of Museum Display*, 212–54.
Ivan Karp and Steven D. Lavine, eds. Washington DC: Smithsonian
Institution Press.

Coffman, Tom. 1998. *Nation Within: The Story of America's Annexation of the
Nation of Hawaii*. Kaneohe HI: EPICenter.

Cohen, Felix S. 1971. *Felix S. Cohen's Handbook of Federal Indian Law*.
Albuquerque: University of New Mexico Press.

Collier, John. 1947. *The Indians of America*. New York: W. W. Norton.

Collins, Susan. 1992. Government Involvement in Colorado Archaeology
and the Art of the State. In *The State of Colorado Archaeology*, 95–108. Philip
Duke and Gary Matlock, eds. Colorado Archaeological Society memoir
5. Denver: Colorado Historical Society.

Conn, Steven. 1998. *Museums and American Intellectual Life, 1876–1926*.
Chicago: University of Chicago Press.

Coughlin, Ellen K. 1994. Returning Indian Remains. *Chronicle of Higher
Education* 40(28): A8, A10, A16.

Courlander, Harold. 1971. *The Fourth World of the Hopis*. Greenwich CT:
Fawcett.

Cushing, Frank Hamilton. 1979[1901]. The Rabbit Huntress and Her
Adventures. In *Zuñi: Selected Writings of Frank Hamilton Cushing*, 392–400.
Jesse Green, ed. and intro. Fred Eggan, foreword. Lincoln: University of
Nebraska Press.

Debo, Angie. 1940. *And Still the Waters Run: The Betrayal of the Five Civilized
Tribes*. Princeton NJ: Princeton University Press.

———. 1941. *The Road to Disappearance*. Norman: University of Oklahoma
Press.

Deloria, Philip J. 1998. *Playing Indian*. New Haven CT: Yale University Press.

Deloria, Vine, Jr.. 1969. *Custer Died for Your Sins: An Indian Manifesto*. New
York: Avon.

————. 1997. *Red Earth, White Lies: Native Americans and the Myth of Scientific Fact*. Golden CO: Fulcrum.

Deloria, Vine, Jr., and Clifford M. Lytle. 1984. *The Nations Within: The Past and Future of American Indian Sovereignty*. Austin: University of Texas Press.

De Meo, Antonia M. 1994. More Effective Protection for Native American Cultural Property through Regulation of Export. *American Indian Law Review* 19(1): 1–72.

Dirks, Nicholas B., Geoff Eley, and Sherry B. Ortner. 1994. Introduction. In *Culture/Power/History: A Reader in Contemporary Social Theory*, 3–45. Nicholas B. Dirks, Geoff Eley, and Sherry B. Ortner, eds. Princeton, NJ: Princeton University Press.

Dirlik, Arif. 1999. The Past as Legacy and Project: Postcolonial Criticism in the Perspective of Indigenous Historicism. In *Contemporary Native American Political Issues*, 73–97. Troy R. Johnson, ed. Walnut Creek CA: Altamira Press.

Dodson, Mick. 1999. The Human Rights Situation of Indigenous Peoples in Australia. *Indigenous Affairs* 1 (March): 32–45. (Copenhagen: International Work Group for Indigenous Affairs)

Dongoske, Kurt E., and Roger Anyon. 1997. Federal Archaeology: Tribes, Diatribes, and Tribulations. In *Native Americans and Archaeologists: Stepping Stones to Common Ground*, 188–96. Nina Swidler, Roger Anyon, Kurt Dongoske, and Alan S. Downer, eds. Walnut Creek CA: Altamira Press.

Downer, Al[an S.]. 1999. A Decade of Change. *Common Ground* (Fall): 14–19.

Downey, Gary Lee, and Juan D. Rogers. 1995. On the Politics of Theorizing in a Postmodern Academy. *American Anthropologist* 97(2): 269–81.

Drug Probe Yields NAGPRA Conviction: Utah Man Admits to Selling Anasazi Skull. 1998. *Common Ground* 3(2/3): 15.

Dubin, Steven C. 1999. *Displays of Power: Memory and Amnesia in the American Museum*. New York: New York University Press.

Ducheneaux, Wayne L. 1990. Memorandum from Wayne L. Ducheneaux, President of the National Congress of American Indians, to Tribal Leaders regarding Repatriation, Reburial and Grave Protection Legislation, 16 February. Mimeograph.

Duke, Philip. 1999. Foreword. In *Affiliation Conference on Ancestral Peoples of the Four Corners Region Held at Fort Lewis College, Durango, CO 81301*, i. A Cooperative Agreement between the National Park Service and Fort Lewis College. Typescripts and papers. Mimeograph.

References

Duke, Philip, and Gary Matlock. 1999. *Points, Pithouses, and Pioneers: Tracing Durango's Archaeological Past*. Niwot CO: University Press of Colorado.

Echo-Hawk, Walter R. 1988. Tribal Efforts to Protect against Mistreatment of Indian Dead: The Quest for Equal Protection of the Laws. *Native American Rights Fund Legal Review* 14(1): 1–5.

Echo-Hawk, Walter R., and Roger C. Echo-Hawk. 1993. Repatriation, Reburial, and Religious Rights. In *Handbook of American Indian Religious Freedom*, 63–80. Christopher Vecsey, ed. New York: Crossroad.

———. 1994. *Battlefields and Burial Grounds: The Indian Struggle to Protect Ancestral Graves in the United States*. Minneapolis: Lerner.

Egan, Timothy. 1996. Tribe Stops Study of Bones That Challenge History. *New York Times*, 30 September.

———. 2001. For Indians, Casinos Are No Golden Goose. *New York Times*, 2 June.

Etienne, Roland, and Françoise Etienne. 1992. *The Search for Ancient Greece*. Anthony Zielonka, trans. New York: Harry N. Abrams.

Fardon, Richard. 1995. Introduction: Counterworks. In *Counterworks: Managing the Diversity of Knowledge*, 1–22. Richard Fardon, ed. New York: Routledge.

Farrell, John Aloysius, and Jim Richardson. 1983. *The New Indian Wars*. Denver: Denver Post.

Farrer, Claire R. 1994. Who Owns the Words? An Anthropological Perspective on Public Law 101–601. *Journal of Arts Management, Law and Society* 23(4): 317–26.

Fausett, Rory Snowarrow. 1990. Indigenous Cultural Rights as Human Rights: Repatriation of Human Skeletal Remains, Burial Artifacts and Cultural Objects and Properties. *IWGIA Newsletter* 62 (December): 112–15. (Copenhagen: International Work Group for Indigenous Affairs)

Felman, Shoshana. 1999. Benjamin's Silence. *Critical Inquiry* 25(2): 201–34.

Fenton, William N. 1989. Return of Eleven Wampum Belts to the Six Nations Iroquois Confederacy on Grand River, Canada. *Ethnohistory* 36(4): 392–410.

Ferguson, T. J. 1991. Return of War Gods Sets Example for Repatriation. In *Zuni History: Victories in the 1990s*, section 2: 13. Zuni History Repatriation Project. Seattle: Institute of the North American West.

Ferguson, T. J., Joe Watkins, and Gordon L. Pullar. 1997. Native Americans and Archaeologists: Commentary and Personal Perspectives. In *Native*

228

Americans and Archaeologists: Stepping Stones to Common Ground, 237–52. Nina Swidler, Kurt E. Dongoske, Roger Anyon, and Alan S. Downer, eds. Walnut Creek CA: Altamira Press.

Fine, Kathleen S. (See also Kathleen S. Fine-Dare). 1988. The Politics of "Interpretation" at Mesa Verde National Park. *Anthropological Quarterly* 61(4): 177–86.

———. 1994. Intellectual Property Rights, the Academy, and the Para-Academy: The Appropriateness of Cultural Appropriation in the Grey Areas of University Teaching and Discourse. Paper presented at the Annual Meeting of the American Anthropological Association, 30 November, Atlanta.

Fine, Kathleen, and Philip Duke. 1993. Native Americans and Archaeology: A Reply to Meighan. Unpublished manuscript submitted to *American Antiquity*.

Fine-Dare, Kathleen S. (See also Kathleen S. Fine). 1997. Disciplinary Renewal out of National Disgrace: Native American Graves Protection and Repatriation Act Compliance in the Academy. *Radical History Review* 68: 25–53.

Fine-Dare, Kathleen S., and W. James Judge. 1995. Anthropological Frameworks for Establishing Cultural Affiliation, Final Report: A Document to Accompany the Inventory of Native American Human Remains and Associated Funerary Objects in the Possession or Control of Mesa Verde National Park. Prepared for Mesa Verde National Park Research and Research Management Division in Partial Fulfillment of Contract #MEVE-R-94-0436.

Flood, Renée Sansom. 1995. *Lost Bird of Wounded Knee: Spirit of the Lakota*. New York: Da Capo Press.

Fort Lewis College, ed. 1999. *Affiliation Conference on Ancestral Peoples of the Four Corners Region*. Vols. 1–3. Transcripts and Papers. January, February, April, 1998. Durango CO. Mimeograph.

Foucault, Michel. 1980. Two Lectures. In *Power/Knowledge: Selected Interviews and Other Writings, 1972–1977*, 78–108. Colin Gordon, ed. and trans. New York: Pantheon.

Fraser, Nancy. 1997. *Justice Interruptus: Critical Reflections on the "Postsocialist" Condition*. New York: Routledge.

Frazier, Ian. 2000. *On the Rez*. New York: Farrar, Straus and Giroux.

Fry, Edward F. 1972. The Dilemmas of the Curator. In *Museums in Crisis*, 103–16. Brian O'Doherty, ed. New York: George Braziller.

References

Garroutte, Eva Marie. 1999. American Indian Science Education: The Second Step. *American Indian Culture and Research Journal* 23(4): 91–114.

Goldberg, Carey. 1999. Pueblo Awaits Its Past in Bones from Harvard. *New York Times*, 20 May.

Gonzalez, Magda Weck, and J. A. Gonzalez. 1982. *Native American Tarot Deck*. NY: U.S. Games Systems.

Graber, Dorothy. 1999. An Indian Artifact Collection in Court: Whose Family Heirlooms? *Wicazo Sa Review* 14(1): 177–96.

Gray, Andrew. 1999. The U.N. Declaration on the Rights of Indigenous Peoples Is Still Intact. In *The Indigenous World*, 1998–99, 355–72. Copenhagen: IWGIA.

Green, Jesse, ed. 1990. *Cushing at Zuni: The Correspondence and Journals of Frank Hamilton Cushing, 1879–1884*. Albuquerque: University of New Mexico Press.

Greenblatt, Stephen. 1991. *Marvelous Possessions: The Wonder of the New World*. Chicago: University of Chicago Press.

Grimshaw, Anna, and Keith Hart. 1994. Anthropology and the Crisis of the Intellectuals. *Critique of Anthropology* 14(3): 227–61.

Guilty Verdict in First NAGPRA Jury Trial. 1996. *Common Ground* 1(2): 9.

Gulliford, Andrew. 2000. *Sacred Objects and Sacred Places: Preserving Tribal Traditions*. Niwot: University Press of Colorado.

Gupta, Akhil. 1992. The Song of the Nonaligned World: Transnational Identities and the Reinscription of Space in Late Capitalism. *Cultural Anthropology* 7(1): 63–79.

Hallowell, A. Irving. 1960. The Beginnings of Anthropology in America. *Selected Papers from the American Anthropologist, 1888–1920*, 1–90. Frederica de Laguna, ed. Evanston IL: Row, Peterson.

Hammil, Jan. 1995. Cultural Imperialism: American Indian Remains in Cardboard Boxes. *World Archaeological Bulletin*, no. 1. Electronic document, www.wac.uct.ac.za/bulletin/bulletin1.contents.html, accessed 4 November 2001.

Hammil, Jan, and Robert Cruz. 1989. Statement of American Indians against Desecration before the World Archaeological Congress. In *Conflict in the Archaeology of Living Traditions*, 195–200. R. Layton, ed. One World Archaeology no. 8. London: Unwin Hyman.

Handler, Richard. 1985. On Having a Culture: Nationalism and the Preservation of Quebec's *Patrimoine*. In *Objects and Others: Essays on*

References

Museums and Material Culture, 192–217. George W. Stocking Jr., ed. Madison: University of Wisconsin Press.

Hansen, Emma. 1998. Powerful Images: Art of the Plains and Southwest. In Powerful Images: Portrayals of Native America, 3–34. Sarah E. Boehme, Gerald T. Conaty, Clifford Crane Bear, Emma I. Hansen, Mike Leslie, and James H. Nottage. Dave Warren, intro. Seattle: University of Washington Press and Museums West.

Harjo, Suzan Shown. 1995. Introduction. In Mending the Circle: A Native American Repatriation Guide, 3–7. Barbara Meister, ed. New York: American Indian Ritual Object Repatriation Foundation.

Harper, Kenn. 2000[1986]. Give Me My Father's Body: The Life of Minik, the New York Eskimo. Kevin Spacey, foreword. New York: Washington Square Press.

Haven, Samuel F. 1974[1856]. The Origin of the Mound Builders. In Readings in the History of Anthropology, 185–205. Regna Darnell, ed. New York: Harper and Row.

Henriksen, John. 1999a. Indigenous Peoples at the United Nations: The Past Thirty Years. Indigenous Affairs 1 (January, February, March): 48–52. (Copenhagen: International Work Group for Indigenous Affairs)

———. 1999b. Introduction to the United Nations and the Process Pertaining to the Establishment of a Permanent Forum for Indigenous Peoples in the United Nations System. In The Permanent Forum for Indigenous Peoples: The Struggle for a New Partnership, 12–29. IWGIA Document 91. Copenhagen: International Work Group for Indigenous Affairs.

Hertzberg, Hazel Whitman. 1988. Indian Rights Movement, 1887–1973. In Handbook of North American Indians. William C. Sturtevant, gen. ed. Vol. 4: History of Indian-White Relations, 305–23. Wilcomb E. Washburn, ed. Washington DC: Smithsonian Institution Press.

Hibbert, Michelle. 1998–99. Galileos or Grave Robbers? Science, the Native American Graves Protection and Repatriation Act, and the First Amendment. American Indian Law Review 23(2): 425–58.

Hill, Richard, Sr. 1996. Reflections of a Native Repatriator. In Mending the Circle: A Native American Repatriation Guide, 81–96. Barbara Meister, ed. New York: American Indian Ritual Object Repatriation Foundation.

Hill, Stephen, and Tim Turpin. 1995. Cultures in Collision: The Emergence of a New Localism in Academic Research. In Shifting Contexts: Transformations in Anthropological Knowledge, 131–52. Marilyn Strathern, ed. New York: Routledge.

References

Hinsley, Curtis M. 1981. *Savages and Scientists: The Smithsonian Institution and the Development of American Anthropology, 1846–1910.* Washington DC: Smithsonian Institution Press.

————. 1989. Zunis and Brahmins: Cultural Ambivalence in the Gilded Age. In *Romantic Motives: Essays on Anthropological Sensibility,* 169–207. George W. Stocking, ed. History of Anthropology, vol. 6. Madison: University of Wisconsin Press.

Hitchens, Christopher (with essays by Robert Browning and Graham Binns). 1997[1987]. *The Elgin Marbles: Should They Be Returned to Greece?* New York: Verso.

Holmes, Steven A. 2001. True Colors: The Confusion over Who We Are. *New York Times,* 3 June.

Hopi Tribe Office of Cultural Preservation and Protection (now named Hopi Cultural Preservation Office). 1995. Protocol for Research, Publications and Recordings: Motion, Visual, Sound, Multimedia and Other Mechanical Devices. August.

Horsman, Reginald. 1988. United States Indian Policies, 1776–1815. In *Handbook of North American Indians. William C. Sturtevant, gen. ed.* Vol. 4: *History of Indian-White Relations,* 29–39. Wilcomb E. Washburn, ed. Washington DC: Smithsonian Institution Press.

Hrdlička, Aleš. 1907. *Skeletal Remains Suggesting or Attributed to Early Man in North America.* Bureau of American Ethnology Bulletin 33. Washington DC: Smithsonian Institution/Government Printing Office.

Hubert, Jane. 1995. The Disposition of the Dead. *World Archaeological Bulletin, no.* 2. Electronic document, www.wac.uct.ac.za/bulletin/wab2/hubert.html, accessed 4 November 2001.

Hustito, Charles. 1991. Why Zuni War Gods Need to Be Returned. In *Zuni History: Victories in the 1990s,* section 2: 12. The Zuni History Newspaper Project. Seattle: Institute of the North American West.

Inouye, Daniel K. 1992. Repatriation: Forging New Relationships. *Arizona State Law Journal* 24: 1–3.

International Indian Treaty Council (IITC). 1974. Declaration of Continuing Independence by the First International Indian Treaty Council at Standing Rock Sioux Indian Country, June 1974. *www.treatycouncil.org/1.html,* accessed 4 November 2001.

International Work Group for Indigenous Affairs. 1987–89. IWGIA *Yearbook, 1986.* IWGIA *Yearbook, 1987.* IWGIA *Yearbook, 1988.* Copenhagen: International Work Group for Indigenous Affairs.

References

————. 1999. *The Permanent Forum for Indigenous Peoples: The Struggle for a New Partnership*. IWGIA Document no. 91. Copenhagen: International Work Group for Indigenous Affairs.

Jacknis, Ira. 2000. Repatriation as Social Drama: The Kwakiutl Indians of British Columbia, 1922–1980. In *Repatriation Reader: Who Owns American Indian Remains?* 266–81. Devon A. Mihesuah, ed. Lincoln: University of Nebraska Press.

Jaimes, M. Annette. 1992. Introduction: Sand Creek: The Morning After. In *The State of Native America: Genocide, Colonization, and Resistance*, 1–12. M. Annette Jaimes, ed. Boston, MA: South End Press.

Jefferson, Thomas. 1964[1785]. *Notes on the State of Virginia*. New York: Harper and Row.

Jemez Remains Reburied. 1999. *Indian Country Today*, 7–14 June.

Jensen, Marianne. 1999. Editorial. *Indigenous Affairs* 1 (March): 1–3. Copenhagen: International Work Group for Indigenous Affairs (March).

Johansen, Bruce E. 1999. Great White Hope? Kennewick Man, the Facts, the Fantasies and the Stakes. *Native Americas* 16(1).

Johnson, Troy, Duane Champagne, and Joane Nagel. 1999. American Indian Activism and Transformation: Lessons from Alcatraz. In *Contemporary Native American Political Issues*, 283–304. Troy R. Johnson, ed. Walnut Creek CA: Altamira Press.

Joseph, Chief. 1991[1879]. My Son, Stop Your Ears. In *Native American Testimony: A Chronicle of Indian-White Relations from Prophecy to the Present, 1492–1992*, 129–33. Peter Nabokov, ed. Vine Deloria Jr., foreword. New York: Viking.

Karakasidou, Anastasia N. 1994. Sacred Scholars, Profane Advocates: Intellectuals Molding National Consciousness in Greece. *Identities* 1(1): 35–61.

Kehoe, Alice Beck. 1998. *The Land of Prehistory: A Critical History of American Archaeology*. New York: Routledge.

Kelley, Klara, and Harris Francis. 1999. Kin Yaa'a, an Anaasazi Ruin with a Diné (Navajo) Story. *Affiliation Conference on Ancestral Peoples of the Four Corners Region*. Vol. 1: Transcripts and Papers, 176–84. 23–24 January 1998. Mimeograph.

Kelly, Alfred H., and Winfred A. Harbison. 1970[1948]. *The American Constitution: Its Origins and Development*. 4th ed. New York: W. W. Norton.

Killion, Thomas W., and Tamara L. Bray. 1994. Looking toward Larsen Bay: Evolving Attitudes at the Smithsonian Institution. In *Reckoning* with the Dead: The Larsen Bay Repatriation and the Smithsonian Institution, 3–9. William W. Fitzhugh, foreword. Washington DC: Smithsonian Institution Press.

Klesert, Anthony L., and Shirley Powell. 1993. A Perspective on Ethics and the Reburial Controversy. *American Antiquity* 58(2): 348–54.

Knickerbocker, Brad. 1999. An Ancient Man's Bones of Contention. *Christian Science Monitor*, 21 October.

Kosslak, Renee M. 1999–2000. The Native American Graves Protection and Repatriation Act: The Death Knell for Scientific Study? *American Indian Law Review* 24(1): 129–51.

Krause, Susan Applegate. 1999. Kinship and Identity: Mixed Bloods in Urban Indian Communities. *American Indian Culture and Research Journal* 23(2): 73–89.

Kubler, George. 1962. *The Art and Architecture of Ancient America: The Mexican 'Maya' and Andean Peoples*. Baltimore: Penguin Books.

LaDuke, Winona. 1996. Sacred Sites, Fishponds, and the National Park Service. *Indian Country Today*, 30 April–7 May.

Lahr, Marta Mirazón. 1997. History in the Bones. *Evolutionary Anthropology* 6(1): 2–6.

Lathrop, Alan K. 1986. Another View of Wounded Knee. *South Dakota History* 16(3): 249–68.

Liberty, David Michael. 1999. Kennewick Man Was Not Alone! Or Corps Confusion in Columbia Park! Paper presented to the World Archaeological Congress 4, at the symposium "Collecting and Repatriation Case Studies," University of Cape Town, 10–14 January 1999.

Lipe, William, Mark D. Varien, and Richard H. Wilshusen, eds. 1999. *Colorado Prehistory: A Context for the Southern Colorado River Basin*. Cortez CO: Colorado Council of Professional Archaeologists, Crow Canyon Archaeological Center.

Little Eagle, Avis. 1996. Ghost Dance Shirt May Be Repatriated. *Indian Country Today*, 23–30 December: C1-C2.

Locke, John. 1952[1690]. *Concerning Civil Government, Second Essay. The Great Books*. Vol. 35: *Locke, Berkeley, and Hume*. Chicago: Encyclopaedia Britannica.

Loring, Stephen, and Miroslav Prokopec. 1994. A Post Peculiar Man: The Life and Times of Aleš Hrdlička. In *Reckoning with the Dead: The Larsen Bay Repatriation and the Smithsonian Institution*, 26–40. Tamara L. Bray and

References

Thomas W. Killion, eds. William W. Fitzhugh, foreword. Washington DC: Smithsonian Institution Press.

Lurie, Nancy Oestreich. 1999[1966]. *Women and the Invention of American Anthropology.* Prospect Heights IL: Waveland Press.

Lux, Laurent. 1999. Le rapatriement de biens culturels dans les relations musées-Amérindiens: L'objet *muséifié* est-il le sujet d'une politique du savoir scientifique ou d'une politisation du savoir? M.A. thesis, l'Université Laval, France.

Macdonald, Theodore, Jr. 1997. Introduction: 25 Years of the Indigenous Movement in the Americas and Australia. *Cultural Survival Quarterly* 21(2): 21–23.

MacLennan, Carol. 1995. Democratic Participation: A View from Anthropology. In *Diagnosing America: Anthropology and Public Engagement,* 51–74. Shepard Forman, ed. Ann Arbor: University of Michigan Press.

Malcomson, Scott L. 2000. The Color of Bones: How a 9,000-Year-Old Skeleton Called Kennewick Man Sparked the Strangest Case of Racial Profiling Yet. *New York Times Magazine,* 2 April: 40–45.

Mankiller, Wilma, and Michael Wallis. 1993. *Mankiller: A Chief and Her People.* New York: St. Martin's Press.

Masayesva, Vernon. 1993. Epilogue. In *Handbook of American Indian Religious Freedom,* 134–36. Christopher Vecsey, ed. New York: Crossroad.

Matlock, Gary, and Philip Duke. 1992. The State of the State: A Critical Review. In *The State of Colorado Archaeology,* 173–205. Philip Duke and Gary Matlock, eds. Memoirs of the Colorado Archaeological Society, no. 5. Denver: Colorado Archaeological Society.

Matthiessen, Peter. 1991[1983]. *In the Spirit of Crazy Horse.* Martin Garbus, afterword. New York: Viking.

McDonald, Kim A. 1998. Researchers Battle for Access to a 9,300-Year-Old Skeleton. *Chronicle of Higher Education,* 22 May.

McGimsey, Charles R., III. 1999. Tributaries: Archaeology Goes to Capitol Hill, 1960–1974. (Headwaters Part 2). *Common Ground* (Winter): 8–15.

McGuire, Randall H. 1992. *A Marxist Archaeology.* Orlando FL: Academic Press.

———. 1997. Why Have Archaeologists Thought the Real Indians Were Dead and What Can We Do about It? In *Indians and Anthropologists: Vine Deloria Jr. and the Critique of Anthropology,* 63–91. Thomas Biolsi and Larry J. Zimmerman, eds. Tucson: University of Arizona Press.

References

McKeown, C. Timothy. 1999. Preservation on the Reservation [Revisited]. *Common Ground* (Fall): 10–13.

Meighan, Clement W. 1992. Some Scholars' Views on Reburial. *American Antiquity* 57(4): 704–10.

Meltzer, David J. 1983. The Antiquity of Man and the Development of American Archaeology. In *Advances in Archaeological Method and Theory*, vol. 6, 1–51. Michael B. Schiffer, ed. New York: Academic Press.

Merenstein, Adele. 1993. The Zuni Quest for Repatriation of the War Gods: An Alternative Basis for Claim. *American Indian Law Review* 17(2): 589–637.

Meriam, Lewis, et al., eds. 1928. *The Problem of Indian Administration: Report of a Survey Made at the Request of Honorable Hubert Work, Secretary of the Interior, and Submitted to Him, February 21, 1928.* Institute for Government Research, Studies in Administration. Baltimore: Johns Hopkins Press.

Merrill, William L., and Richard E. Ahlborn. 1997. Zuni Archangels and Ahayu:da: A Sculpted Chronicle of Power and Identity. In *Exhibiting Dilemmas: Issues of Representation at the Smithsonian*, 176–205. Amy Henderson and Adrienne L. Kaeppler, eds. Washington DC: Smithsonian Institution Press.

Merrill, William L., Edmund J. Ladd, and T. J. Ferguson. 1993. The Return of the Ahayu:da: Lessons for Repatriation from Zuni Pueblo and the Smithsonian Institution. *Current Anthropology* 34(5): 523–67.

Michaelsen, Robert S. 1993. Law and the Limits of Liberty. In *Handbook of American Indian Religious Freedom*, 116–33. Christopher Vecsey, ed. New York: Crossroad.

Mihesuah, Devon A. 2000. Introduction. In *Repatriation Reader: Who Owns American Indian Remains?* 1–15. Devon A. Mihesuah, ed. Lincoln: University of Nebraska Press.

Miller, Bruce G. 1998. Culture as Cultural Defense: An American Indian Sacred Site in Court. *American Indian Quarterly* 22(1/2): 83–97.

Mohawk, John C. 2000. *Utopian Legacies: A History of Conquest and Oppression in the Western World.* Santa Fe NM: Clear Light.

Montana, Cate. 1999. Most Countries Don't Base Repatriation on Ethnicity. *Indian Country Today*, May 24–31.

Mooney, James. 1973[1896]. *The Ghost-Dance Religion and Wounded Knee.* New York: Dover.

Moore, Steven C. 1993. Sacred Sites and Public Lands. In *Handbook of*

American Indian Religious Freedom, 81–99. Christopher Vecsey, ed. New York: Crossroad.

Morsink, Johannes. 1999. *The Universal Declaration of Human Rights: Origins, Drafting, and Intent*. Philadelphia: University of Pennsylvania Press.

Nagel, Joane. 1996. *Native American Ethnic Renewal: Red Power and the Resurgence of Identity and Culture*. New York: Oxford University Press.

NAGPRA News: Implementing the Native American Graves and Repatriation Act. 1996. *Federal Archeology* 8(3/4): 31–35.

Naranjo, Tessie. 1996. Musing on Two World Views. In *Mending the Circle: A Native American Repatriation Guide*, 27–28. Barbara Meister, ed. New York: American Indian Ritual Object Repatriation Foundation.

Nason, James D. 1971. Museums and American Indians: An Inquiry into Relationships. *Western Museums Quarterly* 8(1):13–17.

———. 1999. Museums and Modern Cultural Centers: Traditional Roots, Modern Preservation. *Common Ground* (Fall): 20–25.

National Congress of American Indians. n.d. Army Continues to Parade Wounded Knee "Battle" Streamer. Electronic document, *www.ncai.org/indianissues/CulturalResources/wounkneeban.htm*, accessed 4 November 2001. (Alternative address: http://130.94.214.68/index.asp)

———. 1999. Moving NAGPRA Responsibilities from the National Park Service to the Office of Management, Budget and Policy. Resolution #PSC-99–128. Adopted by the General Assembly during the 1999. Annual Session of the NCAI, Palm Springs Convention Center, CA, October 3–8. www.ncai.org.NAAIResolutions/Palm%20Springs%20Resolutions, accessed 4 November 2001. (Alternative address: http://130.94.214.68/index.asp)

National Museum of the American Indian, ed. 2000. *The Changing Presentation of the American Indian: Museums and Native Cultures*. Washington DC: Smithsonian Institution Press.

Native American Graves Protection and Repatriation Act. 1990. Public Law 101–601; 25 USC 3001–13; 104 Stat. 3042.

Native American Graves Protection and Repatriation Act (NAGPRA) Review Committee. 1992–2001. Minutes of all meetings can be retrieved electronically at www.cast.uark.edu/other/nps/nagpra/rcm.html (accessed 4 November 2001).

Native American Rights Fund (NARF). 1990. Pawnees Repatriate Their Dead for Reburial. Press release, 24 September.

References

————. 1991. Smithsonian to Give Back Indian Human Remains. Press release, 17 April.

————. n.d. Briefing Document: Kansas Unmarked Burial Sites Preservation Act. House Bill No. 2144. Prepared by the Native American Rights Fund on Behalf of the Pawnee Tribe of Oklahoma, Wichita and Affiliated Tribes of Oklahoma, Three Affiliated Tribes of the Fort Berthold Reservation.

Native American Rights Fund, National Congress of American Indians, and Association of American Indian Affairs. 1990. Briefing Document: Protection and Repatriation of Indian Graves, Dead Bodies, and Ceremonial Objects. 16 February 1990. Mimeograph.

Navajo Mask Case Passes Legal Test: Supreme Court Lets Trafficking Conviction Stand. 1998. *Common Ground* 3(2/3): 15.

Navrot, Miguel. 1999. Indians Celebrate Repatriation of Remains. *Albuquerque Journal*, 23 May.

Norrell, Brenda. 1999a. Ishi's Brain in Storage! *Indian Country Today*, 8–15 March: A1, A3.

————. 1999b. Return of Ishi's Brain Delayed: California Legislators and Tribes Want Proper Burial. *Indian Country Today*, 12–19 April: A2.

————. 1999c. Smithsonian to Return Ishi's Brain to California. *Indian Country Today*, 31 May–7 June: A2.

O'Brien, Sharon. 1993. A Legal Analysis of the American Indian Religious Freedom Act. In *Handbook of American Indian Religious Freedom*, 27–43. Christopher Vecsey, ed. New York: Crossroad.

Ooton, Susan. 1992. Ancient Dreams and Stardust Memories: The Amateurs' Impact on Colorado Archaeology. In *The State of Colorado Archaeology*, 109–48. Philip Duke and Gary Matlock, eds. Memoirs of the Colorado Archaeological Society, no. 5. Denver: Colorado Historical Society.

Orchard, William C. 1975. *Beads and Beadwork of the American Indians*. New York: Museum of the American Indian/Heye Foundation.

Ortiz, Alfonso. 1972. Introduction. In *New Perspectives on the Pueblos*, xv–xx. Alfonso Ortiz, ed. Albuquerque: University of New Mexico Press.

————. 1996. American Indian Religious Freedom: First People and the First Amendment. *Cultural Survival Quarterly* 19(4): 26–29.

Osborne, Lawrence. 1999. Greek to Me: How the Elgin Marbles Ruined England. *Lingua Franca* 9(1): 52–59.

Parker, Patricia L., and Thomas F. King. 1990. Guidelines for Evaluating

References

and Documenting Traditional Cultural Properties. *National Register Bulletin* 38 (June). Washington DC: National Park Service.

Paulson, Steven K. 2000. Tribes Reach Agreement on Remains. *Durango Herald*, 18 October.

Pearce, Emma. 1996. Indigenous Chronology. In *Return of the Indian: Conquest and Revival in the Americas*, 194–203. By Phillip Wearne. Rigoberta Menchú, foreword. Philadelphia: Temple University Press.

Pennybacker, Mindy. 1999. Decolonizing the Mind. *Nation*, 4 October: 31–35.

Peregoy, Robert M. 1999. Nebraska's Landmark Repatriation Law: A Study of Cross-Cultural Conflict and Resolution. In *Contemporary Native American Political Issues*, 229–74. Troy R. Johnson, ed. Walnut Creek CA: Altamira Press.

Petersen, Tove Søvndahl. 1999. Preface. In *The Permanent Forum for Indigenous Peoples: The Struggle for a New Partnership*, 8–11. Document no. 91. Copenhagen: International Work Group for Indigenous Affairs.

Pevar, Stephen L. 1992. *The Rights of Indians and Tribes: The Basic American Civil Liberties Union Guide to Indian and Tribal Rights.* 2nd ed. Carbondale: Southern Illinois University Press.

Preston, Douglas J. 1989. Skeletons in Our Museums' Closets: Native Americans Want Their Ancestors' Bones Back. *Harper's Magazine*, February.

Price, H. Marcus, III. 1991. *Disputing the Dead: U.S. Law on Aboriginal Remains and Grave Goods.* Columbia: University of Missouri Press.

Pritchard, Sarah. 2000. The Draft Declaration on the Rights of Indigenous Peoples Remains on Its Troubled Path through the U.N. *The Indigenous World, 1999–2000.* Copenhagen: International Work Group for Indigenous Affairs.

Prucha, Francis Paul. 1988. United States Indian Policies, 1815–1860. In *Handbook of North American Indians*. William C. Sturtevant, gen. ed. Vol. 4: *History of Indian-White Relations*, 40–50. Wilcomb E. Washburn, ed. Washington DC: Smithsonian Institution Press.

Ragsdale, John W., Jr. 1997–98. Anasazi Jurisprudence. *American Indian Law Review* 22(2): 393–444.

Raines, June Camille Bush. 1992. One Is Missing: Native American Graves Protection and Repatriation Act: An Overview and Analysis. *American Indian Law Review* 17(2): 639–65.

Ramos, Alcida Rita. 1994. The Hyperreal Indian. *Critique of Anthropology* 14(2): 153–71.

References

Rappaport, Roy A. 1995. Disorders of Our Own: A Conclusion. In *Diagnosing America: Anthropology and Public Engagement*, 235–94. Shepard Forman, ed. Ann Arbor: University of Michigan Press.

Repatriation Standoff. 1996. *Archaeology* 49(2): 12–13.

Riding In, James. 1992. Without Ethics and Morality: A Historical Overview of Imperial Archaeology and American Indians. *Arizona State Law Journal* 24: 11–34.

Ridington, Robin, and Dennis Hastings (In'aska). 1997. *Blessing for a Long Time: The Sacred Pole of the Omaha Tribe.* Lincoln: University of Nebraska Press.

Robbins, Catherine C. 1999. Pueblo Indians Receive Remains of Ancestors. *New York Times,* 23 May.

Rousseau, Jean Jacques. 1952[1794]. *A Discourse on a Subject Proposed by the Academy of Dijon: What is the Origin of Inequality Among Men, and is it Authorised by Natural Law?* 321–66. In *Great Books of the Western World,* vol. 38. Chicago: Encyclopaedia Britannica.

Rowe, John Howland. 1974[1965]. The Renaissance Foundations of Anthropology. In *Readings in the History of Anthropology,* 61–77. Regna Darnell, ed. New York: Harper and Row.

Rowlandson, Mary. 1982[1676]. A Narrative of the Captivity and Restauration of Mrs. Mary Rowlandson. In *The Portable North American Indian Reader,* 312–59. Frederick W. Turner, ed. New York: Penguin Books.

Rudenstine, David. 2000. Did Elgin Cheat at Marbles? *Nation,* 29 May: 30–35.

Russell, Steve. 1995. The Legacy of Ethnic Cleansing: Implementation of NAGPRA in Texas. *American Indian Culture and Research Journal* 19(4): 193–211.

Sackler, Elizabeth. 1996. About the American Indian Ritual Object Repatriation Foundation. In *Mending the Circle: A Native American Repatriation Guide,* 67–72. Barbara Meister, ed. New York: American Indian Ritual Object Repatriation Foundation.

Salmond, Anne. 1995. Self and Other in Contemporary Anthropology. In *Counterworks: Managing the Diversity of Knowledge,* 23–48. Richard Fardon, ed. New York: Routledge.

Saltzstein, Katherine. 1996a. Sentencing Set for Man Convicted of Selling Masks. *Indian Country Today,* 28 May 28–4 June.

———. 1996b. Yei B'Chei Masks Bring Arizona Man Bad Luck. *Indian Country Today,* 22 July–29 July.

References

Sanders, Douglas. 1988. Government Indian Agencies in Canada. In *Handbook of North American Indians*. William C. Sturtevant, gen. ed. Vol. 4: *History of Indian-White Relations*, 276–83. Wilcomb Washburn, ed. Washington DC: Smithsonian Institution Press.

Schamel, Kathleen, Jill Schaefer, and Loretta Neumann. 1997. Update of Compilation of State Repatriation, Reburial and Grave Protection Laws (July 1997). Prepared for the Natural Resources Conservation Service under order number 40–3A75-7-102. Electronic document, www.arrowheads.com/burials.htm, accessed 4 November 2001.

Scheckel, Susan. 1998. *The Insistence of the Indian: Race and Nationalism in Nineteenth-Century American Culture*. Princeton NJ: Princeton University Press.

Schroeder, Albert H. 1979. Pecos Pueblo. In *Handbook of North American Indians*. Vol. 9: *Southwest*, 430–37. Alfonso Ortiz, ed. Washington DC: Smithsonian Institution Press.

Second Convocation of Indian Scholars. 1974. *Indian Voices: The Native American Today: The Second Convocation of Indian Scholars*. American Indian Historical Society. San Francisco: American Indian Educational Publishers.

Shea, Christopher. 2000. The Return of Ishi's Brain. *Lingua Franca* 10(1): 46–55.

Sider, Gerald. 1994. Identity as History: Ethnohistory, Ethnogenesis and Ethnocide in the Southeastern United States. *Identities* 1(1): 109–22.

Silber, Ilana Friedrich. 1995. Space, Fields, Boundaries: The Rise of Spatial Metaphors in Contemporary Social Theory. *Social Research* 62(2): 323–55.

Smith, Joseph, trans. 1981[1830]. *The Book of Mormon: Another Testament of Jesus Christ*. Salt Lake City UT: Church of Jesus Christ of Latter-day Saints.

Smoak, Gregory E. 1986. The Mormons and the Ghost Dance of 1890. *South Dakota History* 16(3): 269–94.

Society for American Archaeology (SAA). 1986. SAA Policy Concerning the Treatment of Human Remains. Electronic document, www.saa.org/repatriation/repat_policy.html, accessed 4 November 2001.

———. 2000. Position Paper: The Secretary of the Interior's September 21, 2000 Determination of Cultural Affiliation for Kennewick Man. Electronic document, www.saa.org/repatriation/lobby/kennewickC8.html, accessed 4 November 2001.

References

Sotheby Parke Bernet, Inc. 1980. *Fine American Indian Art and Important Books of Related Interest*. Sale Number 4472Y. Illustrated catalog. New York.

South and Mesoamerican Indian Information Center (SAIIC). 1990. Declaration of Quito. *SAIIC Newsletter* 5(3/4):21.

Spalding, Julian. 1999. Bury the Truth at Wounded Knee: Is Restitution Always Right? *Art Newspaper* 95 (September): 21.

Spicer, Edward H. 1983[1969]. *A Short History of the Indians of the United States*. Malabar FL: Robert E. Krieger.

Spivak, Gayatri Chakravorty. 1993. *Outside in the Teaching Machine*. New York: Routledge.

Stannard, David E. 1992. *American Holocaust: The Conquest of the New World*. New York: Oxford University Press.

Stevenson, Katherine H. 2000. Statement of Katherine H. Stevenson, Associate Director, Cultural Resource Stewardship and Partnerships, National Park Service, Department of the Interior, Before the Senate Subcommittee on Indian Affairs Concerning the Oversight of the Native American Graves Protection and Repatriation Act (July 25). Electronic document, www.nps.gov/legal/testimony/106th/nagpra7.htm, accessed 4 November 2001.

Stocking, George W., Jr. 1985. Philanthropoids and Vanishing Cultures: Rockefeller Funding and the End of the Museum Era in Anglo-American Anthropology. In *Objects and Others: Essays on Museums and Material Culture*, 112–45. George W. Stocking Jr., ed. History of Anthropology, vol. 3. Madison: University of Wisconsin Press.

———. 1988. Bones, Bodies, Behavior. In *Bones, Bodies, Behavior: Essays on Biological Anthropology*, 3–17. George W. Stocking Jr., ed. History of Anthropology, vol. 5. Madison: University of Wisconsin Press, 3–17.

Stolcke, Verena. 1995. Talking Culture: New Boundaries, New Rhetorics of Exclusion in Europe. *Current Anthropology* 36:1–24.

Strathern, Marilyn. 1995. The Nice Thing about Culture Is That Everyone Has It. In *Shifting Contexts: Transformations in Anthropological Knowledge*, 153–76. Marilyn Strathern, ed. New York: Routledge.

Sturm, Circe. 1998. Blood Politics, Racial Classification, and Cherokee National Identity: The Trials and Tribulations of the Cherokee Freedmen. *American Indian Quarterly* 22(1/2): 230–58.

Suagee, Dean B., Esq. 1996. Building a Tribal Repatriation Program: Options for Exercising Sovereignty. In *Mending the Circle: A Native American*

Repatriation Guide, 29–44. Barbara Meister, ed. New York: American Indian Ritual Object Repatriation Foundation.

Taliman, Valerie. 1996. Sacred Yei Jish Returned. *Indian Country Today*, 7–14 October.

Tauli-Corpuz, Victoria. 1999. Thirty Years of Lobbying and Advocacy by Indian Peoples. *Indigenous Affairs*: 1 (January, February, March): 4–11. (Copenhagen: IWGIA)

Taylor, Wayne, Jr. 1999. Letter dated 24 September 1999, to Departmental Consulting Archaeologist, National Park Service, from Wayne Taylor Jr., Chairman of the Hopi Tribe.

Thomas, David Hurst. 2000. *Skull Wars: Kennewick Man, Archaeology, and the Battle for Native American Identity*. Vine Deloria Jr., foreword. New York: Basic Books.

Thoms, Alston V. 1999. Protecting Lost Graves: Civil Rights Demand Legislation for all Burial Places. *Discovering Archaeology*, May/June: 100–102.

Thornton, Russell. 1987. *American Indian Holocaust and Survival: A Population History since 1492*. Norman: University of Oklahoma Press.

Trask, Haunani-Kay. 1999. *From a Native Daughter: Colonialism and Sovereignty in Hawaii*. Honolulu: University of Hawaii Press.

Trigger, Bruce. 1989. *A History of Archaeological Thought*. New York: Cambridge University Press.

Trope, Jack F., Esq. 1996a. The Native American Graves Protection and Repatriation Act. In *Mending the Circle: A Native American Repatriation Guide*, 9–19. Barbara Meister, ed. New York: American Indian Ritual Object Repatriation Foundation.

———. 1996b Existing Federal Law and the Protection of Sacred Sites: Possibilities and Limitations. *Cultural Survival Quarterly* 19(4): 30–35.

Tsadiasi, Perry. 1991. I Want Our Fathers Back. *Zuni History: Victories in the 1990s*, section 2:13. Zuni History Newspaper Project. Seattle: Institute of the North American West.

Tsosie, Rebecca. 1997. Indigenous Rights and Archaeology. In *Native Americans and Archaeologists: Stepping Stones to Common Ground*, 64–76. Nina Swidler, Kurt E. Dongoske, Roger Anyon, and Alan S. Downer, eds. Walnut Creek CA: Altamira Press.

United Nations. 1993. Discrimination against Indigenous Peoples: Report of the Working Group on Indigenous Populations on Its Eleventh Session. United Nations Economic and Social Council

Commission on Human Rights Sub-Commission on Prevention of Discrimination and Protection of Minorities. Forty-fifth session, Agenda Item 14. [Fourth World Documentation Project web site version, www.cwis.org/fwdp/International/draft93.txt, accessed 4 November 2001].

U.S. Bureau of the Census. 1998. American Indian Heritage Month: November 1–30. Census Bureau Facts for Features, CB98-FF.13. Electronic document, www.census.gov/Press-Release/cb98ff13.html, accessed 4 November 2001.

U.S. Department of the Interior. 1995. Native American Graves Protection and Repatriation Act Regulations: Final Rule. *Federal Register* 60(232): 62133–62169. Department of the Interior, Office of the Secretary 43. CFR Part 10, RIN 1024-AC07. Electronic document, www.cast.uark.edu/other/nps/nagpra/DOCS/lgm005.html, accessed 4 November 2001.

———. 1997. Native American Graves Protection and Repatriation Act Regulations: Civil Penalties. *Federal Register* 62(8): 1819–1823. Department of the Interior, Office of the Secretary 43. CFR Part 10, RIN 1024-AC48. Electronic document, www.cast.uark.edu/other/nps/nagpra/DOCS/lgm006.html, accessed 4 November 2001.

———. 2000. Museums and Federal Agencies That Have Submitted a NAGPRA Inventory as of March 10, 2000. National Park Service Archaeology and Ethnography Program. NADB-NAGPRA National Archaeological Database. (For a current listing of Notices of Inventory Completion filed by museums or federal agencies and recorded in the National NAGPRA Database, see www.cast.uark.edu/other/nps/nagpra/nic.html, accessed 4 November 2001)

U.S. Senate. 1999. Oversight Hearing before the Senate Committee on Indian Affairs on the Native American Graves Protection and Repatriation Act. Tuesday, 20 April. Electronic document, http:\\indian.senate.gov/1999hrgs/nagpra4.20/nag_wit.htm, accessed 4 November 2001.

Van Slambrouck, Paul. 1999. Native Americans Wield New Political Clout. *Christian Science Monitor*, 27 October.

Wade, Edwin L. 1985. The Ethnic Art Market in the American Southwest, 1880–1980. In *Objects and Others: Essays on Museums and Material Culture,*

167–91. George W. Stocking Jr., ed. History of Anthropology, vol. 3. Madison: University of Wisconsin Press.

Walker, Hollis. 1999. A Return to Grace: Jemez Pueblo Members Receive Apology, Artifacts. *Santa Fe New Mexican,* 21 May.

Walton, Eugene O. 1970. *God Is Alive.* Independence MO.

Wearne, Phillip. 1996. *Return of the Indian: Conquest and Revival in the Americas.* Rigoberta Menchú, foreword. Philadelphia: Temple University Press.

Weiner, James F. 1995. Anthropologists, Historians and the Secret of Social Knowledge. *Anthropology Today* 11(5): 3–6.

Whiteley, Peter M. 1998. *Rethinking Hopi Ethnography.* Washington DC: Smithsonian Institution Press.

Whiteley, Peter M., and Vernon Masayesva. 1998. Paavahu and Paanaqso'a: The Wellsprings of Life and the Slurry of Death. In *Rethinking Hopi Ethnography,* 188–207. By Peter M. Whiteley. Washington DC: Smithsonian Institution Press.

Willinsky, John. 1998. *Learning to Divide the World: Education at Empire's End.* Minneapolis: University of Minnesota Press.

Wilmer, Franke. 1993. *The Indigenous Voice in World Politics: Since Time Immemorial.* Newbury Park CA: Sage.

Willson, Margaret. 1995. Afterword. In *Taboo: Sex, Identity and Erotic Subjectivity in Anthropological Fieldwork,* 251–75. Don Kulick and Margaret Willson, eds. New York: Routledge.

World's Indigenous People Mount Global Campaign for Rights. 2000. *Indian Country Today,* 13 October.

Would-Be Artifact Dealers Sentenced in New Mexico. 1996. *Common Ground* 1(3/4): 9–10.

Young, Kanalu G. Terry. 1998. *Rethinking the Native Hawaiian Past.* New York: Garland.

Zimmerman, Larry J. 1997a. Anthropology and Responses to the Reburial Issue. In *Indians and Anthropologists: Vine Deloria, Jr. and the Critique of Anthropology,* 92–112. Thomas Biolsi and Larry J. Zimmerman, eds. Tucson: University of Arizona Press.

———. 1997b. Remythologizing the Relationship between Indians and Archaeologists. In *Native Americans and Archaeologists: Stepping Stones to Common Ground,* 44–56. Nina Swidler, Kurt E. Dongoske, Roger Anyon, and Alan S. Downer, eds. Walnut Creek CA: Altamira Press.

Index

CPSIA information can be obtained at www.ICGtesting.com
Printed in the USA
LVOW130152050912

297378LV00008B/3/P